Advance Praise for
THE LATINO GUIDE TO PERSONAL MONEY MANAGEMENT
By Laura Castañeda and Laura Castellanos

Foreword by Antonia Hernández, President and General Counsel,
Mexican American Legal Defense and Educational Fund (MALDEF)

"Latinos are a dazzlingly diverse people in America at century's end.
Depending on migration history, level of education, and family background,
the kind of 'money advice' needed is all over the map . . . from starting a first
savings account to high finance. Yet, this book successfully straddles a wide
range of concerns for a wide range of people, with good humor, flair, and
most importantly, without condescension. The information in this book is
required ammunition for building a secure future."
>   —RAY SUAREZ
>   Host of National Public Radio's "Talk of the Nation," and
>   Author of *The Old Neighborhood: What We Lost in the Great
>   Suburban Migration*

"*¡Por fin!* A financial guide for the Latino community that is easy to
understand, useful, and relevant. Laura Castañeda and Laura Castellanos
have created an invaluable tool toward achieving our next goal: economic
empowerment and financial independence. *¡Lealo!*"
>   —ARTURO VARGAS
>   Executive Director
>   National Association of Latino Elected and Appointed Officials
>   (NALEO)

"Despite the fact that the Hispanic community is a $350 billion market and
growing, very little attention has been paid to educating Latinos on how to
manage their money. Clear, accessible, and timely, *The Latino Guide to Personal
Money Management* is a much needed contribution to closing the financial information gap that exists between Hispanics and other Americans."
>   —RAUL YZAGUIRRE
>   President
>   National Council of La Raza (NCLR)

"To be truly successful in the United States, you must be financially secure. This book gives you the road map to that security. Follow it and you'll become the 'Hispanic Millionaire Next Door'!"

　　—LIONEL SOSA
　　President & CEO
　　Spark! KJS Advertising & Author of
　　The American Dream: How Latinos Can Achieve Success
　　　in Business and in Life

"Las Lauras have written a comprehensive yet easy-to-read guide that's packed with useful information and helpful exercises. I know I will refer to it often!"

　　—LAVONNE LUQUIS
　　President, LatinoLink Enterprises, Inc.
　　& USHCC National Hispanic Businesswoman of the Year (1998)

". . . Laura Castañeda and Laura Castellanos have transformed financial victimization into empowerment. Their guide is thorough and easy to follow."

　　—NELY GALAN
　　President of Entertainment
　　Telemundo Network Group

"Congratulations! This book is a valuable source of information for all who want to make sound financial decisions, particularly for women, who are emerging as the primary financial planners in our society. It should be used as a reference for all financial situations."

　　—BELENA B. ROBLES
　　Immediate Past National President
　　League of United Latin American Citizens (LULAC)

"This financial guide provides clear and useful information necessary to move Latinos along the road to greater financial prosperity."

　　—REP. XAVIER BECERRA
　　Member of the United States Congress
　　California, 30th Congressional District

"... a comprehensive blueprint for both new citizens and Latinos who trace their roots for several generations. The authors have conducted much research, and while readers must ultimately make individual judgments about their own financial matters, it will save Latinos valuable time and money. *¡Si vale la pena!*"

> —FEDERICO PEÑA
> Senior Adviser, Vestar Capital Partners
> Former U.S. Secretary of Energy &
> Former U.S. Secretary of Transportation

"... comprehensive, friendly advice on how to protect and grow money at every life stage. Las Lauras help individuals take control of their financial futures by guiding them through money basics while pointing out mistakes and scams. I highly recommend this guide. *¡Vale su tiempo!*"

> —DON M. BLANDIN
> President
> American Savings Education Council
> (www.asec.org)

"At last, a comprehensive work on money management for Latinos and our *familias*. The Lauras show us a clear path to financial health. Read it and take the next steps. Planning—like prevention—works."

> —SANDRA HERNANDEZ, MD
> Chief Executive Officer
> The San Francisco Foundation

"Latinos constitute twelve percent of the U.S. population but have less than one percent of America's available capital. This long overdue financial guide could help close this gap and thereby radically alter the political and economic landscape of America."

> —ROBERT GNAIZDA
> Policy Director
> Greenlining Institute

THE LATINO GUIDE TO PERSONAL MONEY MANAGEMENT

THE LATINO GUIDE TO PERSONAL MONEY MANAGEMENT

Laura Castañeda
Laura Castellanos

FOREWORD BY ANTONIA HERNANDEZ

BLOOMBERG PRESS

PRINCETON

Books are available for bulk purchases at special discounts. Special editions or book excerpts can also be created to specifications. For information, please write: Special Markets Department, Bloomberg Press.

BLOOMBERG, BLOOMBERG NEWS, BLOOMBERG FINANCIAL MARKETS, OPEN BLOOMBERG, BLOOMBERG PERSONAL FINANCE, BLOOMBERG WEALTH MANAGER, NEGOCIOS BLOOMBERG, THE BLOOMBERG FORUM, COMPANY CONNECTION, COMPANY CONNEX, BLOOMBERG PRESS, BLOOMBERG PROFESSIONAL LIBRARY, BLOOMBERG PER-SONAL BOOKSHELF, and BLOOMBERG SMALL BUSINESS are trademarks and service marks of Bloomberg L.P. All rights reserved.

This publication contains the author's opinions and is designed to provide accurate and author-itative information. It is sold with the understanding that the author, publisher, and Bloomberg L.P. are not engaged in rendering legal, accounting, investment-planning, or other professional advice. The reader should seek the services of a qualified professional for such advice; the author, publisher, and Bloomberg L.P. cannot be held responsible for any loss incurred as a result of spe-cific investments or planning decisions made by the reader.

First edition published 1999
1 3 5 7 9 10 8 6 4 2

Castañeda, Laura 1963—
        The latino guide to personal money management / Laura Castañeda,
    Laura Castellanos.

    Foreword by Antonia Hernández
            p.   cm.
        Includes index.
        ISBN 1-57660-058-0
        1. Hispanic Americans - - Finance, Personal. I. Castellanos, Laura,
    1959-   . II. Title.
    HG179.C35 1999
    332.024'0368073 - - dc21   99-13522
                                                                             CIP

Book design by Barbara Diez
Acquired and edited by Jared Kieling

ACKNOWLEDGMENTS

THIS BOOK BEARS our two names, but it would have been impossible to complete without the help of dozens of people who graciously shared their time and expertise. Although we cannot list them all, a few deserve special acknowledgement.

Un abrazo to our hardworking agent, Robert Shepard, who believed in this project with all his heart and held our hands from beginning to end. Roberto, consider yourself an honorary Latino!

Gracias to the talented and enthusiastic staff at Bloomberg Press, especially our editor Jared Kieling, and Lisa Goetz, Melissa Hafner, John Crutcher, Christina Palumbo, Maris Williams, and Barbara Diez. At Bloomberg L.P., thanks to Rich Arent, Ana Castañeda, Emily Hsiung, Jose Morais, and Elsa Shilling.

We are deeply indebted to three Latino financial planning professionals who spent hours discussing financial concepts and Latino attitudes toward money—and never once charged us for their time: Delia Fernández, a fee-only financial planner in Los Alamitos, California; and American Express financial planners Conrad Santiago in Coral Gables, Florida, and Josue González in San Diego, California.

Thanks also go to several experts who generously agreed to review chapters or sections of the book for accuracy. They include Robin Leonard, an attorney and author of several Nolo Press books such as *Credit Repair and Money Troubles: Legal Strategies to Cope With Your Debts*; reporters Arthur Louis and Mark Martínez of *The San Francisco Chronicle*; Lincoln Pain, a Berkeley, California-based certified financial planner specializing in socially responsible investing; Rick Harper, housing director for the Consumer Credit Counseling Service in San Francisco; Dr. Herm Davis, co-author of *College Financial Aid for Dummies* and head of the National College Scholarship Foundation in Rockville, Maryland; Mark Wilson, a financial adviser specializing in retirement plans for small businesses in Newport Beach, California; estate attorneys Alina Laguna in South San Francisco, and Ricardo Pesquera in Orlando, Florida; and a team from the Los Angeles office of Deloitte & Touche including senior tax manager Jess Penilla, partner and CPA Carlos Perez, attorney Renae Welder, tax researcher Nancy Foster, and staff members Martín López and Santos Hernández.

And finally, our heartfelt thanks to the many Latinos from all around the country who shared their stories with us.

This book was truly a labor of love for the both of us. When we began this project, we agreed that as the writer, Laura Casteñeda would tackle the initial research, interviews, and writing; Laura Castellanos would add the voice of the financial professional working with investors in the Latino community, as well as edit and complete the Spanish translations. But we share joint and equal credit for the finished product. We've tried our best to produce the most accurate, up-to-date, and practical guide possible. Of course, we also share joint and equal responsibility for any mistakes or misinterpretations that appear in the book.

Special thanks go to my husband, Art Buckler, for his love, kindness, understanding, and sense of humor. He is the best part of my life. I would also like to thank my parents, Rubén and Socorro Castañeda, for their love and unwavering belief in me, and my brothers Rubén Jr., Jarier, Adrian, and Andy, for their support. Thanks go to all of my former colleagues at *The San Francisco Chronicle*, especially business editor Kathleen Pender, assistant business editor David Tong, managing editor Jerry Roberts, and human resources director Susan Bloch, for giving me time to work on this project. Last, but not least, I would like to thank several friends who provided encouragement and laughter when I needed it the most. They include Julie Amparano, Patricia Bibby, Steven DeSalvo, Ann Buckley Kurz, and Mary McGrath.

—*Laura Castañeda*

Without the love and strength of my family and friends, very little in life would be possible or meaningful. You are the reason I get up each day believing it is possible to make a difference, and go to bed each night knowing I am forgiven when my efforts fall short. *Sin duda,* my partner, Martha I. Jiménez, is the prime example of this blessing in my life. There are no words to express my gratitude to my parents for their courage, humor, compassion, and unconditional love. *Los hijitos quieren a sus padres y los padres a sus hijos.* Finally, a word of thanks to my brother, Alex Castellanos, and to my many friends who supported me not only in this endeavor, but are at my side and in my heart each day.

—*Laura Castellanos*

FOREWORD

As A LITTLE GIRL, on Saturdays and Sundays I accompanied my father to small businesses to sell the *tamales* my mother had made at home the night before. The sights, sounds, and smells of those days are vividly returned to me now in odd places. I remember those days when I am sitting in thickly carpeted boardrooms among other corporate directors. I recall working alongside my father when I testify before the U.S. Senate or I address an assembly of local leaders. I thought again of those times as I read *The Latino Guide to Personal Money Management.* And I felt proud.

I am delighted to have an opportunity to introduce this book to you because it fits so neatly into my very simple lifelong agenda: how do I help the Latino community? How do I serve as a bridge?

For the Latino community to advance, I have always believed that in addition to the traditional emphasis on political involvement, we must also pursue economic empowerment. Financial planning is important. I have always been a business woman, and I believe in bringing economic opportunities to my community. My business now is the business of change. I firmly believe that change begins in our own homes.

If I could name only one basic trait of the Latino character, it would be our work ethic. Yet we have not benefited from our labor in proportion to how hard we work and how much we contribute to the economy. It is critical for Latinos to do more than just work hard; we must also save smart, spend well, and invest wisely.

In this book, las Lauras offer tremendous insights and strategies to help Latinos understand how to budget, save, invest, and build financially strong families that will support even stronger communities. As Latinos become a demographic majority, it is incumbent upon us to become well-educated and to join the financial mainstream. We not only need to solve problems for ourselves, but for and with all our neighbors in the broader community of the United States.

The advice offered in this book isn't some hocus-pocus elixir for becoming an instant millionaire. This is a practical, detailed guide for developing and implementing a financial plan. Any Latino—indeed anybody—can benefit from the resources found in these pages if they only will take action.

And las Lauras have written an engaging book. I smiled as I read some of their observations, because I recognized myself, my family, and my community in these pages. *Gracias* to them for writing it for all of us.

—*Antonia Hernández*
President and General Counsel
Mexican American Legal Defense and
Educational Fund (MALDEF)
and former Director of Federal Reserve Board
of San Francisco, Los Angeles Branch

Controlling Our Destiny

"WHEN MONEY SPEAKS THE REST ARE SILENT" —CUBA

TWO LATINAS ARE ATTENDING A RECEPTION FOR A LATINA MENTOR-ing group. Although these *chicas* have just met, they fall into a serious conversation, which inevitably turns to the challenges they face as they try to *hechar adelante*. Getting ahead, they agree, requires perseverance and education. Then, almost in unison, they add, "and financial stability."

Our two Latinas, it turns out, also share a dream. They both intend to write a book that will help all Latinos save, keep, and grow their money, and teach them how to find and use financial resources. The best way for Latinos to improve the lives of their families and communities, they believe, is by taking control of their financial *destino*.

That's our story. We're those two Latinas, or las Lauras, to our readers, *nuestros amigos*. We wrote *The Latino Guide to Personal Money Management* together because we passionately believe that our success as Latinos in the United States depends on our ability to understand and speak the language of money—*el idioma del dinero*.

In our personal and professional lives, we have each been inspired by stories of how our *gente* have triumphed against the odds. We have also been pained by stories of financial losses stemming from opportunities not taken, bad advice, or simply not knowing whom to ask for help.

Many books provide solid information about financial planning. Some focus on specific readers such as Generation X, Baby Boomers, gays and lesbians, women, African-Americans, retirees—even "dummies" and "idiots"! But none cater to the unique needs of Latinos. At the same time, there is growing demand in the Latino community for financial information.

When Laura the journalist began writing about personal finance for *The San Francisco Chronicle*, for example, she received a steady stream of phone calls and e-mail messages from Latino readers who wanted to know whether any Spanish-language resources existed, and if so, where to find them.

Laura the financial planner was inspired to switch careers after spending years working as a public interest attorney. Why? Whether working on civil rights, education, or small business issues, she too found that more and more Latinos were peppering her with questions about money matters. "Everything is so different here," she was often told. And the same question always arose: "Who can we trust to help us?"

Finding help has never been easy for Latinos. Many financial service firms have long ignored Latinos despite estimates that our community's purchasing power will reach $477 billion by the year 2000, and that we will be the largest minority group in the United States by the year 2010. This lack of attention has taken a heavy toll in our community.

Consider the following: only three out of ten Latinos have basic checking accounts; fewer than five out of ten have passbook savings accounts; fewer than five out of ten have a credit card; half of us have no health insurance; fewer than one out of ten invests in stocks, bonds, or mutual funds; just four out of ten own homes; and about three out of ten have a pension plan.

The Latino Guide to Personal Money Management is our attempt to change what we as Latinos know about finances, and most important, what we do with our money. We tell you how to cut costs and save money by making a budget. We show you how to reduce your insurance premiums. And we teach you how to trim your tax bill.

Did you know, for instance, that you could reduce your insurance premiums by hundreds of dollars by selecting a higher deductible? That every year you can claim a child tax credit of $500 per dependent child under the age of seventeen if you meet certain income requirements? Or that you can save thousands of dollars on funeral costs by joining a nonprofit memorial society?

We also address specific Latino fears and biases about money that few of us talk about. We translate key financial terms and tell you where to find more information *en español*, if it's available. Subjects that are of particular interest to many Latinos include

- ❏ where to find Hispanic-owned banks and savings and loans
- ❏ the most economical ways to send money to foreign countries
- ❏ how to locate members of the Latino Community Development Credit Union Network
- ❏ how to build credit in nontraditional ways
- ❏ what type of auto insurance you need in Mexico
- ❏ where to find low-income or first-time homebuyer programs
- ❏ how to pay for private elementary, junior high, high school, and college tuition
- ❏ where to find free and bilingual help with tax returns
- ❏ understanding special income and estate tax rules for non-U.S. citizens.

In each chapter we explain various concepts and offer our *Consejo*, or advice, on different topics, using specific examples from our personal and professional experiences as illustrations. You can find out how to act on this advice, and where to go for more information on a specific subject, under headings titled *Acción*. Notes, or *Avisos*, are sprinkled throughout the book. Each chapter also concludes with a quick, compact recap, or *Repaso*, and finally, a list of recommended readings that we believe provides clear and objective information about specific topics.

We've tackled a wide range of topics to appeal to the largest number of Latinos. As a result, some portions of the book may interest you more than others. After all, the Latino who is just learning about the dangers of check cashers (Chapter 1) or the ins and outs of establishing credit (Chapter 2) will probably have little in common with the Latino who wants to develop better investment and estate planning strategies (Chapters 4 and 8). So if you come to a subject you believe is too basic, skip ahead. But if you have friends or relatives who may be in need of this basic information, please point it out to them.

We've included many telephone numbers, mailing addresses, and Web site addresses to make it as easy as possible for you to get the help you deserve. If you don't have a computer at home, we encourage you to ask your local library or school if they have computers with Internet access. Excellent financial information is now available instantly—and in many cases for free—on the World Wide Web.

Our goals are simple: To demystify financial topics for Latinos; show you how and where to find help; inspire you to change what you do with your money; and encourage you to pass along what you learn to your family, friends, and community.

DON'T LET THIS BOOK just sit on the shelf looking pretty. Consider it a road map. If used regularly and carefully, it can lead you and your loved ones toward a healthier financial life.

CHAPTER 1

Banks, Savings and Loans, and Credit Unions

"ONE WHO IS PREPARED HAS WON HALF THE BATTLE" —CUBA

WALK THROUGH ALMOST ANY LATINO WORKING-CLASS NEIGHBOR-hood in the United States, and chances are you'll see storefronts with names like Cash-A-Check, C&C Check Cashers, or Checkers International offering check-cashing services, short-term loans, wire transfers, and sometimes even pagers, phone cards, and lottery tickets.

Although these check-cashing stores—dubbed "fringe banks" by John P. Caskey in his book *Fringe Banking: Check Cashing Outlets, Pawnshops, and the Poor*—charge high interest rates and fees, residents regularly turn to them for basic financial services instead of using traditional financial institutions such as banks, savings and loans, and credit unions.

Consider these numbers tracking use of bank services from the U.S. Census Bureau: Only about 33 percent of Latinos have basic checking accounts compared with 48.2 percent of non-Latino whites; 19.3 percent of Latinos have interest-earning checking accounts compared with 39 percent of non-Latino whites; 46 percent of Latinos have passbook savings accounts compared with 62 percent of non-Latino whites; 3.7 percent of Latinos have money-market accounts compared with 13.8 percent of non-Latino whites;

and 4.4 percent of Latinos have certificates of deposit (CDs) compared with 17.7 percent of non-Latino whites.

Why are so many hard-working Latinos willing to pay higher fees in return for often questionable financial services? One explanation is the deep mistrust Latinos have toward financial institutions. Shady Latin American banks that skimmed money from accounts or disappeared with deposits have burned many of us or our families. Volatile economies have also made placing money in Latin American bank accounts as risky as playing *la lotería*—but not nearly as fun. All it takes is one sharp currency fluctuation to lose a lifetime of savings. Many of us either know or have heard of Latinos who stuff their money in jars, under mattresses, or in safe-deposit boxes. *¿Pero nosotros, no, verdad?*

Financial institutions haven't welcomed Latinos with open arms, either. With a few exceptions, banks and savings and loan associations have been pulling out of Latino neighborhoods. Of those that remain, many charge prohibitively expensive fees for products and services, require an intimidating amount of paperwork to open and use accounts, or provide no Spanish-language services.

Unfortunately, these business practices fuel another Latino misconception—that a lot of money is needed to use U.S. banks and credit unions, and that it's impossible to get loans. In reality, some banks and savings and loans *(sociedades de ahorros y préstamos)*, or S&Ls—and almost all credit unions—offer bare-bones accounts that can be opened with small initial deposits, sometimes as little as $1.

Even those of us who are part of the financial mainstream and regularly use the full range of services available to us—checking and savings accounts, credit cards, automated teller machines (ATMs), debit cards, certificates of deposit, and money-market accounts—don't do enough to find the best deals on fees and interest rates.

Ironically, we're excellent savers. A survey by Miami-based Strategy Research Corp. found that the 1.3 million Latino households in the nation's ten largest markets—Los Angeles, New York, Miami, San Francisco–San Jose, Chicago, Houston, San Antonio, McAllen–Brownsville, Dallas, and San Diego—each manage to send an average of $221.21 per month to family members in their countries of origin. That amounts to $3.4 billion a year.

Getting the most out of financial institutions makes economic sense because, if used properly, they are one of many tools we can use to increase our savings. They not only keep our money safe from fire, loss, and theft. Deposits can earn interest. Canceled checks are proof that bills have been paid. Even more important, having a checking or savings account makes it easier to get good deals on credit cards and loans. (Credit is covered in Chapter 2.)

Take Lucy and Gregorio, who used check cashers when they first came to the United States from Mexico in 1980. "We didn't think we needed a bank because we spent everything we earned," explains Lucy. But within a couple of years, they opened a checking account at Bank of America because they got tired of spending so much of their earnings on money orders to pay their bills.

Since then, they've opened a savings account for themselves and their daughter, and they have a certificate of deposit. Lucy and Gregorio have also borrowed money from two smaller neighborhood banks to buy a house and open a small grocery store. They often encourage their Latino customers to find out about services banks are offering.

Edgar, a graphic artist from Guatemala, took his business to the Community Bank of the Bay in Oakland, California, because he was impressed with its full range of financial products, its friendly service, and its commitment to providing credit to individuals, businesses, and nonprofit organizations in the low-income community it serves. "We need to educate Latinos about banking, and show that there are other options," he says.

 Stay away from check-cashing stores and services. *Ni se acerquen.*

The average cost of cashing a paycheck at a check-cashing store in 1997 was 2.3 percent of the amount of the check, according to a survey by the Consumer Federation of America. For a Social Security check, the fee was 2.2 percent. And for a personal check, you had to pay a steep 9.4 percent.

Although that may not sound like much, it adds up. Using these figures, you'd pay a total of $374.50 to cash 50 paychecks worth $320 each. You'd pay $132 to cash 12 Social Security checks worth $500 each. And you'd pay $84.24 to cash 6 personal checks worth $150 each. Since banks and credit unions often don't charge their customers anything to cash a check, using a check-cashing store is just throwing away money. ¡Ay! ¿Y para qué?

Unfortunately, many mainstream banks and financial services companies, including GE Capital, Chase Manhattan, and Citibank, to name a few, have recognized the big profits that can be made with check cashing services and are starting to launch joint ventures with some of the biggest players in the check cashing industry.

Although we're dead set against it, some of you may insist on using check cashers. If so, there are steps to take that can help save money and avoid problems:

- ❏ Find out if your employer, a local supermarket, or other local retailer offers check cashing, which is often less expensive.
- ❏ Get a complete disclosure of charges and fees before using any check cashing service.
- ❏ *Siempre* get a receipt.

Figuring out where to turn for help if you run into trouble with a dishonest check casher can be confusing because different states are regulated by different agencies. If you have a complaint and don't know where to go, call your state consumer affairs office or state attorney general's office.

 Open a savings and checking account with a bank, S&L, or credit union.

Having a savings and checking account at a bank, Savings and Loan (which are also known as thrifts), or credit union *(cooperativa de crédito)* saves you money you would have spent on exorbitant check cashing fees or money orders.

Both banks and S&Ls are for-profit businesses owned by their stockholders. Banks were originally chartered to lend money to businesses and corporations, while S&Ls were chartered to make home loans. Today, there's virtually no difference between the services you receive from banks and S&Ls, except that S&Ls must use at least 65 percent of their assets to provide home loans.

Banks and S&Ls offer savings and checking accounts, certificates of deposit, money market accounts, credit cards, ATMs, debit cards, auto and personal loans, and mortgages. Some banks are also expanding into insurance (explained in Chapter 3) and mutual funds (explained in Chapter 4).

Checking and savings accounts at most banks and S&Ls are federally insured by the Federal Deposit Insurance Corp. (FDIC) for a maximum of $100,000. There's an important caveat: Mutual funds, even those sold by banks, are not insured.

If you have more than $100,000 you can keep it all safe by splitting up your deposits among several different financial institutions or holding the accounts in the names of various individual family members. Of course, if you have that much in liquid assets, you should consider more aggressive investments. (Investing is explained in depth in Chapter 4.)

Banks and S&Ls, especially the bigger ones, can be very convenient. They often have hundreds of branches and ATMs, sometimes across many states. They offer direct deposit, which is the electronic transfer of your paycheck from your employer to your account. Also, many offer on-line banking via your home computer, which can facilitate paying your bills and reconciling your accounts.

But you'll often pay a premium for these conveniences. In recent years, many banks have also been increasing basic fees, or adding new fees. Some banks charge for writing and cashing checks, bouncing checks, making a deposit or withdrawal, falling below the required minimum balance, or even speaking to a live teller.

Opening an account at a bank can also be a bureaucratic nightmare. Most banks typically require two pieces of identification, one with your picture on it, to open an account. You may also need a Social Security number or a credit card, both of which take some effort for recent immigrants to obtain. (For a list of Hispanic-owned banks and S&Ls, see page 10.)

ACCIÓN To check the insurance status of a bank or S&L, call the FDIC at 800-934-3342. A brochure, *Your Insured Deposit/Sus Depósitos Asegurados,* is available for free in English and Spanish by calling the same number, or writing to the FDIC, Office of Consumer Affairs, 5501 17th St. NW, Washington, DC 20429.

Credit unions, nonprofit cooperatives that emphasize saving and education, are typically a low-cost alternative to banks and S&Ls. But they aren't open to the general public. Credit unions are comprised of people who share

HISPANIC-OWNED BANKS AND SAVINGS INSTITUTIONS

CALIFORNIA
Mission National Bank, San Francisco	415-826-3627
Pan American Bank, Los Angeles	323-264-3310

FLORIDA
Capital Bank, Miami	305-536-1500
Continental National Bank of Miami	305-642-2440
Eastern National Bank, Miami	305-995-5800
Gulf Bank, Miami	305-443-4853
Hemisphere National Bank, Miami	305-856-5600
Interamerican FSB, Miami	305-223-1434

MARYLAND
Capital Bank, NA, Rockville	301-279-8900

NEW MEXICO
Centinel Bank of Taos, Taos	505-758-6700
Community Bank, Española	505-753-2383
Interamerica Bank NA, Albuquerque	505-837-9500

NEW YORK
Banco Central Hispano	212-785-0700
New York National Bank, Bronx	718-589-5000

PUERTO RICO
Banco Central Hispano, Hato Rey	787-250-2500
Banco Financiero de Puerto Rico, Ponce	787-840-0050
Banco Popular de Puerto Rico, San Juan	787-765-9800
Doral Federal Savings Bank, Catano	787-788-2626
Eurobank and Trust Co., Hato Rey	787-751-7340
Fajardo Federal Savings Bank, Fajardo	787-863-3555
Firstbank, Santurce	787-729-8200
Oriental Bank, Humacao	787-850-2000

TEXAS
Brownsville National Bank, Brownsville	956-546-4503
Commerce Bank, Laredo	956-724-1616
Falcon National Bank, Laredo	956-723-2265
Falfurrias State Bank, Falfurrias	512-325-5646
International Bank NA, Brownsville	956-982-9661
International Bank of Commerce, Laredo	956-722-7611
International Bank of Commerce, Zapata	956-765-8361
Nueces National Bank, Corpus Christi	512-888-8181

NOTE: We're not endorsing these financial institutions. You should compare their fees and services with other banks, S&Ls, and credit unions.

SOURCE: CREATIVE INVESTMENT RESEARCH, WASHINGTON, D.C., WWW2.ARI.NET/CIRM

a "common bond" such as the same employer, union, association, place of worship, or neighborhood.

Credit unions are owned by their members. If one person qualifies to join, then generally everyone in that person's family can become a member. A small paid staff or even volunteers often run credit unions.

Larger credit unions offer services similar to those of banks and S&Ls. These services include savings and checking accounts (which credit unions call share draft accounts), direct deposit, CDs and money market accounts, credit, ATM and debit cards, auto and personal loans, mortgages, and insurance. Smaller credit unions may offer just savings accounts.

Most credit unions are federally insured by the National Credit Union Administration (NCUA) for a maximum of $100,000. As with a bank or S&L, if you have more than $100,000 you can keep it all safe by splitting up your deposits among several different credit unions or holding the accounts in the names of various individual family members.

ACCIÓN To learn whether a credit union is federally insured, call the National Credit Union Administration at 703-518-6300, or check its Web site at www.ncua.gov/.

Credit unions can be less expensive to use than banks. Since they emphasize education and saving, they tend to spend a lot of time with customers. Loan evaluations may take into consideration your character and reputation as well as your credit record. If you don't have a credit record, they can help you build one.

Although credit unions need to verify your identification before you open an account, they're often more willing to accept a utility bill, paycheck stub or a receipt from government benefits as proof of identification instead of a driver's license, passport, or Social Security number.

But credit unions have some drawbacks. Not everyone is eligible to join. The credit union you are eligible for may not be conveniently located. And most credit unions don't have nearly as many branches or ATMs as commercial banks or S&Ls.

ACCIÓN To find out if you're eligible to join a credit union, call the Credit Union National Association (800-356-965), or write to the group at P.O. Box 431, Madison, WI 53701. Include a stamped, self-addressed envelope. You can also check the association's Web site at www.cuna.org/.

 You may need to establish an Electronic Transfer Account to receive federal benefits.

An immediate and practical reason why Latinos should maintain accounts at banks, S&Ls or credit unions is that the U.S. Treasury on January 2, 1999, stopped sending paper checks for all government payments except tax refunds (many states have also done so). Checks to Social Security and welfare recipients, government workers, and suppliers are now sent electronically to accounts at financial institutions. The only exceptions are consumers who show they have a physical disability, a geographic barrier, or a financial hardship.

The U.S. Treasury Department plans to establish free or low-cost Electronic Transfer Accounts at federally insured financial institutions, but probably not until the year 2000. These accounts will likely permit deposits and withdrawal of funds at ATMs and special terminals. In the meantime, you need to find banks, S&Ls, and credit unions that offer low-cost direct deposit deals (keep reading to find out how).

Many money transfer services and check cashing stores are also developing products to help them retain customers after the government eliminates paper checks. But these products are expensive. Western Union, for example, has introduced Benefits Quick Cash, which lets consumers cash federal benefits checks at its retail outlets for $7.50 per transaction. Not only is this service more expensive than many bank or credit union products, it won't help you establish credit.

 Support a community development bank or credit union.

Community development banks (*bancos comunitarios del desarrollo*) and community development credit unions (*cooperativas de crédito comunitario del*

desarrollo) tend to be located in areas that have traditionally been under-served by mainstream financial institutions, especially in low-income and minority neighborhoods. Some community development credit unions were launched specifically to serve Latinos. These credit unions use most of their deposits to make loans to members and to local community reinvestment projects such as low-income housing.

Community development banks and credit unions serve many people who may be using financial institutions for the very first time. But they also draw more sophisticated clients who prefer to have their deposits used for socially responsible causes and to provide services in underrepresented neighborhoods.

All it takes is a membership fee of $10 and an initial minimum deposit of $50 to open a savings account at the Neighborhood Trust Federal Credit Union in New York City, which serves a largely Dominican community. Personal loans of between $500 and $5,000, with interest rates as low as 8 percent, have been given to members who have no credit histories. Money orders cost just 49¢.

The Delmarva Fife Federal Credit Union in Bridgeville, Delaware, opened a mobile branch to serve the large Mexican, Peruvian, and Guatemalan communities that work in the area's poultry processing industry. Members get free check cashing services if they keep $50 in savings and deposit at least $5 into their checking accounts every time they cash a check.

The Community Trust Federal Credit Union in Apopka, Florida, has three branches serving Mexican and Guatemalan migrant farm workers. Savings accounts can be opened for a $5 annual membership fee and a $10 minimum initial deposit, and a credit card is available for an annual fee of $6. (For members of the Latino Community Development Credit Union Network, see pages 14–15.)

ACCIÓN To find a community development bank near you, check the Social Investment Forum's Web site at www.socialinvest.org/, or call Co-Op America's Fax Information Center at 800-380-FAXX to get information by fax. You can also get a copy of the *Directory of Socially Responsible Investment Services* by sending $2 to the Social Investment Forum, P.O. Box 57216, Washington, DC 20037, or by calling 202-872-5319. To find a

The Latino Community Development Credit Union Network

Arizona

Chicanos Por La Causa, Phoenix	602-257-0700
First American Credit Union, Window Rock	520-871-4767
South Park/Pueblo Gardens Federal Credit Union, Tucson	520-770-9345

California

Comunidades Federal Credit Union, Los Angeles	213-251-2190
El Futuro Credit Union, Porterville	209-784-7901
Episcopal Community Federal Credit Union, Los Angeles	213-482-2040
Family Federal Credit Union, Wilmington	310-835-6132
Mission Area Federal Credit Union, San Francisco	415-431-2268
Santa Cruz Community Credit Union, Santa Cruz	408-425-7708
Watts United Credit Union, Los Angeles	323-564-7854

Colorado

Denver Community Credit Union, Denver	303-292-3910

Delaware

Delmarva Fife Federal Credit Union, Bridgeville	302-422-0155

Florida

Community Trust Credit Union, Apopka	407-880-4300
POC Federal Credit Union, St. Petersburg	813-327-8690

Illinois

Austin/West Garfield Federal Credit Union, Chicago	773-287-2943
Cosmopolitan Federal Credit Union, Chicago	773-536-7212
North Side Community Federal Credit Union, Chicago	773-549-1537

community development credit union near you, contact the National Federation of Community Development Credit Unions by calling 212-809-1850, or sending a self-addressed, stamped envelope to 120 Wall St., 10th Floor, New York, NY 10005.

INDIANA
Near Eastside Community Federal Credit Union,
Indianapolis   317-633-3100

NEW JERSEY
La Casa Federal Credit Union, Newark   973-497-2700

NEW YORK
Bethex Federal Credit Union, Bronx   718-299-3062
Brooklyn Ecumenical Federal Credit Union,
Brooklyn   718-858-8803
Central Brooklyn Federal Credit Union, Brooklyn   718-399-1763
Lower East Side People's Federal Credit Union,
New York   212-529-8197
Neighborhood Trust Federal Credit Union,
New York   212-740-0900
Progressive Neighborhood Federal Credit Union,
Rochester   716-328-5410
Roberto Clemente Federal Credit Union, Bronx   718-992-1220
Transfiguration Parish Federal Credit Union,
Brooklyn   718-388-0729
Union Settlement Federal Credit Union, New York   212-828-6061

NORTH CAROLINA
Victory Masonic Mutual Credit Union, Winston-Salem 910-724-9081

PENNSYLVANIA
Borinquen Federal Credit Union, Philadelphia   215-228-4180

PUERTO RICO
San Juan Community Federal Credit Union, San Juan   956-781-6845

TEXAS
Common Ground Community Credit Union, Dallas   214-421-7224
Weslaco Catholic Federal Credit Union, Weslaco   956-968-8371

SOURCE: NATIONAL FEDERATION OF COMMUNITY DEVELOPMENT CREDIT UNIONS

CONSEJO
T I P

Know what to ask when choosing a financial institution.

The idea of giving your business to the nearest bank or credit union may have a lot of appeal. *Eso es lo más fácil. Pero no lo mejor.* Here are the things you should think about when choosing a financial institution:

Convenience. Nobody wants to spend an hour getting across town to a bank or ATM. Find out whether the financial institution has a branch near your home and one near your place of employment. If you can do most of your banking through the mail or computer, location may not initially be as important, but think about the day you may want to talk to a bank employee in person.

Services. What do you need? If it's just a basic savings and checking account, you may want to stick with a no-frills, low-cost credit union. If you'll need a variety of services—a credit card, an auto loan, or a mortgage—find an institution that offers these services. Are Spanish-language tellers, services, and informational materials available?

Costs and interest rates. Are you more concerned about earning higher interest rates on your accounts, or paying lower fees for services tied to your checking and savings accounts? There's a good possibility you won't be able to get both at a single institution.

Community commitment. The Community Reinvestment Act (CRA) of 1977 was passed by Congress to combat "redlining", the practice of accepting deposits from low-income communities but not making any loans to them. The CRA requires all banks and S&Ls to meet the credit needs of the communities where they do business.

To get a sense of how a financial institution is adhering to the CRA, look at its CRA statement, which defines its community geographically, identifies the community's needs, and explains how it is meeting those needs. Ask for its CRA evaluation rating as well, which is based on its reports of the race, income, and sex of people who apply for and get loans. Both the CRA statement and evaluation are public documents that the institution must give to you upon your request. Some financial institutions may charge a nominal fee for them.

ACCIÓN To get CRA ratings from the FDIC's Web site go to www.fdic.gov/publish, then click on "Community Reinvestment Act," followed by "Automated CRA Ratings Search."

Write down what your ideal financial institution must offer in terms of services and convenience. Then take your "tienen que tener" list

and shop around to find the bank, S&L, or credit union that best suits your needs.

Most of us use banks or credit unions primarily for savings and checking accounts, safe deposit boxes, and to obtain credit. Although all savings and checking accounts provide basically the same type of service, you'll find a wide range of packages, interest rates, and fees at different financial institutions.

With a basic passbook savings account (*cuenta de libreta de ahorros*), all the money you deposit is completely liquid, which means you can get access to the funds whenever you like. *¡Cuidado con eso!* Depending on the financial institution, interest on the money you keep in the account is compounded (*compuesto*) daily, monthly, twice a year, or once a year. With compounding, you earn interest on the interest you've already earned, as well as on the original principal amount. (Two other types of bank savings accounts—money market accounts and CDs—will be discussed later in this chapter.)

With a checking account (*cuenta corriente*), you transfer money from your account to someone else by signing a paper check. Credit unions call them share draft accounts. Checking and share draft accounts are more convenient to use than cash or money orders. They're a good way to keep a record of your expenses. And they provide proof of payment. There must be sufficient funds in your account for the check to clear. If not, the check will bounce and you'll get socked with penalty fees (and possibly *mala fama*).

Shopping for a checking or share draft account can get complicated. Find out what the monthly service fees are, whether there are any charges for writing or cashing checks, what the minimum initial deposit is, what the minimum balance is to avoid some or all fees, and what the interest rate is, if any.

In addition, find out how much it costs if you bounce a check or stop payment on a check, if you request a copy of an old check, if you speak to a customer service representative by telephone, if you see a teller in person, and if you want to have all of your canceled checks returned to you. Ask how long it takes to get access to funds from a check you've deposited.

Fee structures are constantly changing, so periodically shop around to see if you can get a better deal elsewhere.

Many banks are touting so-called "relationship banking" or "linked accounts" that provide free checking or lower-rate loans if you keep all your accounts at one bank. *Cuidado.* You need to analyze these deals carefully. You may be able to save more money by keeping your checking and savings accounts at one institution, and your CDs and money market accounts at another.

> **ACCIÓN** Cut costs by ordering checks directly from check printers instead of the bank. Call Checks in the Mail Inc. at 800-733-4443, The Check Store at 800-424-3257, or Current at 800-426-0822.

Outstanding bad checks, which are checks you've written but didn't have enough money to actually pay, from an old bank account may prevent you from opening a new one at another bank. But in most cases, just paying off the old checks will allow you to open a new checking account.

> **ACCIÓN** To find out if you have any outstanding bad checks call ChexSystems at 800-428-9623 or Equifax Check Services at 800-352-5970.

 Don't use safe deposit boxes to store cash, other people's property, or important documents that you may need in a hurry.

Safe deposit boxes can be rented from financial institutions to store valuable items that you don't want to keep at home in case of fire or theft. These items include jewelry, rare coins, family heirlooms, or important documents such as birth and marriage certificates, mortgages, and citizenship papers.

However, there are certain things that should not be kept in a safe deposit box (unless it's held jointly with someone else in certain states) because it can take a long time to get access to the items if the renter dies. These items include original wills, cemetery deeds, burial instructions, and other people's property. Don't store large sums of cash in a safe deposit box, either, because it may be viewed as a sign of criminal activity or intent to evade income taxes. Plus, you don't earn any interest on money in a safe-deposit box. (See Chapter 8 for more on safe deposit boxes.)

 Avoid interest-bearing checking accounts unless you do the math and know you're coming out ahead on a consistent basis.

Do the math before you get seduced by promises of interest-bearing checking accounts, some of which impose high fees and require you to keep a big minimum balance.

Be aware that credit unions offer even better deals on checking accounts, which they call share draft accounts. And about 64 percent of all credit unions offer free share draft accounts with no minimum balance, compared with just 32 percent of banks that offer free checking, according to the Credit Union National Association (see the table below for comparison).

 Use certificates of deposit and money market accounts only for short-term savings.

SOURCE: BANK RATE MONITOR, CREDIT UNION NATIONAL ASSOCIATION

COST COMPARISONS: BANKS VERSUS CREDIT UNIONS

	BANK	CREDIT UNION
MINIMUM BALANCE (Interest-bearing checking/share account)	$319	$308
MINIMUM BALANCE TO AVOID FEES (Interest-bearing checking/share account)	$1,647	$731
MINIMUM BALANCE (No-interest checking/share account)	$80	$69
MINIMUM BALANCE TO AVOID FEES (No interest checking/share account)	$346	$381

When it comes time for Latinos to branch out from basic savings and checking accounts, certificates of deposit and money market accounts are often the first, sometimes the only, products we use. *Somos un poco cobardes.* There's nothing inherently wrong with this strategy, but it's important to remember that CDs and money market accounts should only be used for cash reserves and short-term savings—no more than five years. (For longer-term investing see Chapter 4.)

When you put your money in a CD, you're lending money to the bank or financial institution for a certain period of time in return for a specific interest rate during that period. Generally, the longer you agree to leave your money, the higher the interest rate. Periods range from three months to five years.

The initial minimum investment for a CD can be as low as $500 and as high as $100,000. If a CD is a bank product, it's federally insured for up to $100,000. Other institutions such as mutual fund firms or financial services companies may offer CDs with higher rates or lower minimum deposits, but they're not federally insured. Be aware that some banks impose penalties for cashing in your CD before it expires (early withdrawal), so ask about their policies.

Pero cuidado con una cosa. When your CD matures, be sure to tell your financial institution whether you intend to collect the money or roll the money over into another CD. If you don't give instructions, the financial institution will automatically put the money into another CD. Most financial institutions will tell you when a CD is about to mature. But to be on the safe side you may also want to make a note of it on your calendar.

Money market accounts are a hybrid of the traditional savings account and a standard checking account. They pay higher interest rates than other bank accounts do, but often require a minimum balance of between $2,000 and $25,000. The interest rate, which can change from day to day, is also referred to as the return and must be stated as an annual percentage yield (APY). The annual percentage rate (APR), on the other hand, is the effective rate you'll pay for credit agreements, such as car loans.

You have easy access to the money in your money market account, but the number of monthly and/or annual transactions is usually restricted. If you go over the limit you'll be charged a fee. Money market accounts from banks, S&Ls, or credit unions are federally insured for up to $100,000.

(These accounts are different from money market mutual funds, which we describe in Chapter 4.)

Financial planners (including one of your Lauras) recommend using both CDs and money market accounts. But if you don't have a lot of money to start with and are trying to choose between a CD or a money market account, you need to think about what kind of liquidity you need, what the interest rates are, and what your short-term goals are.

If the money you're setting aside is purely a cash reserve that's to be used in emergencies, keep it in a money market account so you have easy and fast access to the funds. If you know the money you're saving won't be needed for a specific period of time, a CD may be better because you'll be likely to get a higher interest rate.

However, you can also use a combination of CDs with different maturity dates—a technique known as laddering *(escalonando)*—to maintain some liquidity and take advantage of changing interest rates.

For example, instead of putting $6,000 in a five-year CD, divide the money into six CDs that will mature every other month starting three months from now. With CDs expiring at regular intervals, you can check interest rates and either transfer the money to a money market account or roll it over into another CD.

ACCIÓN To compare interest rates for CDs, money market accounts, and other banking products, check the BanxQuote Web site at www.banx.com/. For global CD interest rates go to Treasury Worldwide's Web site at www.treasuryworldwide.com/. CD and money market rates also appear every Wednesday in *The Wall Street Journal*. They may also appear in your local newspaper's business section.

 **Learn the differences between ATM cards and debit cards.**

Automated teller machine cards let you deposit and withdraw money, transfer funds between accounts, and sometimes even get a cash advance on your credit card by using an ATM machine and a personal identification number (PIN).

For security purposes, never use your Social Security number or birthday as your PIN. Instead, why not spell out a four-letter word in Spanish?

The biggest advantage of using ATM cards is the convenience. There are thousands of ATM machines across the country (and in some foreign countries), and they're open twenty-four hours a day, seven days a week.

But ATM cards can be expensive. If you have an account at Bank A, but use Bank B's ATM machine, Bank B may charge you for this transaction. Your own bank may charge you for using its own ATMs or another bank's ATM. There may be weekly, monthly, or annual fees to gain access to the ATM system. There's a one-time fee to obtain an ATM card, and another fee to replace it if it's lost or stolen. There are also fees to use ATM systems that are part of national or international networks.

Y una cosa más: For ATM cards and debit cards, the "available balance" section at the ATM window often inflates the amount in your account by hundreds or thousands of dollars by adding your credit line (cash advance). To know exactly how much money is in your account, you must know your credit line amount, and subtract it.

ACCIÓN To avoid getting hit with ATM surcharges, find out whether your bank or credit union belongs to a network of financial institutions that don't charge ATM fees to customers and non-customers.

Like ATM cards, debit cards are used to withdraw cash directly from bank accounts. But unlike ATM cards, you can make purchases with debit cards. Using a debit card to make a purchase from a store or gas station may seem like using a credit card, but with a debit card the cost of what you buy comes straight out of your checking account. You also may not need a PIN, which makes it easier for *ladrones* to clean out your accounts if your debit card is lost or stolen.

As with ATM cards, debit cards make it imperative that you keep track of exactly how much money you have in your accounts. If you're not sure how much money you actually have, and you make a big purchase with a debit card that pushes you over the limit, you'll get hit with penalty fees when your charges bounce. Be sure to enter your ATM and debit card withdrawals into your check register, just as you would with checks.

Another drawback is that debit cards are regulated by the federal Electronic Funds Transfer Act, which states that while your liability is limited to $50 if you notify the bank within two days of discovering the loss or theft, you're liable for up to $500 if the bank is notified after two days, and liable for a potentially unlimited amount if the bank isn't notified within sixty days.

Fortunately, several banks as well as Visa U.S.A. and MasterCard International, two big debit card issuers, have agreed to limit lost or stolen debit card liability to $50. Even so, find out exactly what the policy is of the bank or company that issues your debit card. (The same rules apply to the loss of ATM cards.)

You can also take steps to avoid debit card liability headaches by following some basic rules (these guidelines also apply to credit cards, which we talk about in Chapter 2):

❏ Never give your debit card number to a salesperson over the phone or over the Internet if the initial contact was unsolicited.

❏ When you get a debit card in the mail, immediately sign the back in ink.

❏ Be sure you get your debit card and receipt back after making a purchase.

❏ Keep debit card receipts in a safe place to cross-check your statements to make sure all purchases are yours.

❏ If you receive an unsolicited debit card, *rómpela a pedacitos.*

❏ Keep a list of your account numbers at home in case you ever need to report a loss or theft.

❏ Never loan your debit card to anyone.

❏ With both ATMs and debit cards, never carry your PIN in your purse or wallet, or write it on the card or on a deposit slip or envelope.

❏ Never tell your PIN to anyone; bank employees are never supposed to ask you for it.

 Read your monthly bank, S&L, or credit union statements carefully within two days of receipt.

Many of us glance at our monthly bank or credit union statements, then toss them into a drawer. These statements typically itemize all deposits, withdrawals, ATM activities, and fees. It's very important to carefully read these monthly statements within two days to make sure they match your own records.

Checking accounts usually have a form on the back that you can use to reconcile, or balance, your checkbook. The form helps you identify transactions that are outstanding—not yet processed by the bank or credit union—and see if they explain the difference between the balance in your checkbook and the balance on the statement from your bank or credit union.

If the figures don't add up, compute your figures again to make sure you haven't made a mathematical error. If you still can't determine where the problem is, contact the financial institution for help. These statements should be filed away in a safe place for at least one year.

 Weigh all your options for sending money to other countries.

There are three ways to send money to Latin America: wire transfers from a bank, credit union, U.S. post office, or service such as Western Union or MoneyGram; money orders; and a combination money order/express mail service. Each varies in price, and has its own set of benefits and drawbacks. *Vamos a ver.*

Wire transfers can be expensive, depending on which service you use. With most services, all fees are paid up front by the sender. The person who receives the money can usually pick up the funds for free. The best part is you get the peace of mind knowing that your funds have arrived, usually within minutes.

Western Union's fees are based on the amount sent, and where it's sent. The standard charge for transfers between $200.01 and $300 is $29 ($27 to Mexico). The price increases to $34 ($32 to Mexico) for amounts between $300.01 and $400. Some banks offer wire transfers, but only to their own customers. Bank of America, for example, charges a flat rate of $30 per transaction.

One of the least expensive ways to send money electronically to Latin America is through the U.S. Post Office's Dinero Seguro program. The biggest drawback is that this program can only be used to transfer money to and from California, Texas, or Chicago, and Mexico. But the program may be expanded to other U.S. cities and Latin American countries.

With Dinero Seguro, you can send up to $3,000 to a branch of Bancomer, one of Mexico's largest retail banks. The recipient can simply pick up the money from Bancomer, without having to maintain an account there. Fees range from $12 for transfers of up to $350 to $60 for transfers of between $2,251 to $3000.

At least one credit union is experimenting with wire transfers to Latin America, and many others may soon follow. The Mission Area Federal Credit Union in San Francisco has a program that allows its members to send money electronically to El Salvador's national credit union for a flat fee of just $6.50 per transaction.

International money orders are another option. Money orders cost $3 each, and can be purchased in denominations of up to $500. They can be sent to most of Latin America. The main problem is the unreliability of the mail system in many of these countries.

To address these concerns, the U.S. Post Office introduced Giro Express, international money orders sent via express mail. In most cases, Giro Express arrives within three days. You pay the $3 money order charges, plus a $15 express mail fee. However, the service is available only to Mexico.

 **Handling money wisely includes saving as much as you can. Start by figuring out what your income and expenses are.**

Before you can systematically save money, you need to determine what your income and expenses are. You need to know, on a monthly and annual basis, how much money is coming in, how much money is going out, and how much money, if any, you should have left over. One of the first things Laura the financial planner asks her clients to do is to prepare a budget.

Make a list of expenses for: groceries, school expenses, laundry, medical/dental charges or supplies, personal care, child care, entertainment, beverages, tobacco, household items, clothes, telephone, utilities, rent or mortgage, insurance, taxes, charitable contributions, bus or train fare, auto costs (loan payments, maintenance, gas, and oil), money sent to Latin America, and savings.

MAKING A BUDGET

MONTHLY INCOME:

Wages	$____	Self-employment income	$____
Dividends from stocks,		Real property income	$____
mutual funds, etc.	$____	Other pensions, royalties,	
Interest on savings accounts,		etc.	$____
CD's, bonds, etc.	$____	**Total monthly income**	**$____**

MONTHLY EXPENSES:

Mortgage payment or rent	$____	Pre-tax retirement	
Vacation home mortgage	$____	contributions	$____
Real estate taxes	$____	After-tax retirement	
Homeowners or renters	$____	contributions	$____
insurance premiums		Systematic savings	$____
Condominium fees	$____	Household maintenance	
Personal loans		cleaning, repair, painting,	
(e.g. school)	$____	gardening	$____
Charge accounts	$____	Minor home improvements	
Automobile loan	$____	(decorating)	$____
Auto maintenance (gas,		Gas and electricity	$____
license, repairs)	$____	Cable/direct/Web/TV/	
Transportation (AAA; bus,		Internet	$____
train or subway fares;		Telephone, including	
parking, tolls	$____	cellular and beeper	
Auto Insurance	$____	Answering service	$____

Write down what you actually spend on these items, then total the amounts. Think about once-a-year expenses, like a vacation or auto registration. Divide these expenses by 12 and work them into your monthly budget. Now subtract these expenses from your monthly income. Then take a look at the bottom line. *¡Coraje!* (See the exercise above for help.)

Water and garbage $____
Food and staples $____
Medical premiums (medical,
dental, vision) Pre-tax? $____
Medical expenses (not
   covered by medical
   insurance, e.g., drugs &
   alternative therapies) $____
Personal Care (massages,
   hair cuts, gym/personal
   trainer) $____
Clothing (new purchases
   and dry cleaning) $____
Pets (food, grooming,
   kennels, vet.) $____
Entertainment (dining out,
   movies, theater/opera,

concerts, sports events) $____
Travel and leisure (trans-
   portation, lodging, food,
   entertainment) $____
Education expenses $____
Child care $____
   Names:
Charitable contributions $____
Miscellaneous expenses
   (newspapers, magazines,
   books, CDs) $____
Disability insurance
   premiums $____
Life insurance premiums $____
Gifts (holidays, birthdays,
   anniversary) $____
Total monthly expenses $____

◎ **TOTAL MONTHLY INCOME, EXPENSES & DISCRETIONARY INCOME:**

TOTAL MONTHLY INCOME $____   **DISCRETIONARY MONTHLY INCOME**
TOTAL MONTHLY EXPENSES $____   **(INCOME MINUS EXPENSES)** $____

 Develop a savings plan.

If you're over budget you have two choices: Earn more by getting a higher paying job or a second job, or spend less by trimming costs. ¿Esto no es gran sorpresa, eh? The second thing may seem just as hard as the first, but economizing is more within your control.

Say you stop going out for lunch a couple of days a week and bring your food from home instead. That can save you at least $10 a week. It may not sound like much, but it adds up to a total of $520 in just one year. Also, try to save every bonus or raise instead of spending it.

ACCIÓN A brochure titled *66 Ways to Save Money/66 Formas de Ahorrar Dinero* is available free in both English and Spanish by sending a self-addressed stamped envelope to Consumer Action, 116 New Montgomery St., Suite 233, San Francisco, CA 94105.

 Pay yourself first.

Saving money is a lot like losing weight or kicking a bad habit: We know we should do it, but we don't seem to get beyond talking about it until we're forced to do so because of an emergency.

As children, Latinos are taught that patience is a great virtue. And patience is exactly what it takes to save even just a few *pesos* on a regular basis. (After all, we won't reap the rewards of our savings until a future date.) No wonder we're such good savers once we start.

The first rule of any savings plan is to pay yourself first. That means figuring out how much money you can reasonably save, and then putting that amount away in a savings account before you pay any bills or make any purchases.

A good goal is to try to save at least 10 percent of your gross income, and eventually build an emergency cash reserve that's big enough to sustain you and your family for between three and six months.

This may be difficult, especially if you've got a large family to support or are sending money back to Latin America. You may feel at times that you're being selfish by saving when there are immediate needs around you. But the best way to protect your family in the future is to save a little each day.

 Sign up for automatic payroll deposit and deduction if it's available.

Automatic payroll deposit and deduction is one of the least painful ways to cut costs and start saving for a rainy day or a sunny holiday. Ask your employer if this service is available. Many banks offer free or low-cost checking with direct deposit because the electronic transfer of funds saves them money over processing the paper check. You can set it up so that most of your pay goes into a checking account to pay your bills, while the rest goes directly into a savings account. Since you never see the amount you're putting into savings, *ni lo notan, amigos.*

ACCIÓN For a free budgeting kit called *Money Helps* in English or Spanish, write to the National Center for Financial Education, P.O. Box 34570, San Diego, CA 92163, or check the Web site at www.ncfe.org/.

 Beware of scams by phony financial institutions.

In recent years, there's been at least one case where Latinos were the main victims of fraudulent financial companies. In Washington, D.C., in the 1980s and 1990s, a company set up shop in a Salvadoran neighborhood and operated as a bank, even though it was never licensed as one. When it went under, an estimated 2,500 depositors lost $6.5 million.

If you have any questions about a company that promotes itself as a bank, call the FDIC to make sure that it's legitimate and that its deposits are insured for up to $100,000. And if you have a complaint about a financial institution that you haven't been able to resolve, there are many organizations you can call.

ACCIÓN To complain about a national bank, call the Office of the Comptroller of the Currency at 202-874-5000; for S&Ls, call the Office of Thrift Supervision at 800-842-6929; for credit unions, call the National Credit Union Administration at 703-518-6429; for state banks that are regulated by the Federal Reserve Board of Governors, call 202-452-3693; for state banks that are regulated by the FDIC, call 800-934-3342; for private financial institutions such as check-cashing stores, call your state banking commissioner or state attorney general's office. A brochure called *Tip Sheet for Resolving Credit and Banking Complaints/Resolviendo Quejas Tocante Crédito y Asuntos Bancarios* is available for free in English and Spanish by calling the U.S. Department of Commerce at 202-482-5001, or writing to the department's Office of Consumer Affairs at 14th St. and Constitution Ave. NW, Room 5718, Washington, DC 20230.

❏ Stay away from check cashing stores.
❏ Open an account at a bank or credit union. Shop around to find one that best suits your needs and pocketbook.
❏ Compare financial products such as savings, checking and money-market accounts, and CDs to get the best fees and interest rates.
❏ Use CDs and money market accounts only for cash reserves and short-term savings vehicles.
❏ Learn the differences between ATM and debit cards.
❏ Carefully read your monthly statements from your bank, S&L, or credit union.
❏ Know your options for sending money to another country.
❏ Figure out what your income and expenses are.
❏ Develop a savings plan.
❏ Sign up for automatic payroll deposit and deduction if it's available.

ADDITIONAL RESOURCES

Recommended Books

The Budget Kit: The Common Cents Money Management Workbook, by Judy Lawrence (Chicago: Dearborn Trade, 1997).

Your Money or Your Life: Transforming Your Relationship With Money and Achieving Financial Independence, by Joe Domínguez and Vicki Robin (New York: Penguin Books, 1993). Also available in Spanish: *La Bolsa O la Vida: Como Dejar de Ser Esclavo del Dinero y Mejorar la Calidad de la Vida* (New York: Penguin Ediciones, 1997).

Credit and Debt

"PAY WHAT YOU OWE AND YOU WILL BE CURED OF YOUR COMPLAINT" —PERU

A GOOD CREDIT RECORD IN THE UNITED STATES MAKES IT EASIER TO rent an apartment, to get lower interest rates on auto and home loans, to qualify for affordable insurance plans, and even to get some jobs. But credit used improperly can hurt as much as it helps.

Rafael, a city employee in Corpus Cristi, Texas, learned the hard way. When he started a new job after a stint in the U.S. Marine Corps, he didn't want any credit cards. "I don't like being in debt," he says. Yet he knew he and his wife had to establish a credit record to eventually qualify for a home loan.

The couple started small, with one department store credit card. Within a few years, they had five cards, all of which they used to buy household goods such as television sets and furniture. Before they knew it, their debts totaled more than $10,000.

"We were living a champagne lifestyle on a Kool-Aid budget," says Rafael, who blames the strain of financial problems for the breakup of his marriage. "There were times when my car was on empty and I had no money in the bank. I didn't know how I was going to make it home."

Credit can make life easier if it's used correctly. Juan, a dishwasher from Mexico, was able to obtain a personal loan of $800 from the Community Trust Federal Credit Union in Apopka, Florida, after establishing a nontraditional credit history (explained later). After paying off that loan, he was able to get a credit card with a $500 limit. "I hope to get a car loan someday," he says.

About 46.7 percent of all U.S. Latinos have some sort of credit card, compared with 75.2 percent of non-Latino whites, according to Miami-based Strategy Research Corp. More U.S.-born Latinos have credit cards than foreign-born Latinos, 62 percent versus 42 percent.

Although fewer Latinos have credit cards, those who do may be following in Rafael's footsteps and carrying high-interest debt over every month instead of settling bills as soon as possible. Lower-income Latinos often fall victim to finance companies, check cashers, used car salesmen, rent-to-own stores, and even loan sharks, all offering credit at outrageously high interest rates.

Latinos from all walks of life—U.S.-born and immigrants—are also ruining their credit records by co-signing loans or credit cards for relatives. We all want to help our families. But we need to be sure we can afford to assume other people's debt before we co-sign for them. *Al fin no ayudamos a la familia si solamente compartimos la miseria de deudas.*

For some immigrants, part of the problem is simply a lack of familiarity with the concept of credit. Many Latin American countries are cash-based societies, with credit available only to the wealthy.

While it's important to establish and maintain a good credit record, at the same time we must learn how to use credit, where to shop for the best deals, which lenders to avoid, what to do if we can't pay our bills, how to rebuild a bad credit record, and where to go for help if we can't solve our own problems.

 Understand how your credit report is compiled.

Credit reports (*registros de crédito*) are compiled by three major credit bureaus: Experian (formerly TRW), Equifax, and TransUnion. There are two types of credit reports: a standard credit report contains your financial history and is used by a lender before deciding whether or not to give you credit; an investigative report, including employment reports, may contain more information about your lifestyle, and is usually prepared if you're taking out a large insurance policy or are a candidate for a high-level job.

Your credit report contains your name, address, previous addresses, date of birth, Social Security number, the names and addresses of your current and previous employers, and perhaps your phone number. If you're married, your spouse's name and Social Security number may also appear.

In addition, your credit report contains a list of your credit accounts, when they were opened, whether you've paid your accounts on time, how much money you still owe on the accounts, and whether the accounts are held jointly with another person.

Public record information, such as a bankruptcy, state or federal tax liens (legal claims attached to property of an individual who is delinquent in tax payments), court cases to which you are a party, court judgments when you lose a lawsuit, divorces, and even criminal arrests and convictions also appear. So will a listing of everyone who's asked to see your credit report within the previous two years.

For a standard report, credit bureaus don't collect personal information such as race, religious preference, medical history, political preference, friends, criminal record, or any other type of information that's unrelated to your credit. However, information about your personal life may be compiled for an investigative report.

Potential and current employers are allowed to see a modified version of your credit report, called an employment report, for hiring and promoting purposes. This type of report lists your current employer, your financial obligations, public-record information, and past-due accounts. Under federal law, no one can obtain your employment report without first getting your written permission.

Creditors generally look at the "three Cs" when deciding whether you're creditworthy or not: credit history, or how responsible you are about paying back your bills; capacity, or your ability to pay back loans based on your income; and collateral, or what property creditors can seize from you if you don't pay back the loan.

Some creditors will look at your application and use their own judgment when deciding whether to approve credit. But most use a system known as credit scoring (*puntuación de crédito*), a mathematical calculation based on the information in your credit report. The actual number won't appear on your credit report.

References that can improve your credit score include a regular job, checking and savings accounts, other accounts held in your own name, and timely payment of credit card and department store bills, mortgages, and car loans. On the other hand, your credit score can be lowered by late payments, bankruptcies, or loans from finance companies, which we explain later in this chapter.

Other factors that can prevent you from obtaining credit are having too many credit cards, being close to or over your credit limit, having too many inquiries from lenders on your credit report (applying for a lot of credit may be a warning sign of financial problems), and a low income-to-debt ratio (*razón ingresos-deudas*), a measurement of how much debt you have compared with your income.

There is no such thing as a good score or a bad score on your credit report. That's because each lender will look at the data differently and use its own model to come up with a number. One may decide to extend credit to you based on the number it comes up with, while another won't.

If you're turned down for credit based on information in a credit report, the creditor must tell you the name and address of the credit bureau that supplied the report. It must also disclose the reason for the denial if you request it in writing.

You can obtain a free copy of your credit report if you ask for it within 60 days of being denied credit, insurance, employment, or rental housing because of information in the report, or if you suffer an "adverse action" such as a decrease in your credit limit or an increased interest rate. A free copy of your credit report is also available if you've been unemployed, but are returning to work; you believe you've been a victim of fraud; you receive public assistance; or you live in Colorado, Georgia, Maryland, Massachusetts, New Jersey, or Vermont.

ACCIÓN A brochure called *Fair Credit Reporting Act/Ley Sobre Justa Información de Crédito* is available for free in English and Spanish by calling the Federal Deposit Insurance Corp. at 800-934-3342, or writing to the FDIC's Office of Consumer Affairs at 550 17th St. NW, Washington, DC 20429.

If you have no credit record whatsoever, build a nontraditional credit record.

You may be able to obtain credit for the very first time by building a non-traditional credit record. *Todo el mundo tiene que empezar por un lado.* First, try to hold a steady job and live at the same address for at least six months. At the same time, open a checking and savings account, and make regular deposits to the savings account, no matter how small. Pay your utility and telephone bills on time.

Next, find out if you can use records showing timely payment of your rent and other bills to obtain credit from clothing, furniture, appliance, or jewelry stores in your neighborhood. Although interest rates may be higher than bank credit cards, small local merchants often let you pay off your purchases over time if you can prove financial responsibility. Just be sure the creditor reports your payment history to a credit bureau. Pay these bills *en total y pronto.* You want the credit, not the debt.

Many credit unions, and even some banks, are also willing to provide small personal loans and car loans to people with good nontraditional credit histories. By paying off these bank and credit union loans regularly, you will establish a good credit record, making it much easier for you to obtain credit cards and other loans.

When trying to establish a nontraditional credit history, be sure all of the bills are in your name only. If you're sharing a home with several people you can take turns and put all the bills in your name, then switch them to another person's name once you've established credit. Or you can act as a co-signer for others in the household after you've established credit. *Pero siempre tenga cuidado con lo que firma—entienda bien a que se compromete.*

 **Get a secured credit card or small personal loan to build a traditional credit record, but shop around for the best deal.**

The easiest and best way to establish a traditional credit record is to obtain a major credit card, use it regularly, and pay off all or most of the balance every month for at least six months. If you don't have any credit history, or are rebuilding a bad credit history, you may have to start with a secured credit card *(tarjeta de crédito garantizada con cuenta de ahorros)* backed by a collateral deposit *(depósito colateral)* in the bank or credit union that issues the card. Your deposit will be kept in the bank or credit union for as long you own the credit card. If you don't pay your bill, the bank or credit union will take the payment from your deposit. Try to find a secured credit card that lets you convert it to a regular credit card after a few years if you use it correctly.

When shopping around for a secured credit card, look for one that has no or low annual fees, a low interest rate, no application fee, and pays interest on your deposit. (We'll tell you how to find good deals later in this chapter.) Also, make sure the issuer of the secured card reports your payment record to a credit bureau. It's better if the issuer doesn't tell the credit bureau that your account is a secured card.

Passbook loans are another option. By putting a few hundred dollars in a bank or credit union, you can get a loan for the same amount, then pay it all back. However, if you have enough money to do this, you might as well get a secured credit card. You can also establish credit by getting a co-signed or guaranteed credit card *(cuenta de tarjeta de crédito garantizada)* in which the co-signer promises to repay the charges if you don't.

ACCIÓN A brochure called *Establishing Good Credit/Como Establecer Buen Crédito* is available in English and Spanish by sending a self-addressed, stamped envelope to Consumer Action, 116 New Montgomery St., Suite 233, San Francisco, CA 94105.

 Learn how to shop around for the best credit card deals.

Be aware of the many hidden charges that some credit cards are levying. Factors to consider when choosing a credit card include:

Finance charges. The finance charge, or interest rate, is the commission you pay the credit card issuer for lending you the money. With most credit cards, if you pay off your bill in full every month, you avoid a finance charge. If you don't pay the full amount due, you'll owe finance charges on the amount you carry over to the next month.

The finance charge is listed on the monthly statement as the annual percentage rate (*tasa porcentual anual*), or APR, and the monthly periodic rate (*tasa periódica mensual*), which is the APR divided by 12. For example, if you maintain a balance of $1,000 on a credit card with an annual APR of 19.8 percent, you'll pay about $198 per year, or $16.50 of interest per month. What's a good deal? Interest rates change often. To find the best deals at any given moment, see the next *Acción* in this chapter.

Some credit card companies have "teaser" rates that offer low APRs. *Tengan cuidado.* Many of these rates are "introductory," applying for only a short period of time, and may be voided if you make a late payment. Others apply only to cash advances or balances that are transferred from other credit cards. Read the application carefully because sometimes you'll get charged the regular rate instead of the teaser rate.

Switching to a "teaser" rate may be a wise way to lower your interest payments as part of a plan to systematically pay down your debt. But you must be aware of what the rules and time frames are for the "teaser," and you need to be disciplined about paying the debt off.

Balance calculation method. The method a credit card issuer uses to calculate finance charges can have a big effect on how much your credit cards cost. Like grace periods, this can also be *complicadísimo.* Suffice it to say, stick with cards that say they use the average daily balance, which averages each day's debt, and charges you interest on that amount.

Grace periods. A grace period is the time between the closing date of the billing cycle and the date you have to pay the balance in full to avoid finance charges. Definitely get a card with a grace period. Otherwise, you'll be paying interest on all of your purchases even if you pay your bill immediately. *Esta es la clave:* You can only take advantage of a grace period by paying off your bills in full each month.

Annual fees. Some credit cards require holders to pay an annual fee to maintain the card, but many cards have no annual fee. There's often a trade-off between no annual fees and low interest rates (although you may be able to find a card with both if you shop around). Which you choose depends on how you use your card. If you pay your bills off every month, which is what we advise, you don't have to worry about what your interest rate is as long as your card has a grace period. In that case, get a no-fee card. If you tend to carry over a lot of debt, you may want to think about finding a credit card with the lowest possible interest rate, even if it has an annual fee.

Other fees. Cash advance fees *(cargos de efectivo por adelantado)* are usually a percentage of the amount of money you borrow. They are usually very high. Late fees are charges for late payment of bills. Over-the-limit fees are imposed for going over your credit limit. Transaction fees are levied every time you use your card. Unbelievably, some cards are now charging fees for paying off your entire bill every month. Always read the small print. Some banks will also charge you a fee if you close your account, if you don't use your credit card often enough, or if you make too many inquiries about your account such as what your account balance is or how much available credit you have.

Minimum payments. Some cards require smaller minimum payments than others. All this does, however, is stretch your payments out even longer. If you're paying a high interest rate to begin with, this only adds to your overall cost. Always try to pay more than the minimum amount.

Fuzzy interest rates. Tiered-rate cards charge lower rates for higher balances, and higher rates for lower balances. Variable-rate *(tasa variable)* cards change interest rates quarterly or semi-annually depending on the credit card company. Even "fixed-rate" credit cards aren't always fixed. Again, read the fine print and know the exact terms of the credit. The creditors need only to give you 15 days notice before changing the rate.

Rewards. Credit cards that promise money back or frequent flier miles every time you use them often come with annual fees or high interest rates. You often have to charge hundreds, if not thousands, of dollars to collect on the rewards. *Piénsenlo bien.* Before you sign up for one of these, take a hard look at how you are going to use the card and pay for the charges. Then balance these costs against what you will "earn" in points or cash back. To be frank, cards that offer rewards work well only if you pay off your entire bill every month.

Affinity cards. Credit cards featuring pictures painted by celebrities or photographs of a city or your alma mater may sound nifty, especially when they promise to contribute money to a charity every time you make a purchase. But these cards often charge high interest rates and fees, which means your debt can quickly add up unless you pay it off every month. A smarter move is to find a low-interest, no-fee credit card, and just make your own tax-deductible charitable contributions directly. (See Chapter 9 for tips on donations and taxes.) Credit card issuers must give you details about credit card costs in an easy-to-read box format that can usually be found at the bottom of credit card applications, solicitations, and billing statements.

ACCIÓN For comprehensive lists of low-rate credit cards, send $5 to CardWeb, P.O. Box 3966, Gettysburg, PA 17325, call 800-344-7714, or check the Web site at www.cardweb.com. You can also get a free list of credit cards with no annual fees by sending a self-addressed stamped envelope to Consumer Action, Credit Card Survey, 116 New Montgomery St., Suite 233, San Francisco, CA 94105. The following Web sites also provide lists of low-rate credit cards: HSH Associates at www.hsh.com/; and GetSmart at www.getsmart.com/. Bank Rate Monitor provides news and rates in English and Spanish for credit cards, mortgages, home equity loans, auto loans, and checking and saving accounts. For English go to www.bankrate. com/; for Spanish go to www.bankrate.com/esp.

 Pay off your credit card balance each month if you can, and no more than three months later if you can't.

Many of us make the mistake of thinking of credit cards as *dinero plástico* that can be used to supplement our income and pay for things we can't afford right now. *¡Un error enorme!* Credit cards are really "plastic debt" and should only be used as a convenience or for emergencies.

To avoid getting too far into debt, try keeping your credit cards at home when you go out to shop. Studies show that consumers spend up to 30 percent more when they use credit cards instead of cash or checks. If you do use a credit card to make a purchase, pay it off before the payment due date on your monthly statement, or no more than three months later if at all possible. If you're itching to make a big credit card purchase, or another one of those small credit card purchases that don't seem like much at the time, ask yourself if you'd be willing to go to the bank and ask for a loan for this particular item. If you need a car or a new roof on your house, then the answer may be yes. But if all you want is dinner or a new pair of jeans, the answer is no.

Some of us may find it hard to write a big check to a credit card issuer every month and instead find it more palatable to send in the minimum payment. One way to pay off credit card bills a little faster is to authorize your bank or credit union to deduct a certain amount from your account every month and send it in to the credit card issuer.

In general, try to stick with no more than two major credit cards such as Visa and MasterCard, and no more than two department store cards. Charge cards, such as the ones offered by American Express, technically aren't credit cards because they require that you pay off your bill in full every month. The annual fees can be steep, depending on the card you get. But it might be worth it if you have a tendency to let your bills roll over month after month, because a charge card issuer simply won't let you do that.

ACCIÓN If you think you've been unfairly denied credit, contact your state attorney general's office. Complaints against financial institutions that have already extended credit to you must be made to the proper regulatory agencies: To complain about a national bank, call the Office of the Comptroller of the Currency at 202-874-5000; for S&Ls, call the Office of Thrift Supervision at 800-842-6929; for credit unions, call the NCUA at 703-518-6429; for state banks that are regulated by the Federal Reserve Board of Governors, call 202-452-3693; for state banks that are regulated by the FDIC, call 800-934-3342; for a gasoline company, department store or other creditor, or a credit bureau, write to the Federal Trade Commission at 6th & Pennsylvania Ave., N.W., Washington, DC 20580, or call 202-326-2222.

 Credit records require special precautions in the event of marriage, divorce, or death.

If you're a newlywed, you and your spouse may want to keep your accounts separate for a while rather than immediately signing on to each other's accounts. The reason? If you start having marital difficulties, one spouse may close the accounts, leaving the other without credit. Or an irresponsible spouse may build up a large debt, leaving the other to foot at least half the bill.

If you change your name when you get married, you have to decide whether to notify the credit bureaus and make the same changes on your credit record. You're legally entitled to obtain credit in your own name, your married name, or a combination of the two. *Pero no se hagan la vida más complicada de lo necesario.* For simplicity's sake, keep all your accounts in a single name, whatever you choose.

If you've been legally married (or registered as a domestic partner where that's available) for years and have used your spouse's credit cards, you may not have a credit record of your own. If this is the case, find out if you can be added to a couple of accounts as a co-signer or joint applicant. After a few months you may be able to get a credit card in your own name. If not, consider getting a secured credit card. In the event of a divorce, you and your spouse will both be held liable by creditors for any debts incurred while married if you live in a community property state (Arizona, California, Idaho, Louisiana, Nevada, New Mexico, Texas, Washington, Wisconsin, and Puerto Rico). In common law states (all the rest), you're not liable if your name isn't on the account. The first thing to do is to close any joint credit card accounts, notify creditors that you'll no longer be liable for your spouse's bills, and see if creditors will provide you with separate accounts. They may refuse to do so until the balance on the joint account is paid off.

If your spouse dies, and you were a co-signer on his or her accounts, or the account was a joint account, tell creditors that the accounts will now be held in your name only. If your financial situation is good enough that you could obtain credit on your own, there should be no problem keeping the credit you already have.

ACCIÓN A brochure called *Equal Credit Opportunity for Women/Igual Oportunidad de Crédito Para Mujeres* is available for free in English and Spanish by calling the Federal Deposit Insurance Corp. at 800-934-3342, or by writing to the FDIC's Office of Consumer Affairs at 550 17th St. NW, Washington, DC 20429.

 Be careful when co-signing a loan for a relative or friend.

When you co-sign a loan or credit card you are agreeing to pay back the entire debt if the person you are co-signing for fails to do so. If the person you co-signed for doesn't pay the debt, or makes late payments, it will show up as a negative mark on your credit report. Even if the co-signer pays the debt on time every month, you may find it difficult to obtain more credit for yourself. That's because the amount of the loan you co-signed for will appear on your credit report as though you had borrowed the money yourself. Some creditors will take into account that amount, and decide that you already have too much credit.

The issue of co-signing can be *muy delicado*. You may want to help your extended family, but you shouldn't do so in a way that hurts your own financial standing. Before co-signing, determine whether the person you're helping is responsible. Also consider whether you can repay the debt if the person defaults. There are some other options besides co-signing. Offer to loan the person enough money to get a secured credit card and build up a credit history. If you have a good credit record, you can also obtain a loan yourself and make the other person the co-signer. This way, the bills will come to you and you don't have to worry about ruining your credit record if the co-signer skips bills or pays late.

ACCIÓN A brochure called *Co-Signing a Loan/Co-Firmando un Préstamo* is available for free in English and Spanish by writing to the Federal Trade Commission's Consumer Response Center at 6th St. and Pennsylvania Ave. NW, Washington, DC 20580.

 Take the initiative yourself to correct mistakes on your credit record or to rebuild a negative credit record.

You can correct mistakes on your credit record, and even rebuild a bad credit record, on your own. You don't have to resort to unscrupulous credit "clinics" or "doctors" that charge hundreds, perhaps thousands, of dollars. Start by getting a copy of your credit record from Experian, Equifax, or TransUnion (see *Acción* below for toll-free telephone numbers). One copy from a single agency should be enough, unless you plan to make a major purchase soon, such as a house. In this case, compare all three reports.The price charged by each agency for a report varies by state. Typically, the cost is $8 per report (more if you and your spouse have a joint report). But you're entitled to one free copy if you've been denied credit, employment, or insurance within the past sixty days; you've been a victim of fraud; you receive public assistance; or you live in Colorado, Georgia, Maryland, Massachusetts, New Jersey, or Vermont.

If you spot outdated or incorrect information on your report, contact the credit bureau and ask for a correction. You can do this by completing a "request for reinvestigation form" that the credit bureau should have included with your credit report. If there's no form enclosed, simply write a letter.

The credit bureau is supposed to check with the source of the data and send you the results within thirty days after getting your complaint. Any changes it makes will be passed on to the other two credit bureaus. Be sure your Social Security number and other identifying information are correct. If the credit bureau refuses to remove the bad reference, try discussing the matter with the creditor. Under federal law, creditors must not report information they know to be incorrect. If talking doesn't fix the problem, you can add a statement of 100 words or less to your credit report to explain your side of the story. Adding your own statement may not change the ultimate report, but ¿qué daño va a hacer?

To start rebuilding a bad credit record, pay off your outstanding bills. If you can't afford to pay the entire balance, try negotiating a payment plan with your creditors. At the very least, try to catch up on overdue or delinquent bills. It's okay to have a balance due. But you don't want a credit record that says you're behind on payments. After correcting any mistakes and getting current on your accounts, the next step is to start adding positive references. That means regularly using a major credit card, secured or unsecured, and paying off all or most of the balance every month. Manténgase positivo en todo aspecto.

ACCIÓN To obtain a copy of your credit report, call Equifax at 800-685-1111; Experian (formerly TRW) at 800-682-7654; or TransUnion at 800-916-8800. For a compilation of all three credit reports in one easy-to-read format for $30.95, call First American Credco at 800-443-9342. A brochure called *Rebuilding Good Credit/Como Reconstruir su Buen Crédito* is available for free in

English and Spanish by sending a self-addressed, stamped envelope to Consumer Action, 116 New Montgomery St., Suite 233,
San Francisco, CA 94105.

 If you're having money troubles, stop using your credit cards.

We all know the *señales* of money troubles. Bills get paid late. Credit card cash advances are used to pay for daily expenses. Creditors call or write about overdue bills. Minimum payments consistently are made on credit card bills. We put off medical or dental visits because we can't afford them. If this sounds like you, stop using your credit cards and pay cash. Don't accept any offers for new credit cards, either. And review your recent credit card state-ments to make sure you really owe what your creditors claim you owe.

Try contacting your creditors to let them know you're having trouble making your payments. Tell them what caused the problem (a medical emer-gency, a job loss, etc.). Ask if you can work out a new payment schedule. Some creditors may be willing to work with you. Remember your budget from Chapter 1? Take another look at it and see what types of optional expenses you can reduce in order to pay down your debts faster. Unnecessary expenses include entertainment, vacation, and impulse purchases such as compact discs or shoes. No more Luis Miguel compact discs.

If you've got any savings stashed away, especially money that's sitting in a low-interest account, now's a good time to use it to reduce your high-inter-est debt. What sense does it make to keep $1,000 in an account that's earn-ing 2 percent interest if the interest rate on your debts is significantly higher than that? If you've got several debts with many different interest rates, try to first pay off debts that have higher interest rates. It's just good sense to try to pay off a credit card bill with a 19 percent interest rate before you pay off a car loan with a 7 percent interest rate. One option is to sell an asset, such as a car, and use the proceeds to settle your bills. Another is to ask for help from your extended family. Pat, a credit counselor in Corpus Cristi, says she was stunned when an indebted consumer with $1,000 in monthly bills was able to reduce his payments to less than $300 thanks to contributions from siblings, cousins, and even *Abuelita*.

You may also want to consider a debt consolidation loan, in which you take one big one loan, pay off all of your other debts, and are left with one monthly payment. The easiest way to consolidate is to transfer your balances to a low-interest credit card, then pay off the debt as quickly as possible. You can also get a personal loan. But there are some caveats. The goal of a loan consolidation is to reduce your overall debt burden, so be sure the loan's interest rate is less than the average rate of your current loans. Also, watch out for expensive fees or costs attached to the loan, or monthly payments so low that they stretch the length of your debt by several years.

ACCIÓN A brochure called *Managing Your Debts: How to Regain Financial Health/Como Administrar Sus Deudas y Recuperar el Bienestar Economico* is available in both English and Spanish by sending a self-addressed, stamped envelope to Consumer Action, 116 New Montgomery Street, Suite 233, San Francisco, CA 94105.

 Stay away from payday loans, finance companies, bill-paying services, rent-to-own stores, title loans, and pawn shops.

The credit that's the easiest to obtain is usually the most expensive, with extremely high interest rates and other large fees that effectively put the interest rate into the stratosphere.

Some check cashers, and even banks, offer payday loans (*préstamos de día de pago*), which are also known as cash advances or deferred deposit loans. For example, if you need $100, you'd write a personal check for that amount, plus a fee of perhaps $15, to the check casher or bank in return for a loan of $100. Your check is postdated, usually to your next payday, which means it can't be cashed until you think you'll have enough money in your account to cover the $115 check. Come payday, you can do one of three things:

1. You can allow the check casher or bank to cash your check.

2. You can get your check back by paying cash to cover the loan and the fee.

3. If you can't pay off the loan, you can "roll it over" by paying an additional fee to extend it for another week or two. Payday loans are a terrible idea. Their fees translate into effective triple-digit annual percentage rates.

The rates for $100 payday loans on checks held seven days range from 521 percent to 1,820 percent, according to a survey of check cashers in twenty-three cities by the Consumer Federation of America. On checks held fourteen days, the rates ranged from 261 percent to 913 percent, the survey says.

There are three big reasons to stay away from finance companies *(compañías financieras)*, which are companies other than banks or credit unions that provide loans. First, the consolidation loans they offer carry very high interest rates of up to 25 percent, along with high application fees and low minimum monthly payments, all of which can push you deeper into debt. Second, a loan from a finance company is often considered a negative reference on your credit record. Third, finance companies often add costly insurance features to loans without telling you about it until it's too late. For example, credit life insurance and credit disability insurance will pay off your loan if you die or become disabled, respectively. Credit life insurance is sometimes required for major loans such as for homes or cars. But avoid it for smaller loans. As insurance goes, this kind of coverage is very expensive for what you get. If you need life insurance, for example, you should buy a more comprehensive policy on your own (see Chapter 3).

If you're already locked into paying insurance premiums on your loan, see if you can eliminate them after you've reduced the debt on your loan. Beware also of bill-paying services. They often sound like finance companies offering help with loan consolidation, but all they do is pay your bills for you each month. There's no refinancing at all. What you do is send in a check to the firm every month, and the firm then pays each creditor. Bill-paying services often charge high annual or monthly fees for their services. Rent-to-own stores *(las tiendas de alquiler para la compra)* are another "service" you should stay away from. When you rent something from a rent-to-own store, you sign a contract agreeing to make weekly payments for as long as you want the item. These items are usually large consumer goods such as refrigerators or television sets. You have the option to buy the item if you make all the required weekly payments, usually for a year or more.

Rent-to-own stores often target low-income consumers who can't afford to buy the item outright and are lured by offers of low weekly payments with no down payment. Many rent-to-own stores don't disclose what the annual percentage rate is, either. Some have been known to list used items as new, charge expensive "service" fees, and repossess items if a payment is late just one day. Rent-to-own stores offer notoriously bad deals. Interest rates on televisions and refrigerators charged by 124 rent-to-own stores in seventeen states averaged 100 percent, and ran as high as 275 percent, according to a study by the U.S. Public Interest Research Group, a nonprofit consumer advocacy group. Title loans (*préstamos de título*) should also be avoided. With a title loan you exchange the title of your car for a loan that typically amounts to just 20 percent of the car's value. The "fee" for the loan is essentially an interest rate, which can be as high as 260 percent annually. If you miss a payment, the lender takes possession of your car, and turns around and sells it for a tidy profit, leaving you with *nada*. Pawn shops (*casa de empeño*) provide small loans that are secured by personal items such as jewelry. The loans are often a fraction of the value of these personal items. If you can't repay the loan, the pawn shop turns around and sells your personal items at a profit. If you do repay the loan, the personal items you retrieve may be damaged, but you probably have no recourse against the pawnshop.

ACCIÓN A brochure called *Rent-to-Own: Know Your Rights/Alquiler Para la Compra: Conozca Sus Derechos* is available in English and Spanish by sending a self-addressed, stamped envelope to Consumer Action, 116 New Montgomery St., Suite 233, San Francisco, CA 94105.

 If you can't solve your problems by yourself, seek the advice of a reputable nonprofit credit counseling service.

Two excellent credit counseling groups are the Consumer Credit Counseling Service, a nonprofit agency affiliated with the National Foundation for Consumer Credit, and Debt Counselors of America. Counselors from these two groups are trained in money management. They can help you develop a budget in a friendly, supportive environment, and they are skilled at negotiating financial management plans with creditors that can help you pay off your debts in three to five years. Under these plans, creditors often agree to reduce payments, lower or drop interest rates and finance charges, and waive late-payment and over-the-limit fees.

When you start the plan you'll probably deposit money every month with the counseling service, which then pays your creditors. In some cities, the CCCS also offers most of its services in Spanish, including budget counseling; a credit report review; personal finance presentations to adult groups, students, and employees; and a housing program to teach consumers about the home-buying process.

> **ACCIÓN** To reach Debt Counselors of America, call 800-680-3328, or check the Web site at www.dca.org/; to reach the National Foundation for Consumer Credit, call 800-388-2227 to speak English or 800-682-9832 to speak Spanish, or check the Web site at www.nfcc.org/.

 Use bankruptcy only as a last-ditch option.

Bankruptcy is a court procedure that allows erasing all or most debts or repaying some debts. But it isn't a panacea. No matter what kind of bankruptcy you file for, some debts can't be wiped out, including alimony, child support, most taxes, recent student loans, fines, penalties for breaking the law, and debts for personal injury or death caused by driving while intoxicated. Bankruptcy stays on your credit report for seven to ten years, which can make it difficult to get credit in the future. A bad credit record, in turn, can make it hard to get a job, a mortgage, a car loan, an apartment rental, and even insurance. There are two basic kinds of bankruptcy: Chapter 7 (liquidation) and Chapter 13 (reorganization). The "chapters" refer to the legal codes where the two types of bankruptcy are found. There are also two other bankruptcies that you probably don't have to worry about: Chapter 11 is for businesses or for individuals with more than $1 million of debt, and Chapter 12 is for debt coming primarily from a family farm.

A Chapter 7 bankruptcy allows you to wipe out your debts by selling the assets you own that are considered "non-exempt." These non-exempt assets vary from state to state, but very few people lose property in a Chapter 7 bankruptcy. Creditors often get nothing, or pennies, on the dollar. This is one reason why creditors are often willing to accept reduced payments instead of forcing a debtor into bankruptcy. Under Chapter 7 you typically give up non-residential real estate, second or vacation homes, recreational vehicles, second cars or trucks, expensive musical instruments (unless you're a professional musician), stamp, coin, and other collections, and family heirlooms. Depending on the state, you'll probably lose your stocks and bonds, and other cash deposits. If you have that kind of money, you're best off using it to pay bills rather than to risk losing it all in bankruptcy. Certain assets are exempt in Chapter 7 bankruptcies, which means you can keep them. There's a federal list of the property you can keep, and all states have their own lists, too. In seventeen states, you can choose between the federal and state lists. In all other states, you must choose the state list. In general, exempt property includes some of the equity in a motor vehicle, clothing, household furnishings, goods and appliances, jewelry up to a certain value, personal effects, life insurance with no or limited cash value, part of the equity of a residence, tools of a trade or profession to a certain value, a portion of unpaid but earned wages, and public benefits.

With a Chapter 13 bankruptcy you don't have to sell your assets. Instead, you file a plan with the bankruptcy court proposing how you will repay your creditors within three to five years. This is often referred to as the "wage earner's plan" because you must be employed or have regular income to qualify. A Chapter 7 bankruptcy stays on your credit record for ten years, and you can file Chapter 7 every six years. A Chapter 13 bankruptcy stays on your record for seven years, but you can file for Chapter 13 as often as you want as long as the previous Chapter 13 has been discharged, or concluded. There's no easy formula to determine whether bankruptcy is for you. If you don't see any way of having enough income to pay off your debts in three to five years, even with a negotiated payment plan, it may be time to talk to a bankruptcy attorney. Significant bankruptcy reforms have been proposed, but at this writing, no decisions have been made. Three books published by Nolo Press can help you figure out whether bankruptcy is an option: *How to File for Bankruptcy*, by Stephen Elias, Albin Renauer, and Robin Leonard; *Chapter 13 Bankruptcy; Repay Your Debts*, by Robin Leonard; and *Bankruptcy: Is It the Right Solution to Your Debt Problems?* by Robin Leonard and Twila Slesnick.

ACCIÓN A brochure called *Advertisements Offering Debt Relief May Be Offering Bankruptcy/Propaganda Prometedora al Alivio de Deudas Puede Estar Ofreciendo la Quiebra* is available for free in English and Spanish from the Federal Trade Commission's Consumer Response Center by writing to 6th St. and Pennsylvania Ave. NW, Washington, DC 20580.

 Beware of guaranteed credit offers, and of bogus credit repair, advance loan, and credit counseling services.

Stay away from companies that "guarantee" they can get you a credit card no matter how bad your credit record may be. These companies often require a large up-front fee, then disappear before giving you a credit card. Some companies may also ask you to dial an expensive "900" number for information. Watch out for companies that discourage you from contacting a credit bureau directly, tell you to dispute all information in your credit report, or suggest creating a new identity. It's a federal crime to make false statements on a loan or credit application, or to obtain a fake Social Security number. Many consumers who try to rebuild their credit records fall prey to scam artists who claim they can erase bad credit. Many of these crooks advertise via newspapers, radio, mail, and the Internet, and charge a lot of money for their services. These credit repair companies just bombard credit bureaus with requests to verify information. If a credit bureau can't verify an entry within 60 days, it will remove the information from the report. But if it's later verified, it will go back into your report.

Some of these companies also require payment up front before providing any services. This is another big warning sign, because it's a crime for telemarketers who offer credit repair to require payment until six months after services have been delivered. Advance loan companies should also be avoided. These companies offer to give you a loan no matter what shape your credit history is in. The catch is that you have to pay a large fee just to apply. Some companies disappear after receiving the application fee. Be on the lookout for firms with names that sound similar to the legitimate Consumer Credit Counseling Service, which provides debt counseling free of charge. These other companies may be nonprofits, but that doesn't mean they're *legítimo*. To check the background of a company, ask about its fees, get names and phone numbers of customers, and contact major creditors with whom the company has worked. If you run into trouble, contact your local consumer affairs office, the state attorney general's office, or the National Fraud Information Center.

> **ACCIÓN** To file a complaint against a credit repair company or credit bureau, call the National Fraud Information Center at 800-876-7060, or check the Web site at www.fraud.org/. A brochure called *Don't Be Fooled by Misleading Credit Repair Scams/No Se Deje Engañar Por Declaraciónes Falsas de Reparación de Crédito* is available for free in English and Spanish by sending a self-addressed, stamped envelope to Consumer Action, 116 New Montgomery St., Suite 233, San Francisco, CA 94105.

- ❑ If you have no credit record whatsoever, try establishing a credit history using nontraditional means.
- ❑ Get a secured credit card or small personal loan to help you build a traditional credit record, but shop around for the best deal.
- ❑ Pay off your credit card balance each month if you can, and no more than three months later if you can't.
- ❑ Check your own credit record before applying for a big loan.
- ❑ Take the initiative to correct mistakes on your credit record, or rebuild a negative credit record on your own.
- ❑ If you start having money troubles, stop using your credit cards, don't accept new credit card offers, try to negotiate a new payment plan with creditors, and use your savings to pay down high-interest debt.
- ❑ Stay away from payday loans, finance companies, bill-paying services, rent-to-own stores, title loans, and pawnshops.
- ❑ If you can't solve your problems on your own, seek the services of a reputable debt counseling service.
- ❑ Consider bankruptcy only as a last-ditch option.
- ❑ Beware of guaranteed credit offers and bogus credit repair, credit counseling, and advance loan companies.

ADDITIONAL RESOURCES

Recommended Books

Bankruptcy: Is It the Right Solution to Your Debt Problems?, by Robin Leonard and Twila Slesnick (Berkeley: Nolo Press, 1998).

Chapter 13 Bankruptcy: Repay Your Debts, by Robin Leonard (Berkeley: Nolo Press, 1998).

Credit Repair, by Robin Leonard and Shae Irving (Berkeley: Nolo Press, 1998).

How to File for Chapter 7 Bankruptcy, by Stephen Elias, Albin Renauer, and Robin Leonard (Berkeley: Nolo Press, 1999).

Money Troubles: Legal Strategies to Cope With Your Debts, by Robin Leonard (Berkeley: Nolo Press, 1997).

Surviving Debt: A Guide for Consumers in Financial Stress, by Jonathan Sheldon and Gary Klein (Boston: National Consumer Law Center, 1996).

The Ultimate Credit Handbook, by Gerri Detweiler (New York: Plume Books, 1997).

Insurance

"THOSE WHO ABANDON THEIR FAMILIES, GOD FORSAKES" —VENEZUELA

U NA PREGUNTA: WHAT WOULD HAPPEN IF YOUR FAMILY'S PRIMARY breadwinner died or became disabled? Some of us have relatives willing to provide financial support. But many others don't, or would prefer to handle the situation themselves. One way to reduce the potentially life-shattering impact of an unexpected loss is to buy insurance.

An insurance policy (*póliza de seguro*) is a contract that guarantees you'll be financially compensated for death, disability, illness, disaster, or accident, among other things. The charge you pay is called a premium (*prima*). The higher the probability of suffering such a loss, the bigger the premium.

Insurance issues can seem overly complicated to anyone, but Latinos face some special obstacles. Few insurance companies provide bilingual services, materials, and agents. Many Latinos work in lower-paying sectors of the economy that historically haven't provided fringe benefits such as health or disability insurance. Other Latinos work one or more part-time jobs that don't provide benefits, either.

Some newly arrived immigrants may not be familiar with the concept of medical insurance because medical care is provided by the government in many Latin American countries. Other types of non-governmental insurance, such as auto and life insurance, are prohibitively expensive in Latin America.

For many of us, the most logical place to turn to in an emergency is *la familia*. We'll gladly chip in and provide financial support to parents, children, siblings, and members of the extended family if it's needed, and expect the same in return if we run into trouble.

The numbers bear this out. A 1998 survey by Miami-based Strategy Research Corp. of the top ten Latino markets—Los Angeles, New York, Miami, San Francisco–San Jose, Chicago, Houston, San Antonio, McAllen–Brownsville, Dallas–Fort Worth, and San Diego—found that 62 percent of Latinos have no life insurance, 50 percent have no health insurance, and 26 percent have no auto insurance.

Nationwide, more Latinos proportionately lack basic health insurance than any other ethnic group in the United States. About 33.5 percent of Latinos had no health insurance throughout the first half of 1996, compared with 13.1 percent for non-Latino whites, according to the U.S. Department of Health and Human Services.

The importance of health insurance became apparent to Elda at an early age. When she was 15 she was living in Homestead, Florida, with her parents, grandmother, and an uncle. They had moved to the United States from Venezuela a few years earlier.

One day, when her uncle Osvaldo was driving to his morning job, he fell asleep at the wheel, ran a stop sign, and was hit by a van, suffering severe head injuries that left him with the mental capacity of an eight-year-old child. He also had a broken pelvis and had to learn to walk again. His auto insurance covered only about $10,000 of his $100,000 medical bill.

"My uncle never expected anything to happen, so why have insurance?" says Elda, who is now a counselor in her early 20s. "But you need to have insurance. Even a minor accident can end up being really expensive if you can't work. It's your responsibility to make sure you've provided for your family."

 Buy insurance to protect against losses that you're required to cover, that could result in bankruptcy, or that would force you to borrow money.

If you own a home, you're required by the lender to buy homeowners insurance. If you own a car, you're required by state law to have auto insurance. Other important types of policies may not be required, but should be considered because they can save you from financial ruin. These policies include disability insurance, life insurance, long-term care insurance, disaster insurance, and renters insurance.

Skip insurance for losses you can pay for out-of-pocket from existing assets, current income, or other insurance policies.

There's no need to buy dread disease insurance for cancer if you have a good health plan, for example. With some exceptions, needless insurance includes life insurance for young children; extended-service car contracts; mortgage protection; life and disability coverage that only covers loan payments; coverage of expenses for legal services, towing, canceled trips, bad weather, weddings, pets, adoptions, and child support payments.

Also avoid "extended warranties" and "optional service plans" that promise to repair or replace malfunctioning items. Salespeople earn hefty sales commissions on these warranties, and most consumers never use them. In addition, most new items are covered by an "implied" or "expressed" manufacturer's warranty for at least ninety days.

Shop around for the best insurance deals.

There are three basic steps you can take to get the best deal. *Primero que nada*, contact a few agents to see what kind of plans they offer. Independent agents sell plans from several different insurance companies, while captive agents usually work for just one insurance company.

If you need help in Spanish, look for an agent in your neighborhood, or ask for referrals from friends and family. Also look for insurance companies that provide written materials in Spanish. One way to find them is to be on the lookout for Spanish-language advertisements on radio and television, and in magazines and newspapers.

Second, if you're relatively healthy and have enough money in savings, you

HIGHER DEDUCTIBLES MEAN LOWER PREMIUMS

You can save money on your auto insurance by choosing a higher deductible, and by lowering coverage limits. Some companies offer discounts based on your membership in a group or professional organization.

Here's an example* of how rates go down with higher deductibles for a 30-year-old male who lives in Los Angeles County, has a clean driving record, and drives a 1997 Honda Civic:

Coverage / Limits	$100 deductible	$250 deductible	$500 deductible
BODILY INJURY/PROPERTY DAMAGE ($25,000/$50,000/$10,000)	$597	$597	$597
MEDICAL PAYMENTS ($5,000)	$146	$146	$146
UNINSURED MOTORIST/UNDERINSURED MOTORIST COVERAGE ($25,000/$50,000)	$91	$91	$91
UNINSURED MOTORIST PROPERTY DAMAGE ($3,500)	$13	$13	$13
COMPREHENSIVE INSURANCE	$170	$141	$116
COLLISION INSURANCE	$540	$491	$383
TOTAL SIX-MONTH PREMIUM:	**$1,557**	**$1,479**	**$1,346**

*Amounts are based on rates as of April 1998. Actual rates vary, and all rates are subject to change.

should select the highest deductible *(importe deducible)* you could afford to pay. A deductible is the amount of money you have to pay toward a loss before your insurance company starts picking up the tab (see chart above).

Finally, contact insurance companies that cut out the middleman and sell policies directly to the public. There are also many quote services that can give you free insurance quotes over the telephone or Internet. These plans often cost less than those sold by agents. On the downside, customer service representatives may not be able to help you figure out what you need. (See "Direct-Market Insurers," at right.)

DIRECT-MARKET INSURERS

AETNA: Life and health. Bilingual	800-584-6001
ALLSTATE: Auto, home, renters, and life insurance. Bilingual	800-777-3900
AMICA: Renters, home, life, disability health, and long-term care insurance	800-992-6422
AMERICAN EXPRESS CO.: Auto, homeowners, and life insurance	800-535-2001
AMERITAS: Life and disability insurance	800-552-3553
AMERICAN LIFE OF NEW YORK: Life insurance	800-872-5963
GEICO: Auto and home insurance	800-841-3000
PROVIDENT: Disability and life insurance	800-843-3426
UNUM: Life, disability, and long-term care insurance	800-227-8138
USAA: Life, health, auto, home, and renters insurance (limited to members of the military and their families)	800-531-8080
WHOLESALE INSURANCE NETWORK: Life insurance	800-808-5810

TELEPHONE AND/OR ON-LINE INSURANCE QUOTES

DIRECTQUOTE: Life insurance	800-845-3853
INSTAQUOTE: Life insurance (www.instaquote.com/)	888-223-2220
INSURANCEQUOTE SERVICES: Life, long-term care and disability insurance (www.iquote.com/)	800-972-1104
INSURANCE INFORMATION INC.: Life insurance	800-472-5800
MASTERQUOTE: Life insurance (www.masterquote.com/)	800-627-LIFE
PREFERRED QUOTES INSURANCE SERVICES: Life insurance via e-mail at quotes@pqins.com (fax at 888-333-3750)	800-333-3750
PROGRESSIVE INSURANCE CORP.: Auto insurance. Life and disability insurance also sold	800-288-6776
QUOTESMITH: Life insurance (www.quotesmith.com/)	800-431-1147
QUICKQUOTE: Life insurance. Bilingual (www.quickquote.com/)	800-390-8271
SELECTQUOTE: Life insurance	800-343-1985
TERMQUOTE: Life insurance	800-444-8376

ACCIÓN Call the Independent Insurance Agents of America at 800-221-7917 to find an independent agent, or visit their Web site at www.iiaa.org/.

Before buying any insurance policy, check the licensing status of the insurance agent and insurance carrier, as well as the rating of the carrier.

All insurance agents and insurance companies must be licensed in the states where they do business. By law, agents must also print their license numbers on their business cards. To confirm that an agent or insurance company really is licensed—and to find out if any consumer complaints have been filed against them—call your state's insurance department. (For a list of state insurance departments, see pages 60–61.)

Licensed insurance companies are required to contribute to a pool of "guarantee funds" that will provide consumers with at least some financial protection if the company goes bankrupt. But you should also find out what kind of financial stability ratings (*calificaciones*) the insurance company has received from various agencies. Not all ratings are equal. For example, an "A" rating from A.M. Best is the equivalent of a "B+" from Weiss. Stick with companies rated "Superior" or "Excellent." (See "Insurance Company Ratings," at right.)

ACCIÓN An agent can send you the ratings and full reports on the insurance company. To check the rating of an insurance company yourself, go to the library and ask for *Best's Insurance Reports.* You can also contact the rating companies directly. A.M. Best charges $4.95 per rating through its on-line service at www.ambest.com, or by calling 908-439-2200, ext. 5742. Duff & Phelps at 312-368-3198 provides free ratings. Moody's at 212-553-0377 provides up to four free ratings per call. Standard & Poor's at 212-208-1527 provides ratings for free. Weiss Ratings at 800-289-9222 provides ratings for $15 each.

ne s

INSURANCE COMPANY RATINGS

The following insurance rating agencies use the listed financial ratings*, which measure the ability of a company to pay claims:

A.M. BEST	STANDARD & POOR'S	DUFF & PHELPS	MOODY'S	WEISS
All of the following are considered superior or excellent ratings.				
A++	AAA	AAA	Aaa	A
A+	AA	AA+	Aa	
A		AA		
A-		AA-		
All of the following are considered good ratings.				
B++	A	A+	A	B
B+		A		
B		A-		
B-				
All of the following are considered fair or average ratings.				
C++	BBB		Baa	C
C+	BB			

*Only buy insurance from companies rated "Superior" or "Excellent" in the ratings above.

NOTE: Parallel ratings are not strictly equivalent. Any ratings below those illustrated are below acceptable quality.

SOURCE: STAYING WEALTHY: STRATEGIES FOR PROTECTING YOUR ASSETS, BY BRIAN H. BREUEL (BLOOMBERG PRESS). PG. 213.

 CONSEJO TIP

Call your state's insurance department if you think you've been unfairly denied insurance coverage.

Some insurance companies have been accused of discriminating against Latino and African-American consumers by charging more for insurance, offering less coverage, and denying certain types of coverage. Agents that work for these companies sometimes treat minorities badly when meeting with them. If you think you've been unfairly denied insurance coverage contact your state insurance department. *No sufras en silencio.*

STATE INSURANCE DEPARTMENTS

This is list of insurance departments for all 50 states, the District of Columbia, and Puerto Rico. Calls to an 800 number are free when made within the respective states:

ALABAMA	(334-269-3550) auto, FAIR plan, beach and windstorm, health
ALASKA	(907-269-7900) auto, health
ARIZONA	(602-912-8400) auto
ARKANSAS	(800-247-3261/501-371-2600) auto, health
CALIFORNIA	(800-927-HELP/213-897-8921), auto, FAIR plan, disability, health, long-term care
COLORADO	(303-894-7490) auto, health
CONNECTICUT	(860-297-3800) auto, FAIR plan, health, long-term care
DELAWARE	(800-282-8611/302-739-4251) auto
DISTRICT OF COLUMBIA	(202-727-8000) auto, FAIR plan, health
FLORIDA	(800-342-2762/850-922-3100) auto, FAIR plan, beach and windstorm, health
GEORGIA	(404-656-2070) auto, FAIR plan, health
HAWAII	(808-586-2790) auto, FAIR plan, disability, health
IDAHO	(800-721-3272/208-334-4250, auto
ILLINOIS	(217-782-4515) auto, FAIR plan, health, long-term care
INDIANA	(800-622-4461/317-232-2385) auto, FAIR plan, health, long-term care
IOWA	(515-281-5705) auto, FAIR plan, health, long-term care
KANSAS	(800-432-2484/913-296-7829) auto, FAIR plan, health
KENTUCKY	(800-595-6053/502-564-3630) auto, FAIR plan
LOUISIANA	(800-259-5301/504-342-1259) auto, FAIR plan, beach and windstorm, health
MAINE	(800-300-5000/207-624-8475) auto
MARYLAND	(800-492-6116/410-468-2000) auto, FAIR plan, health, long-term care
MASSACHUSETTS	(617-521-7777) auto, FAIR plan, health
MICHIGAN	(517-373-9273) auto, FAIR plan, health
MINNESOTA	(800-657-3602/612-296-2488) auto, FAIR plan, health

MISSISSIPPI	(800-562-2957/601-359-3569) auto, FAIR plan, beach and windstorm, health
MISSOURI	(800-726-7390/573-751-2640) auto, FAIR plan, health
MONTANA	(800-332-6148/406-444-2040) auto, health
NEBRASKA	(402-471-2201) auto, health
NEVADA	(800-992-0900/702-687-4270) auto
NEW HAMPSHIRE	(800-852-3416/603-271-2261) auto, health
NEW JERSEY	(609-882-4400) auto, FAIR plan, disability, health
NEW MEXICO	(800-947-4722/505-827-4601) auto, FAIR plan, health
NEW YORK	(800-342-3736/212-480-6400) auto, FAIR plan, disability, health, long-term care
NORTH CAROLINA	(800-546-5664/919-733-7349) auto, beach and windstorm
NORTH DAKOTA	(800-247-0560/701-328-2440) auto, health
OHIO	(800-686-1526/614-644-2658) auto, FAIR plan
OKLAHOMA	(800-522-0071/405-521-2828) auto, health
OREGON	(503-947-7984) auto, FAIR plan, health
PENNSYLVANIA	(717-787-7000) auto, FAIR plan, health
PUERTO RICO	(787-722-8686) auto, FAIR plan, disability
RHODE ISLAND	(401-277-2223) auto, FAIR plan, disability, health
SOUTH CAROLINA	(800-768-3467/803-737-6160) auto, FAIR plan, beach and windstorm, health
SOUTH DAKOTA	(605-773-3563) auto
TENNESSEE	(800-342-4029/615-741-2705) auto, health
TEXAS	(800-578-4677/512-463-6169) auto, FAIR plan, beach and windstorm, health
UTAH	(800-439-3805/801-538-3800) auto, health
VERMONT	(802-828-3301) auto, health
VIRGINIA	(800-552-7945/804-371-9741) auto, FAIR plan, health
WASHINGTON	(800-562-6900/360-753-7300) auto, FAIR plan, health, long-term care
WEST VIRGINIA	(800-642-9004/304-558-3386) auto
WISCONSIN	(800-236-8517/608-266-0103) auto, FAIR plan, health
WYOMING	(800-438-5768/307-777-7401) auto, health

Don't go without health insurance.

If you work for a large company, chances are your employer provides some type of coverage, and may even pay a portion of your premium. However, if you're self-employed or work for a small company, you may have to buy an individual policy, which can be hard to find and expensive.

There are two types of health plans: fee-for-service plans and managed care plans. With a fee-for-service plan (*plan de servicio por honorarios*), which is also called an indemnity plan, you can see any doctor you like. You're required to pay an annual deductible. Once you've paid out that amount for medical costs, your insurance will start picking up some of your medical bills, usually about 80 percent. The remaining 20 percent that you're responsible for is called the co-payment.

Managed care plans are less expensive than fee-for-service plans, but you don't have as many choices. Typically, you're given a list of doctors to choose from, and you have to pay more out-of-pocket if you use someone who's not on the list. Managed care plans often have no deductibles and smaller co-payments, sometimes as low as $5 per visit. Here's what the many different types of managed care plans mean to you, the patient:

Health Maintenance Organization (HMO). HMOs offer prepaid, comprehensive health coverage for hospital and doctor services. An HMO contracts with certain health care providers. As a member, you must use only these providers for all services.

Group Practice HMO. A group practice HMO contracts with a multi-specialty physicians group to provide care for HMO members. As a member, you must get your medical care from a group doctor unless a referral is made outside the network.

Network HMO. A network HMO contracts with two or more independent group practices to provide health care services. As a member, you must get your medical care from an independent group practice unless a referral is made outside the network.

Federally qualified HMOs. These HMOs must apply to the federal government for qualification and meet certain federally stipulated provisions aimed at protecting consumers. As with regular HMOs, you must get your medical care from the HMO's providers for all services if you're a member.

Independent Practice Associates (IPA). An IPA is a business formed and directed by doctors in private practice to contract on their behalf with HMOs to provide care for managed-care enrollees. As a member, you can seek care only from IPA providers, and you won't be reimbursed for expenses if you go outside the network for services.

Preferred Provider Organization (PPO). A PPO is a health care arrangement between purchasers of care (employers, insurance companies) and providers that give you incentives such as lower deductibles and co-payments to use providers within the network. As a member, you'll pay more if you use services outside the network.

Point-of-Service (POS). POS plans are also known as open-ended HMOs. They encourage, but don't require, you to choose a primary care physician who will act as a gatekeeper when making referrals. In other words, you may have to see your primary care physician first before seeing anyone else. You can see providers outside of the network, but deductibles and co-payments will be higher.

Exclusive Provider Organization (EPO). An EPO is similar to a PPO. You can seek care only from network providers, and you won't be reimbursed for expenses if you go outside the network for services.

What type of plan should you choose? It depends on what you think the health care needs for you and your dependents are likely to be in the near future. If you're planning to start a family or have another child, you may want to choose a plan that has good coverage for fertility treatments, prenatal care, and pediatrics. If you're older, on the other hand, you may want a plan that offers good deals on prescription drugs and durable equipment, such as wheelchairs.

To find out what the health care coverage will cost, calculate the total cost of coverage, including monthly premiums, co-payments, deductibles, and other out-of-pocket expenses for the various plans to try to get a sense of what you can really afford.

Review the ratings of the various health plans. The easiest thing may be to look at the surveys from magazines such as *Health Pages*, *Consumer Reports*, and *Consumer's Checkbook*.

ACCIÓN To obtain a free accreditation report on managed care plans, call the National Committee for Quality Assurance at 800-839-6487.

If you're happy with your current doctor, find out which health plan he or she belongs to. If you're looking for a doctor, ask family and friends for referrals. Make sure the doctor's office is located nearby and has convenient hours. Learn how to get a referral to see a specialist.

Find out where you're supposed to go for emergency and urgent care if you're traveling, and how much it will cost if you go to the wrong place. By law, a medical plan must cover treatment for an emergency, no matter where you go, as long as you meet the "reasonable person" standard. That means a plan can't refuse to pay for an emergency room visit if you were having chest pains and thought you were having a heart attack, but really had indigestion.

Determine what is and isn't covered by the plan. Are there limits on mental health care, alcohol and drug abuse programs, chiropractic care, and alternative medicine such as acupuncture? Are wellness programs included, such as weight reduction, nutrition training, smoking cessation, stress management, and even health club memberships?

Does the plan cover existing conditions? Federally qualified HMOs are prohibited from having any exclusions or limitations on coverage for pre-existing conditions such as cancer or lupus. But some states have six-month or twelve-month "look back" periods in which health insurers can exclude or limit coverage for conditions you have been treated for in the past year.

To be sure you're adequately protected by your policy, check to see that it provides coverage for at least 80 percent of your medical expenses; caps your annual co-payments; has a lifetime benefit of at least $1 million; and is guaranteed renewable. Guaranteed renewable means the insurer can't raise your premiums or cancel your policy if you get sick, and you can renew your policy as often as you like.

Many states provide health insurance to people who can't get insurance any other way because of a pre-existing condition. Some states also offer special programs for lower-income pregnant women, and children of the working poor through the Children's Health Insurance Program. Call your state insurance department to find out what's offered (pages 60–61).

Latinos who are concerned about finding doctors who speak Spanish and are culturally sensitive to their needs are being served by a growing number of Independent Practice Associates (IPAs), which are formed by doctors in private practice and contracted by HMOs to provide care for managed-care enrollees. One of the most successful, Latino Health Care in Los Angeles, currently serves Southern California only, but it has plans to expand to other states.

ACCIÓN For a free guide called *Choosing and Using a Health Care Plan,* write to the Health Insurance Association of America at 555 13th St. N.W., Washington, DC 20004, or call 888-844-2782. To reach Latino Health Care, call 800-284-3236.

 If you're unemployed or self-employed, you can find an affordable individual health plan by shopping around.

Start by looking at government options. If you quit your job, get fired, or lose your health insurance coverage because of reduced hours, you can buy group coverage for yourself and your family under your former employer's plan for limited periods, thanks to the federal Consolidated Omnibus Budget Reconciliation Act of 1986, or COBRA.

Federal COBRA coverage is offered to employees of companies with twenty or more workers. It typically lasts between 18 and 36 months. After your employer sends you a notice telling you about your COBRA eligibility, you have 60 days to decide whether to join. You must pay the total cost of the plan, which is your former employer's group rate plus a maximum of 2 percent.

In addition to federal COBRA coverage, California and Florida also require small companies with fewer than 20 employees to offer similar COBRA plans if they provide health insurance benefits. This isn't all that common, however, because many small companies can't afford to offer benefits.

Another option is to join a professional, industry, or fraternal organization that offers health insurance to its members at group rates, which can be less expensive than individual rates. These groups include the National Association for the Self-Employed, and many local chambers of commerce.

Many health care providers sell health insurance policies directly to consumers. Independent insurance agents, who typically work with several different carriers, can quickly provide information about many plans. There are also many insurance Web sites including:

❏ Quicken InsureMarket: www.insuremarket.com/
❏ Insurance News Network: www.insure.com/
❏ Insweb: www.insweb.com/
❏ SafeTnet: www.safetnet.com/

ACCIÓN For bilingual information about health plans, call the National Insurance Consumer Helpline at 800-942-4242.

 Don't go without disability insurance.

Disability insurance, also known as income replacement insurance, replaces lost income if you're ill or injured. Many insurance experts and financial planners (including Laura) believe this type of insurance is just as important as life insurance, especially if you're self-employed or your family's primary breadwinner.

¿Por qué? Believe it or not, your chance of becoming disabled before age 65 is three times higher than your likelihood of dying. Disability insurance can protect your home, your car, your children's education, your business, your entire way of life, if you become incapacitated.

Many large companies offer disability insurance to their employees at group rates, which are hard to beat. If not, you have to shop for an individual disability policy. As with individual health plans, the best thing to do is to see if you can join a professional, industry, or fraternal organization that offers disability policies to its members at a group rate. You can also purchase disability insurance directly from an insurance carrier.

Although it's impossible to know how much money you'll need when disabled, generally you should try to buy enough coverage to provide at least 60 percent of your current income. If you've got disability insurance through your employer, but it doesn't cover this amount, you can buy supplemental disability insurance.

What you'll pay for this coverage depends on your age, health, occupation, and waiting period. In general, the younger you are when you buy disability insurance, the healthier you are, and the safer your job, the less expensive the premiums will be.

If you don't have a lot of money, you may want to get an annual renewable disability income policy, where premiums rise as you get older. A longer waiting period—the time between the day you become disabled and the day you begin to receive benefits—can also cut costs. Be sure to ask about discounts for non-smokers.

Most states offer worker's compensation, which provides benefits to employees who get injured on the job. Five states—California, Hawaii, New Jersey, New York, and Rhode Island—also provide short-term disability funds for non-work related illnesses or injuries.

Key features when buying a policy:

Definition of disability. Own-occupation coverage *(cobertura ocupacional propia)* will pay benefits if you can't work at your specific job. Any-occupation coverage *(cobertura de cualquier ocupación)* pays if you're unable to work at any occupation you're educated and trained to do. What you want is an income replacement policy, which pays benefits if you lose income.

Benefit period. Some policies pay benefits for only a few years. Ideally, you want a plan that will cover you until you're eligible for Social Security benefits at age 65.

Residual benefits. Be sure your plan includes residual benefits, which pay a portion of your benefits if you're partially disabled and can only work part-time or in a less demanding job.

Non-cancelable versus guaranteed renewable. With a non-cancelable plan, your premiums remain fixed. With a guaranteed renewable plan, your premiums are subject to general rate increases. Neither plan can cancel your policy if you file a claim.

ACCIÓN For a free copy of *Guide to Disability Income Insurance,* and a directory of companies that offer individual disability or income replacement policies, write to the Health Insurance Association of America at 555 13th St. N.W., Washington, DC 20004, or call 888-844-2782.

Find out what kind of medical and disability benefits you're entitled to from government agencies.

Medicare, the nation's largest health insurance program, provides low-cost benefits to people aged 65 or older, the disabled, and people with permanent kidney failure. It has two parts: Part A is hospital insurance and Part B is medical insurance.

Hospital insurance covers inpatient hospital services, skilled nursing facilities, home health services, and hospice care. Medical insurance covers the cost of physician services, outpatient hospital services, medical equipment and supplies, and other health services and supplies.

Medicaid provides medical assistance for the financially needy and is funded jointly by federal and state governments. Each state establishes its own eligibility standards; determines the type, amount, duration, and scope of services; sets the rate of payment for services; and administers its own program. There's a good chance that Medicare and Medicaid programs will be substantially reduced at some point in the future. *Mejor no depender mucho de estos servicios.*

Private policies called Medigap insurance plans are available to cover expenses that are only partially covered by Medicare. All states (except for Minnesota, Massachusetts, and Wisconsin), as well as Puerto Rico and the District of Columbia, limit to ten the variety of Medigap policies that can be sold; each plan has a letter designation from "A" to "J." Plan A is the most basic benefit package. Each of the other nine plans includes the basic benefit package plus some other benefits. If you live in Minnesota, Massachusetts, or Wisconsin, contact your state insurance department to find out what alternative Medigap coverage is offered.

Federal laws guarantee that for a period of six months from the date you are enrolled in Medicare Part B (medical insurance) you have a right, if you are at least age 65, to buy the Medigap policy of your choice regardless of any health problems you have. Premiums vary from insurance company to insurance company and state to state.

Another Medicare supplement health insurance product is Medicare SELECT. This plan is the same as any Medigap insurance policy. The only difference is that, except for emergencies, with Medicare SELECT you must go to specific hospitals and often see specific doctors to be eligible for full benefits.

Trying to navigate the government health insurance maze can be overwhelming. Fortunately, there's the Health Insurance Counseling and Advocacy Program (HICAP), a government program that offers free bilingual advice on health insurance, including long-term care insurance, through its Eldercare Locator service.

 Some immigrants cannot receive Medicaid.

There is a mandatory five-year ban on Medicaid eligibility for qualified immigrants who were admitted to the United States on or after August 22, 1996. The only exceptions are refugees, people who have been granted asylum, individuals whose deportation is being withheld by the Immigration and Naturalization Service (INS), lawful permanent residents, and honorably discharged U.S. military veterans. After the five-year ban expires, an immigrant's access to Medicaid is up to the state. Immigrants are eligible for emergency services under Medicaid at any time.

Social Security also offers two disability programs: disability insurance and Supplemental Security Income (SSI). Workers pay for disability insurance with their Social Security taxes. Eligibility is based on your work history, and the benefits are determined by your earnings. SSI is financed through general tax revenues. Benefits are paid to people with low income and limited resources.

If you're a U.S. citizen, you can get your Social Security benefits in another country once you've been away for at least thirty days in a row. You're considered to be outside the United States until you return and stay in the U.S. for at least thirty days in a row.

In addition, there are nineteen countries where you can continue to receive benefits as long as you're eligible no matter how long you stay outside the United States, and there are fifty-three countries where you may receive your benefits unless you're receiving benefits as a dependent or survivor. In that case, you must meet additional requirements. However, you cannot receive Social Security payments if you're in some countries, including Cuba.

To receive benefits if you're living outside the United States, you will need to regularly fill out a questionnaire to notify the government of any changes that could affect your payments. Things that must be reported include work outside the United States, marriage, and adoption of a child.

ACCIÓN For bilingual information on government Medicare, SSI, and disability benefits, call the Social Security Administration at 800-772-1213. For information on Medicaid benefits, call your state insurance department (pages 60–61). For more information about benefits if you're outside the United States, contact the nearest U.S. embassy, consulate, or U.S. Social Security office. For a brochure called *Medicare, Medigap and Managed Care: Consumer Update,* send $3 to United Seniors Health Cooperative, 1331 H St. NW, Washington, DC 20005. To reach HICAP and other local agencies that provide a wide range of consumer services, call the Eldercare Locator Service at 800-677-1116.

 Don't go without auto insurance, and get the right coverage.

If you own a *carrito,* you must have auto insurance. How much coverage you get depends on several factors including your state's requirements, the type of car you have, what type of health insurance you have, and your assets. When you buy auto insurance, you're paying for three basic features: liability, medical payments, and collision and comprehensive coverage.

Bodily injury liability *(responsabilidad por lesiones corporales)* covers any passengers in your car who are hurt or injured in an accident, and people in the other car or cars if you're at fault for the accident. Property-damage liability *(responsabilidad por daños a la propiedad)* covers damage to cars and other property, such as a storefront.

This type of liability coverage is sold in what's known as a "split limit" format, which tells you the maximum amount paid for each person hurt in an accident, the total maximum amount paid per accident, and the total maximum amount paid for property damage.

In California, the legal minimum is 15-30-5, or $15,000 per person,

$30,000 per accident, and $5,000 for property damage. But you can be sued for more, so you may want to buy more insurance than what's legally required. Many experts recommend a split limit of at least 100/300/100.

Medical payments (*pagos médicos*) coverage takes care of medical and hospital bills for you and your passengers up to a certain amount. Whether or not you're required to buy medical payments coverage depends on the state you live in. In a "no-fault" state, you or your insurance company pays for all injuries and damage in a car accident no matter who's at fault. In this case, you're probably required to buy a minimum amount of medical payments coverage, which is also called personal injury or no-fault insurance.

In a "fault" or "tort" state, the person who caused the accident, or the person's insurance company, pays for all injuries and damage. Medical payments coverage in "tort" states is not required. Determining who's at fault can often lead to long and expensive lawsuits. And if you get hit by an uninsured motorist, you're out of luck.

There are currently eleven no-fault states: Massachusetts, Florida, Georgia, New York, Minnesota, Hawaii, Colorado, Michigan, Utah, Kansas, and North Dakota. In three other states, Kentucky, Pennsylvania, and New Jersey, drivers can choose between the no-fault and tort system.

Collision (*colisión*) insurance covers the cost to repair or replace your car if you have an accident. Comprehensive (*comprensivo*) coverage pays for damage caused by fire, flood, theft, windstorms, and other non-collision damage. Collision and comprehensive is not usually required by law, but it may be required if you have a car loan or lease.

If your car is new or still worth a lot of money, you should get collision and comprehensive coverage. But you may want to drop the coverage if the cost to repair your car would surpass its blue book (retail) value, and if the premium amounts to more than 10 percent of the value of the car.

 **Buy uninsured and underinsured motorist coverage.**

Uninsured motorist coverage, which is required in some states, pays the medical expenses for you and your passengers if you're hit by a motorist who doesn't have any insurance. Underinsured motorist coverage protects you and your passengers if you get hit by a driver who doesn't have enough insurance.

Skip rental car insurance if you already have auto insurance for your own car.

If you don't own a car and have no auto insurance, buy coverage from the rental agency. But if you already have insurance for your own car, it may already include coverage for rental vehicles. If so, there's no need to buy extra coverage. Collision coverage is also offered free of charge by some credit card companies if you use their credit card to pay for the rental.

 You must be covered by a licensed Mexican insurance company if you drive in Mexico.

There's a chance that your regular U.S. insurance policy can be extended as long as you remain within 25 miles of the U.S. border. Some insurance companies issue endorsements, which add on to your policy, to cover such trips. However, there's no guarantee that Mexican authorities will recognize coverage provided by U.S. insurance companies. And if you drive beyond 25 miles of the U.S. border, you must purchase coverage from a licensed Mexican insurance company.

While auto insurance is not required in Mexico, having an accident in Mexico is very serious and is considered a criminal offense. Mexican authorities can detain you until they determine who was at fault. And you must be able to prove that you have the financial ability to pay for damages either with cash or an approved Mexican insurance policy.

To play it safe, we recommend buying insurance from a licensed Mexican insurance company before leaving the United States no matter how far you plan to travel. Policies can be purchased along the U.S.Mexican border. Most states also make finding a legitimate Mexican insurance company pretty easy.

The Texas and New Mexico state insurance departments provide lists of Mexican insurance companies that are licensed to sell auto policies in those two states. The Arizona state insurance department provides names of licensed agents who are authorized to sell Mexican auto insurance. In California all you can get is confirmation that an insurance agent is properly licensed, but it's better than nothing (pages 60–61).

The cost of Mexican insurance depends on the value of your car, how many people will be traveling with you, the length of your stay, and where you plan to travel. Some agents will charge broker fees as high as $100 to sell you such a policy, so compare costs before making a purchase. A final caveat: any insurance policy becomes invalid if the driver is under the influence of alcohol or drugs.

ACCIÓN If you speak Spanish you can verify the licenses of companies selling insurance in Mexico by calling the Comision Nacional de Seguros y Finanzas at 011-525-724-7436 or 011-525-724-7597.

 Cut costs by selecting a high deductible, and asking for all your discounts.

Lo que paga depende de quien es. Auto insurance premiums are based on many factors including your age, place of residence, gender, driving record, number of miles driven, make and year of car, and even your credit record. You may be able to cut these costs by getting a special group rate if you're a member of a professional organization, request the proper discounts, and carry the highest deductible you can afford.

Discounts are given for safety factors: air bags and anti-lock brakes; anti-theft devices, such as a car alarm; having taken defensive driving courses; using carpools; insuring more than one car with the same company; and even making good grades, if you're a student.

Ask about installment plans, which are available to drivers who can't pay premiums all at once. Fees for these so-called premium pricing plans are usually pretty low. But some can be just as high as the fees charged for credit cards, so shop around.

If you've got a really bad driving record and are having a hard time finding insurance, don't give up and go without. At least one company, Progressive Insurance Corp., specializes in coverage of high-risk drivers (and it provides free auto insurance quotes from several different insurance companies). Many states also offer insurance to high-risk drivers (pages 60–61).

Consumer Reports magazine also offers an Auto Insurance Price Service to drivers in Arizona, California, Colorado, Connecticut, Florida, Georgia,

Idaho, Illinois, Louisiana, Michigan, Mississippi, Missouri, Nevada, New Jersey, New York, North Carolina, Ohio, Pennsylvania, Tennessee, Texas, Virginia, Washington, and Wisconsin. The service will fax or mail you a personal report the same day. Reports cost $12 for the first vehicle, and $8 for each additional vehicle on the same call.

ACCIÓN For bilingual information about auto insurance, call the National Insurance Consumer Helpline at 800-942-4242. To reach Consumer Reports Auto Insurance Price Service, call 800-224-9495. To reach Progressive Insurance Corp., call 800-288-6776.

 Buy life insurance after you learn about the different types of policies available, and you understand what you really need.

Life insurance pays benefits to your heirs when you die. Pretty simple. What's confusing is figuring out who needs life insurance, how much coverage to get, and what type of policy to buy. Single people without any dependents usually don't need life insurance. However, Laura the financial planner has found in her practice that many Latinos provide financial assistance to family, so life insurance may be something to consider no matter what your marital status.

There are two types of life insurance plans, term *(seguro temporal)* and cash value *(seguro con valor en efectivo)*. With term life insurance you pay a regular premium for a fixed amount of time, usually from one to twenty years. When the term expires, you can renew the policy and start over. When you die, the insurance company pays a specific amount of money to your beneficiaries. This is called a death benefit. With term life insurance, premiums are typically pretty low at first, but they rise as you get older.

There are two kinds of term life insurance policies: annual renewable *(seguro a plazo renovable por anualidades)* and level premium *(prima nivelada)*. Annual renewable term insurance doesn't require a medical exam for renewal, but the premiums will usually rise. A level premium policy lets you lock in a premium for a specific period of time. When the time is up you usually have to pass a medical exam to renew at a good rate. Some term life policies will let you convert to cash value policies later on.

Cash value life insurance is also known as "permanent insurance." A cash value policy uses your premium in two ways. Some of it goes to pay for the insurance portion of the policy. The rest goes to an investment portion. The cash value in the investment portion builds, tax-deferred. You can cash in the amount that's grown in the investment portion or use the cash value as collateral for different types of loans. Cash value policies are either participating, which means they pay dividends, or nonparticipating, which means they don't pay dividends.

There are three kinds of cash value life insurance policies: whole life, universal life, and variable life. Whole life (*vida entera*) policies generally have fixed death benefits and premiums, and the cash value is invested in fixed-income instruments such as bonds or money market accounts that usually guarantee a minimum return. However, the insurance company is not required to tell you what effective rate of interest you're earning on your policy.

Universal life (*vida universal*) policies have adjustable death benefits, flexible insurance premiums, and higher costs and fees than whole life. The return on the cash value depends on the insurance company's performance and the return on its investment portfolio.

The cash value and death benefits of variable life (*vida variable*) policies fluctuate with the return on a portfolio of investments that includes mutual funds. In fact, variable life policies are considered securities contracts. Premium payments are flexible. Fees and costs are higher than those for whole life policies.

 Think twice before buying a cash value life insurance policy.

Most consumer groups recommend term life insurance, especially if you're younger, because it's a lot less expensive than cash value life insurance. Unfortunately, some insurance agents push cash value life insurance policies because of the high commissions they earn on these plans.

While it's true that the cash value portion of your policy grows tax-free until withdrawal, you don't get any up-front tax deductions as you do if you contribute to a 401(k), SEP-IRA, or Keogh. (For more information on these retirement plans see Chapter 7.) So, be sure you've contributed the maximum allowable limit to these retirement accounts first.

With proper planning, however, a cash value policy can come in handy by making the proceeds paid to your beneficiaries exempt from estate taxes. Of course, you'll need a big estate at the time of your death to take advantage of this benefit. (See Chapter 8 for more information on estate planning.)

We strongly recommend two things if you're tempted to buy a cash value policy. First, get a comprehensive financial analysis from an objective financial planner, not an insurance agent who makes his or her living by selling these plans. Second, compare prices by calling insurers that sell so-called no-load policies directly to the public. These plans are cheaper because agents don't charge sales commissions. (For a list of direct-market insurers, see page 57.)

 Be sure you buy the right amount of life insurance coverage.

The National Endowment for Financial Education recommends buying a policy that has a face value of 8 to 14 times your annual earnings and other liquid assets for people aged 40 or younger. If you're older than 40, multiply your earnings 4 to 10 times. Be sure to consider the number of your dependents, college tuition for children, mortgage payments, and the lifetime income needs of the surviving spouse.

ACCIÓN For bilingual information about life insurance, call the National Insurance Consumer Helpline at 800-942-4242. For a free booklet called *What You Should Know About Buying Life Insurance,* call the American Council of Life Insurance at 800-338-4471.

 Get an unbiased opinion if you're thinking of switching life insurance policies or buying second-to-die policies.

"Churning" *(voltear)* is the term used when an insurance agent convinces a customer to switch from one cash-value life insurance policy to another policy. Ugly word. Uglier practice. This usually generates a hefty commission for the agent but costs the consumer lots of money in surrender charges, taxes, and other fees. A good agent or planner should offer to show you a written comparison of the replacement policy and your existing policy. Some states now require agents to do so.

Second-to-die policies *(pólizas de segundo en fallecer)* cover two people, but pay benefits only after the second person dies. These plans are usually bought by wealthier people who want to make sure their beneficiaries don't have to sell any assets they've received to pay for estate taxes.

To get an unbiased opinion about a life insurance or second-to-die policy, contact the Consumer Federation of America's Insurance Group. The group offers a Life Insurance Rate of Return service that tells you whether your current life insurance plan is worth keeping. It can also compare your current life insurance policy with new ones, and analyze second-to-die insurance policies.

An analysis of a life insurance plan costs $40 for the first policy, and $30 for each additional plan submitted at the same time for a comparison. Illustrations of second-to-die plans cost $75 for the first one, and $30 for each additional plan submitted at the same time for a comparison.

The American Society of Chartered Life Underwriters & Chartered Financial Consultants also offers a free worksheet to help you evaluate the pros and cons of changing life insurance plans.

ACCIÓN To reach the Consumer Federation of America's Rate of Return service, call 202-387-6121. To reach the American Society of Chartered Life Underwriters, call 800-392-6900.

 Learn how to tap into your life insurance policy to obtain cash.

Whether you own term life insurance, which we recommend in most cases, or a cash value policy, there are several ways you can tap into your policy to get some money if you're terminally ill or elderly:

Viatical settlements. A viatical settlement company will typically pay you a lump sum of 60 percent to 90 percent of the face value of the policy, depending on your life expectancy. After you die, the viatical company receives all the benefits from your life insurance policy.

The sicker you are, the more money you'll get. You'll get an average of 90 percent of the face value of your life insurance policy if you have three months to live, for example, but just 60 percent if you have 24 months to live. Viatical settlements are best for people who don't feel the need to leave money to heirs.

If you want a viatical settlement, you should deal only with a licensed broker or settlement company. (Your state insurance department should keep a list.) A broker will handle the whole transaction for you for an average commission of 6 percent of the face value of the policy. You can also sell your policy directly to a viatical settlement company on your own if you have the strength and time.

Accelerated death benefits. Also known as living benefits, these are available through some insurance companies on some policies. To qualify, you generally must have a short life expectancy: between six months and twelve months. The payment you get ranges from 25 percent to 95 percent of the policy's face value. (Most offer 50 percent.)

The remainder of the policy's value will be paid to your beneficiaries after you die. The insurance company doesn't make any money on ADBs, unless the policy lapses after you get your lump sum payment and it no longer has to pay the remaining death benefits to your heirs. The only reason to take an ADB instead of a viatical settlement is if you don't need all the money up front, and want to make sure something is left to your heirs.

Policy loans. You can get cash for your whole and universal life insurance policy by borrowing against its cash value. (This option is generally not available on a term or group insurance policy.) The interest rate you'll owe on the loan can be fixed or variable, and will depend on the policy you have and the insurance company from which it was purchased.

The death benefit will be restored to you if you repay the loan and interest. If not, the loan and interest will be subtracted from the death benefit, and your heirs will get the rest. Policy loans are good deals if you have enough cash value because you can borrow as much as you want, and your heirs get the death benefits when you die. Most people, however, don't have enough cash value in their policies to take out a loan.

Mix and match policies. It's sometimes possible to "mix and match," or receive a combination of viatical settlements, ADBs, and loans, on the same policy. If you have multiple life insurance policies, you can always sell one or more and keep the others so you can leave some money to your heirs.

ACCIÓN For a free brochure called *What You Should Know About Accelerated Death Benefits* and a list of insurance companies that offer these policies, call the National Insurance Consumer Helpline at 800-942-4242.

 Carefully consider long-term care insurance.

A year in a U.S. nursing home costs about $35,000. That number is expected to rise an average of 7 percent annually, according to the U.S. Congressional Study on Aging. At the same time, many fear that Medicare, which helps pay for the care of the elderly and poor, will be slashed.

As a result, a huge market has developed for long-term care insurance, which pays for all or part of nursing home or in-home care. Premiums for some long-term care insurance qualify as a tax deduction if these costs, plus other medical expenses, exceed 7.5 percent of your adjusted gross income. Benefits from long-term care insurance payments are also excluded from taxable income.

However, long-term care insurance is expensive and complicated. Basically, these policies are for people who have substantial assets, but not enough money to pay for long-term care without being wiped out financially. Also, these policies must be purchased before you actually need the care. Many insurance companies won't sell long-term care insurance plans to people over the age of 85, or to individuals with certain pre-existing medical conditions.

Some states, however, offer more-affordable long-term care insurance plans to low- to moderate-income people through a national pilot program called Partnership for Long-Term Care. Premiums vary depending on where you live. Also, the program will provide only a maximum of five years of care. The following states have Partnership for Long-Term Care insurance policies:

California	800-CARE-445
Connecticut	800-547-3443
Illinois	800-548-9034
Indiana	800-452-4800
New York	888-697-7582
Washington	800-397-4422

How do you figure out if long-term care insurance is for you? One rule of thumb is that your premiums should never exceed 5 percent of your annual income. But if your assets are less than the cost of one year in a nursing home, long-term care insurance may not be for you. Why? It doesn't make sense to buy an expensive policy to protect a small estate.

Among the key questions to ask before buying a long-term care policy:

❏ Is both home care and nursing home care covered?
❏ What is the daily benefit?
❏ How long do these benefits last?
❏ What's the deductible and elimination period?
❏ Do premiums increase every year?
❏ Is there a maximum lifetime benefit?
❏ Is there inflation protection to cover the rising cost of care?
❏ Is there a grace period for late payments?
❏ Are there age limits or specific health conditions that would prohibit you from purchasing a policy?
❏ How long is the waiting period for pre-existing conditions?
❏ Are there any injuries or diseases that aren't covered, such as mental illness?

ACCIÓN For a free copy of the *Guide to Long-Term Care,* and a directory of insurance companies that provide these policies, write to the Health Insurance Association of America at 555 13th St. N.W., Washington, DC 20004, or call 888-844-2782.

 Buy homeowners insurance if you own a home, or renters insurance if you are a renter.

If you own a home and have a mortgage, chances are your lender will require you to get homeowners insurance *(seguro para propietarios de vivienda)*, which protects the structure and contents of your home. It also protects you if you're held liable for injuring someone or damaging another person's property.

When purchasing insurance, get enough coverage to rebuild your home and replace the contents of your home, which is known as the replacement cost *(costo de reemplazo)*. There's absolutely no need to insure your land.

Different types of homes require different types of insurance. In most states, a basic homeowners insurance policy is known as HO-1. Fancier homeowners policies are labeled HO-2 and HO-3. Renters insurance is called HO-4; HO-6 is for co-ops and condominiums; and HO-8 is for older homes. For some strange reason, there's no HO-5 or HO-7 policy available.

You can figure out the replacement cost of your personal property by making an inventory of everything you own, then estimating how much it would cost to replace these items. If you can, include the purchase date and price of your belongings, receipts, and the serial and model numbers of appliances.

Liability protection *(cobertura de responsabilidad)* covers you if someone falls down the stairs at your house and decides to sue you. Most policies provide up to $100,000 in coverage, but you may want more if your assets—home, car, investments—are worth more than that.

Liability coverage is what makes having renters insurance so important. The plan will also pay for the contents of your apartment if they're damaged or lost due to fire or theft. But the biggest reason to get this coverage is to protect your assets in case you get sued.

You can trim the cost of your homeowners insurance bill by making sure you're given a discount for things such as dead-bolt locks, fire alarms and extinguishers, and security systems. You may get a discount if you buy your auto and homeowners insurance policies from the same company.

If you can't get homeowners insurance you may be able to get some coverage from your state through a FAIR (Fair Access to Insurance Requirements) program (pages 60–61).

ACCIÓN For bilingual information about homeowners insurance, call the National Insurance Consumer Helpline at 800-942-4242.

 Consider an umbrella policy.

Instead of buying more homeowners and auto insurance if you have a lot of assets to protect, it may be more economical to get an umbrella liability policy. This type of policy will cover you for damages not included in your homeowners and auto insurance policies, such as slander. The cost is usually pretty reasonable. Most policies provide $1 million of coverage for between $200 to $300 per year.

 Consider disaster insurance for floods, earthquakes, tornadoes, and the like.

Homeowners insurance excludes floods and earthquakes. If you're at risk for either of these natural disasters you need a special policy. Flood insurance is available through the National Flood Insurance Program, which is operated through the Federal Emergency Management Agency. Earthquake insurance can be hard to get and expensive. If you can't find it you may need to resort to the state's FAIR program (pages 60–61).

ACCIÓN To reach the National Flood Insurance Program call 800-638-6620.

❑ Buy insurance to protect against losses that could result in bankruptcy, or when it is required by law.
❑ If you can afford it, buy insurance to protect against losses that would force you to borrow money.
❑ Skip insurance for losses you can pay for out-of-pocket from existing assets or current income.

❏ Investigate the health of an insurance company by calling a rating company such as A.M. Best, Duff & Phelps, Moody's, Standard & Poor's, and Weiss Ratings.

❏ Investigate the credentials of an insurance agent and an insurance carrier by calling your state insurance department.

❏ Reassess your insurance needs with every major change in your life, such as a marriage or the birth of a child.

❏ Shop around for the best insurance rates by calling free telephone quote services, direct-market insurance companies, and insurance agents, both independent and captive.

❏ Keep insurance costs down by getting a high deductible, and making sure you get the discounts you're entitled to.

❏ Find out what kind of benefits you're entitled to from government agencies.

❏ Consider getting an unbiased second opinion before buying or changing insurance policies.

❏ If you're having trouble getting coverage, call your state insurance department to see what types of insurance plans they offer.

ADDITIONAL RESOURCES

Recommended Books

Choosing and Using an HMO, by Ellyn Spragins (Princeton, New Jersey: Bloomberg Press, 1998).

How to Insure Your Home, ed. Silver Lake Editors (Santa Monica, California: Merritt Publishing, 1996).

How to Insure Your Income, ed. Silver Lake Editors (Santa Monica, California: Merritt Publishing, 1997).

How to Insure Your Life, by Wilson, Reg, and the Merritt Editors (Santa Monica, California: Merritt Publishing, 1996).

Smarter Insurance Solutions, by Janet Bamford (Princeton, New Jersey: Bloomberg Press, 1996).

CHAPTER 4

Investing

"ONE WHO DOES NOT VENTURE HAS NO LUCK"   —MEXICO

DELIA WAS RAISED IN A WORKING CLASS MEXICAN-AMERICAN FAMILY that survived from paycheck to paycheck and never talked about money. "It was rude to ask how much you made, it was rude to ask how much you paid for something, it was rude to ask anything about money," says the retired health care administrator from San Francisco. And investing? "It was never part of our language or thinking."

To be sure, some Latinos are very sophisticated investors. Many of us contribute to 401(k) plans and individual retirement accounts (IRAs), or have received stock from the companies we work for (although we may not be sure exactly how these investments work).

Unfortunately, most of us miss some opportunities or even avoid investing altogether because we don't understand how it works, have no idea where to get help, or are uncomfortable discussing money. For example, 16 percent of Latinos own individual stocks and mutual fund shares compared with 23 percent of non-Latinos, according to the U.S. Census Bureau.

¿Por qué no invertimos? One big reason is simply a lack of exposure. If our parents were investors who perused the financial pages over breakfast,

chances are we'll be investors, too. If not, the learning curve is a lot steeper.

There aren't many brokerages in Latino neighborhoods, let alone ones that provide bilingual educational materials or brokers. Laura the financial planner is a rarity. In-depth coverage of financial topics in many Latino-oriented newspapers, magazines, and TV and radio programs is thin or inconsistent. Outside our neighborhoods and communities it is hard to know whom to trust.

Latinos often grapple with cultural barriers to investing as well. Many of us grew up in households like Delia's where any serious discussion of money was frowned upon. Both as a journalist and a financial planner, las Lauras have found that money is a taboo subject for many Latinos. Our friends, clients, and fellow Latino financial planners have told us that it's easier to talk about birth control than it is to talk about money!

As immigrants, or the children of immigrants, many Latinos tend to steer clear of "intangible" investments such as stocks, bonds, and mutual funds and lean toward things we can literally lay our hands on, such as a home, a piece of land, or the family business.

Financial-services companies have tended to ignore the Latino market, thinking we don't have any money to invest. It's true that Latinos are often younger and have larger families, than other population segments, both of which can mean having less money to invest. The U.S. Census bureau says the median age of Latinos is 26 years, while the median age for non-Hispanic whites is 37.3. The average number of people residing in a Hispanic household is 3.45, compared to 2.49 for non-Hispanic whites, according to the *Hispanic Market Handbook,* by M. Isabel Valdes and Marta H. Seoane. However, Valdes and Seoane also note that the fastest growing segment of the Latino market is households with annual income of $50,000 or more.

Changing our ideas and behavior about investing isn't easy. It won't happen overnight. But educating ourselves about investing basics is among the most important things we can do to build a solid financial future for ourselves, for the people we love, and for our communities.

Those of us who are *solteras* need to have the knowledge and confidence to make our own decisions. Financial education is particularly important for women. Since women outlive men an average of seven years, there's a good chance that many women who are married will end up handling the *familias'* finances at some point.

Las Amigas Investment Corp. is an all-female investment club from San Antonio with twelve members between the ages of 45 and 65. The group used to gather once a week to *chismosear* over lunch. But as more members of their circle became widowed or divorced, they decided to form an investment club to learn about finance in a friendly, supportive atmosphere.

The club now owns six stocks that have posted a total one-year return of about 10 percent, which is well below the overall market performance for the same period. The main goal, however, is to gain confidence, not get rich. "I feel we've really gotten a handle on this," says Yolanda, a member of Las Amigas, adding that the club wants to show the next generation how important it is to start early.

Some of us have the time, temperament, and talent to learn about investing and do it all ourselves. Others will prefer to work with a financial planner (see Chapter 10). But even if you hire an adviser, you need to take the time to learn the basics so that you can understand the advice you get, ask the right questions, and evaluate the progress of your investments.

 Never buy an investment unless you understand exactly how it works.

Lots of new investments are being introduced every day. As a beginning investor, focus on the fundamentals: stocks, bonds, and mutual funds. We'll review how you can use them to build a strong portfolio *(cartera de valores)*. (For a discussion about variable annuities, which are mutual funds with an insurance component, go to Chapter 7.)

Stocks. A share of stock *(acciones)* is a small share of ownership in a company. If you buy a company's stock, you're a shareholder of that company. The more stock you buy, the more of the company you own. What you pay for a share is known as the stock price, or price per share. Stock can be purchased from a brokerage firm, or sometimes directly from the company whose stock you want to buy.

Stock can be owned directly by holding an actual stock certificate that's issued in your name, or by holding the stock in "street name," which means it's registered in the name of your brokerage. In this case, all records are computerized and you won't get a stock certificate. But you can track your holdings through regular statements specifying what you own. Stock can also be owned indirectly through a mutual fund *(fondo mutuo)*, which is a pool of stocks, bonds, and cash (more on mutual funds later in this chapter).

There are two ways you can make money investing in stocks. First, some companies pay part of their earnings, or profits, to their stockholders as a dividend *(dividendo)*, usually every quarter. The other way to make money on a stock is to sell it for more than you paid. The difference is called a capital gain *(ganancia de capital)*.

Stock prices are sometimes referred to in points *(puntos)*, one point equalling $1. A stock's total return *(rendimiento total)* is the increase in stock value plus any dividends. Say you buy a stock at $10 a share, and each share pays a $.10 cent dividend for the year. If the price rises to $11 a share, then your total return on that stock is $1.10 per share, or 11 percent.

There are two kinds of stock: Common stock *(acciones ordinarias)*, which gives you a vote on the selection of directors and other important matters, but you aren't guaranteed any dividends. Preferred stock *(acciones de preferencia)* guarantees a dividend even if the company loses money, but it doesn't give you voting rights.

When investors talk about the stock market—or simply the market *(la bolsa)*—they're usually referring to the Dow Jones Industrial Average, an index that tracks the performance of 30 large U.S. companies such as Coca-Cola and Exxon. There are other market indexes as well. The Standard & Poor's (S&P) 500 tracks stock prices of 500 large U.S. companies. The Russell 2000 tracks 2,000 smaller U.S. stocks. The Wilshire 5000 tracks stocks from the U.S. companies of all sizes. The Morgan Stanley EAFE index tracks prices of stocks in other major countries of the world. The Morgan Stanley Emerging Markets index follows stocks in countries with economies that are still developing.

Stocks are bought and sold on stock exchanges. The main U.S. exchanges are the New York Stock Exchange (NYSE), which focuses on some of the largest publicly traded companies, and the American Stock Exchange (AMEX), which focuses on small- to medium-sized companies. Both the NYSE and the AMEX have trading floors in New York. Stocks can also be traded "over the counter" (OTC) through a computer network of stock-brokers called Nasdaq (National Association of Security Dealers Automated Quotation System). Nasdaq has no physical location. (Amex and Nasdaq merged in late 1998, but continue to operate separately and independently.) There are many regional exchanges as well. If you buy or sell individual stocks, in most cases you'll need a stockbroker *(corredor de bolsa)*. We'll talk about different kinds of brokers later in this chapter.

Stocks can be extremely volatile *(volátil)*, which means their prices can shift quickly and unpredictably in the short term. But their long-term returns are hard to beat. For example, the one-year return from investing in large-company U.S. stocks between 1926 and 1996 has ranged from a 43.3 percent loss to a 54 percent gain. But the average compound annual return of stocks, including reinvested dividends over the same 70-year period, has been 10.7 percent, according to Ibbotson Associates, a Chicago-based research firm.

Piensen en esto: If during this period you had invested $1 in the stock market and held it for just one year, you could have ended up with a loss of 43 cents, or as much as $1.54 at the end of that year. But if you invested $1 in the stock market in 1926 and reinvested the dividends for seventy years, you would have ended up with $1,370.95 in 1996.

That's why you shouldn't buy stocks if you think you might need the money in less than five years. The chance of losing money is too great. But if you hold stocks for more than five years—the longer the better—the chance of turning a profit is very good. Ideally, you should try to hold stocks for at least seven years.

Nobody can predict when stock prices will go up or when they'll go down. That's why "timing the market"—buying stocks when you think prices are at a low point and selling them when you think prices are at a high—is a bad idea. *Ni los profesionales pueden* even with their fancy college degrees and research staffs to help them. And that includes las Lauras. Instead of jumping in and out of the stock market, the best strategy is to "buy and hold."

Bonds. A bond is an IOU, with you acting as the lender. The borrower is either the federal, state, or municipal government, or a corporation. These borrowers use your money for a specific period of time, or term *(plazo)*, to finance their day-to-day operations and special projects. In return for your investment, borrowers promise to pay you a certain amount of interest *(interés)* and to return the bond's face value *(valor nominal)*—the amount originally paid for the bond—on a specific date, called the maturity date *(fecha de* *vencimiento).* The face value, also called par value, of a bond is usually $1,000. Bonds are called fixed-income securities *(valores de ingreso fijo),* because the rate of return on your investment is set.

Most bonds are coupon bonds *(bono con cupones),* which pay regular interest, generally every month or quarter. A coupon is a detachable printed statement on a bond specifying the interest due at a given time. There also are zero coupon bonds, which pay no regular interest. Instead, zero coupon bonds are sold at a discount price much lower than their face value, and your gain or loss consists of the difference when you redeem or sell the bond.

Most bonds are fully negotiable, which means they can be sold before maturity, or before the term is up, to other investors on the secondary market *(mercado secundario),* which is run by brokerage houses. The market value of a bond, or the price you get if you sell it before maturity, might be more or less than your original investment, depending on what's happened to interest rates and inflation since the bond was first issued. A change in the financial condition of the bond issuer can also affect a bond's price.

Interest rates play a big part in determining a bond market's value. When interest rates fall, prices of existing bonds rise. That's because the old bonds are still paying the older, higher interest rates, which makes them more attractive than newly issued bonds. Conversely, when interest rates rise, prices of existing bonds fall.

The closer a bond is to maturity, however, the less its price will fluctuate in reaction to changing interest rates. Because bond prices fluctuate, when you buy a bond you're likely to pay either more than the bond's face value, which is known as paying a premium *(prima),* or less than the face value, which is known as buying it at a discount. That means your actual return, or yield *(rendimiento),* will be less or more than the stated interest rate, or coupon rate, of the bond.

Let's say you buy a bond with a $1,000 face value, a 10 percent coupon rate, and a 10-year maturity. Each year, you'll receive $100 in interest (10 percent of $1,000). If you paid the face value, then your actual yield would indeed be 10 percent. But if you paid $1,100 for the bond, then your yield would be 9.1 percent ($100 divided by $1,100). If you paid only $900 your yield would be 11.1 percent ($100 divided by $900).

Short-term bonds mature in one to three years. Intermediate-term bonds mature in three to ten years. Long-term bonds mature in ten to thirty years.

Long-term bonds have higher yields than short-term bonds, but they're riskier because there's a longer period of time in which something can go wrong that lowers the value of a bond. Interest rates may rise. The borrower may go bankrupt. With some bonds, the borrower can decide on its own to pay back, or "call," the bond, before the maturity date, and so deprive you of years of high interest rates.

Because a bond can be bought and sold by many different investors during its lifetime, it's possible to buy a bond that was sold, say, 29 years ago with a 30-year term. That means the bond will mature in one year. So even though it started off as a long-term bond, it now behaves like a short-term bond—with a lower yield and a lower risk.

Treasury securities (*valores de tesorería*), also called Treasuries, are fully backed by the U.S. government and are considered to be the safest of all fixed-income securities. Treasury bills are issued in amounts of $1,000, are sold at a discount or reduced price, and mature in three months to one year. Treasury notes are securities that pay semiannual interest and mature in two to ten years. Treasury bonds are securities that pay semiannual interest and mature in 30 years.

Corporate bonds are issued by companies, large and small. Municipal bonds are issued by local school districts, cities, states, and local government agencies. Mortgage-backed bonds (*bonos respaldados por hipotecas*) are backed by pools of mortgage loans. Adjustable rate mortgage bonds are mortgage-backed bonds whose payments rise along with the inflation rate. Junk bonds (*bonos de calidad inferior*) offer higher yields, but have the highest risk among bonds because the borrower isn't considered financially strong. Convertible bonds issued by companies let you convert your bond into the issuer's common stock at a pre-determined price. U.S. savings bonds, or series EE bonds, are issued by the federal government and require a minimum investment of $25. (For more on savings bonds go to Chapter 6.)

Certain bonds have tax advantages. Interest paid on Treasury bonds is usually exempt from state and local income taxes, but isn't exempt from federal income taxes. Interest paid on municipal bonds is usually exempt from federal income taxes, and in some cases, from state and local income taxes. However, capital gains on municipal bonds are subject to federal income taxes, and possibly state and local income taxes.

Find out the credit rating of a bond before you buy it.

A bond's credit rating is a measure of its credit quality—the likelihood that the borrower will make all the scheduled payments on time. There are several independent bond-rating agencies. The two biggest are Standard & Poor's Corp. and Moody's Investor Service. The lowest-risk (highest-quality) bonds are rated Aaa by Moody's, and AAA by Standard & Poor's Corp. The highest-risk (lowest quality) bonds are rated C by both agencies (a D rating means the bond is in default). A broker who sells you a bond can tell you its credit rating. *Si no se lo dicen, no lo compren.*

Remember that a lower risk usually means a lower return, and a higher risk usually means a higher return. So bonds rated Aaa or AAA such as U.S. Treasury bonds will yield less than bonds that carry a C rating. That's why another name for a junk bond is a high-yield bond.

In general, bonds are considered to be lower-risk investments than stocks, which means the return on bonds is generally lower than the return on stocks over the long term. But this isn't necessarily bad. Bonds can be used to balance the higher risk of stocks.

For example, between 1926 and 1996, the compound annual return including reinvested dividends was 5.1 percent for long-term U.S. government bonds; 5.6 percent for long-term U.S. corporate bonds; 5.2 percent for intermediate-term U.S. government bonds; and 3.7 percent for 30-day Treasury bills, according to Ibbotson Associates.

You can buy and sell bonds through the same brokers who handle stock transactions. Treasuries can be purchased through the federal government to save money on broker commissions. (For a list of Federal Reserve banks and telephone numbers, see pages 94–95.)

Also, try to buy bonds with varying maturity dates, which is known as "laddering." Laddering sounds like a sophisticated concept, but it's really a matter of using common sense and a calendar. *Vamos a decir que tiene* $40,000 to invest in bonds, instead of placing all those *pesos en un bono grande*, break the investments into $10,000 chunks, and invest them at different rates of returns with mixed maturities.

ACCIÓN For a free brochure called *Fixed-Income Investments,* call Charles Schwab & Co. at 800-435-4000. A Spanish-language version called *Inversiones de Renta Fija* is also available from Schwab's Centro Latinoamericano at 800-362-1774.

Mutual funds. A mutual fund is an investment vehicle that pools together money from thousands of people. A fund manager is in charge of deciding where to invest the money, which usually goes into stocks, bonds, or money market instruments *(instrumento del mercado monetario)*; short-term, credit-worthy securities such as bank certificates of deposit; and short-term corporate and government debt, or a combination of the three. You invest in a mutual fund by buying units known as shares *(acciones)*. In effect, you buy shares in a product that in turn buys shares of stocks and other securities.

Most mutual funds are open-end *(ilimitados)*, which means they're either open to new investors, or closed to new investors but still issuing shares to existing shareholders. You can buy shares in an open-end fund from a mutual fund company such as Fidelity Investments and the Vanguard Group, which each manage dozens of mutual funds. One of the benefits of an open-end fund is that you can redeem your shares whenever you like.

When you buy or redeem shares in an open-end fund, the price you pay is equal to the fund's net asset value *(valor de activo neto)*, or NAV—the total value of the fund's holdings divided by the number of shares held by investors. The NAV is calculated at the end of every trading day and is published in many newspapers the next morning. When you buy some funds, you must also pay a sales charge on top of the NAV per share.

A closed-end *(limitados)* fund issues a fixed amount of shares in an initial public offering *(oferta pública inicial)*, or IPO. After that, no new shares are issued, even to existing shareholders. In addition, the manager of a closed-end fund is not required to redeem shares from investors. A closed-end fund's shares usually trade on a stock exchange at a price that can fluctuate above or below the fund's NAV.

There are many different types of mutual funds, and some are more volatile than others. Money market funds and bond funds tend to provide the greatest security of principal. Money market funds invest only in money market instruments. Bond funds invest in individual bonds issued from

BUYING TREASURIES THROUGH TREASURY DIRECT

Treasury bills, notes, and bonds can be purchased through the Treasury Department's Treasury Direct program.

A Treasury Direct account can be opened in person or by mail at your nearest Federal Reserve Bank. You'll need your bank account number, the interbank routing number (which your bank can provide), and your Social Security number or Individual Taxpayer Identification Number.

The Pay Direct feature allows you to purchase Treasury securities by having your bank checking account debited and the money transferred to your Treasury Direct account. The minimum purchase is $1,000, and additional amounts can be purchased in increments of $1,000.

More information about Treasury Direct is available from the Bureau of Public Debt's Web site at www.publicdebt.treas.gov/. You can also buy securities over the Web. Here's a list of the regional Federal Reserve Banks:

ATLANTA	404-521-8653
BALTIMORE	410-576-3300
BIRMINGHAM	205-731-8708
BOSTON	617-973-3810
BUFFALO	716-849-5000
CHARLOTTE	704-358-2100
CHICAGO	612-322-5369
CINCINNATI	513-721-4794, ext. 334
CLEVELAND	216-579-2000
DALLAS	214-922-6100
DENVER	303-572-2470 / 2473

either foreign or U.S. governments and corporations. The difference between individual bonds and bond funds is that individual bonds have set interest rates and fixed maturity dates, while most bonds funds, being comprised of many different bonds, don't.

Stock mutual funds are heavily weighted with stocks and tend to drop and rise sharply. There are many different stock and bond mutual funds, with each category reflecting a different strategy. Income (*ingreso*) funds are designed to deliver a steady stream of income through dividends. Balanced (*equilibrado*) funds combine stocks and bonds to try to produce both capital

DETROIT	313-964-6157
EL PASO	915-521-8272
HOUSTON	713-659-4433
JACKSONVILLE	904-632-1179
KANSAS CITY	816-881-2883
LITTLE ROCK	501-324-8272
LOS ANGELES	213-624-7398
LOUISVILLE	502-568-9238
MEMPHIS	901-523-7171
MIAMI	305-471-6497
MINNEAPOLIS	612-204-5000
NASHVILLE	615-251-7100
NEW ORLEANS	504-593-3200
NEW YORK	212-720-6619
OKLAHOMA CITY	405-270-8652
OMAHA	402-221-5636
PHILADELPHIA	215-574-6680
PITTSBURGH	412-261-7802
PORTLAND	503-221-5932
RICHMOND	804-697-8372
SALT LAKE CITY	801-322-7882
SAN ANTONIO	210-224-2141
SAN FRANCISCO	415-974-2330
SEATTLE	206-343-3605
ST. LOUIS	314-444-8703
WASHINGTON, D.C.	202-874-4000

gains and steady income. Growth funds *(fondos de apreciación)* invest in stocks of more established companies whose earnings are expected to rise over the long run. Aggressive growth funds invest in stocks of new, innovative, or small companies trying to garner the highest returns in the shortest amount of time. Emerging market funds seek out countries with economies that are on the verge of breaking through to market success. Global funds invest in U.S. and foreign companies. International stock funds invest only in foreign companies.

Specialty funds, such as index funds, try to mimic the performance of stocks in a given index, such as the Standard & Poor's 500. (There are also bond index funds, which try to match the returns of the total U.S. bond market, or a particular segment of the market.) With asset allocation funds, managers move funds between different asset classes in response to the market. Socially responsible funds apply moral and ethical screens when selecting securities. Sector funds invest in a single sector of the economy such as utilities or airlines.

Mutual funds distribute their income to stockholders in the form of dividends and capital gains distributions. The dividends represent the dividends and interest that the fund earns from the securities it owns, minus the fund's operating expenses. Mutual funds distribute dividends monthly, quarterly, semiannually, or annually, depending on the fund. Capital gain distributions represent the profit a mutual fund makes when it sells securities for more than it paid. You can choose to receive dividends and capital gain distributions in cash, or ask the fund to reinvest them automatically to buy additional shares of the mutual fund.

There's a common misconception among Latinos that a lot of money is needed to invest in mutual funds. However, some mutual funds can be purchased for as little as $100 or with agreements to make monthly contributions of at least $25.

ACCIÓN For free brochures on mutual funds from the Vanguard Group's *Plain Talk* library, call 800-662-7447. A free Spanish-language brochure on mutual funds called *Fondos Mutuos* is available from Schwab's Centro Latinoamericano at 800-362-1774. Free brochures on mutual funds are also available in English and Spanish from the Investment Company Institute by writing to P.O. Box 27850, Washington, DC 20038-7850.

 Strategy is important. Before you invest, determine your financial goals and how much risk you're willing to take to achieve them.

¡Buenas noticias! Using the right mix of stocks, bonds, and mutual funds can give you a higher return on your investment than a plain old bank CD or savings account. *Y aquí va el pero.* But unlike bank and money market

accounts, these investments aren't federally insured—and they all have some risk of volatility.

If you're *muy conservador,* you're probably concerned with protecting the safety of your principal investment, not with making the principal grow. In this case, you might be better off with more money market funds and bonds than stocks. In general, the older you are, the more conservative you should be with your investments.

If you're a little more *comedido* as an investor, may want a more even distribution between stocks and fixed income investments in your portfolio. If you're an aggressive investor, you're probably willing to accept a reasonably high degree of risk to get the returns you want. That means holding more stocks than anything else. Typically, the longer you can wait until you need the money, the more aggressive you should be.

Since you can lose money by being either too conservative or too aggressive, it's important to figure out how much risk you can stomach (and how much you should try to stomach given your situation) before launching any sort of investment plan. (For a risk tolerance quiz, see pages 98–99.)

 There are inherent risks involved with any investment, and it's important to understand what they are.

If you buy the stock or a bond of an individual company, you're taking the risk that the company's financial health may deteriorate because of a business problem. This would lower the market value of the stock or the bond.

If you own a corporate bond, and the issuer's financial problem is severe enough, the company might not be able to make the interest payments that it owes you. But in general, a stock's price will fluctuate more in reaction to bad news about a company than a bond's price will. That's why stock prices are more volatile than bond prices.

The problems a company has may not be limited to that one firm. You're also taking the chance that the industry may suffer a downturn—or the entire country's economy, or even the worldwide economy, could go into a recession.

And even if the economy and the company you invested in are doing fine, you are always taking a chance that the entire stock market or bond market

RISK TOLERANCE QUIZ

Below we have devised five questions to help you determine your risk tolerance. Be honest—answer what you really would do, not what you think the right answer should be. And remember, this is only a test. Really, this is just meant to get you thinking about risk. You also need to evaluate how much you earn; how much you can save; what your objectives are; and last, but not least, how much time you have to save.

1. As a child, when you earned extra pesos or got a "special" envelope from a family member, which did you do?
   a. Hide the money under your mattress.
   b. Spend every last penny before a month had passed.
   c. Spend some of the money on things you had been saving for.

2. At this very moment, you keep your savings:
   a. Under the mattress.
   b. All your savings go to your retirement plan or mutual funds—you like "being in the market."
   c. In a money market fund or bank account.

3. In June you invested $2,000 in a Roth IRA of international mutual funds. Now it's October, and your investment is valued at $1,800. You decide to:
   a. Sell and put the money back under the mattress.
   b. Leave everything as is because you believe in the fund and are confident it will increase in value over the next five years.

will lose value. Sometimes, the stock and bond markets will go up and down for reasons that aren't apparent or don't seem rational.

 Diversify your portfolio.

c. Give it through the end of the year, but vow never to tell anyone.

4. Your brother asks if your family wants to go with theirs on a trip to Cancun. The vacation would cost $1,500 more than you have saved. You:
   a. Take an extra job and save the money (maybe even under the mattress).
   b. Ask him, "When do we leave?" and plan to charge the trip on a credit card.
   c. Go on a less expensive trip with the money you have saved.

5. You received a huge tax refund this year—again. Immediately, you:
   a. Put the money with last year's refund. . . yes, under the mattress.
   b. Buy presents for your family and new clothes for yourself.
   c. Pay your property taxes, as planned.

There are no right or wrong answers, although clearly some are wiser choices than others. Obviously, "a" responses suggest a low-risk investor, while "b" responses describe a person very comfortable with "taking a chance." And for those of you who consistently went with "c", well, you may truly be practical investors who are willing to take a risk if the potential reward can be reasonably calculated or planned.

By this time, all this talk of economic disaster and risk (*riesgo*) may have a lot of Latinos nervous. One way to reduce risk to a level that you can live with and, more than likely, to produce the returns you need to meet your objectives is called diversifying your portfolio.

Simply put: Don't put all your eggs in one basket. With investing, it's much safer to spread your money across different types of investments. The idea is to build variety into your portfolio so that if one type of investment drops, the others will remain strong and lessen the pain of the loss.

For example, instead of owning nothing but a mutual fund that buys stocks of small technology start-up companies, the money you invest in the stock market—whether directly or through mutual funds—should go into small, medium, and large companies in many different industries, such as retailing, health care, or energy. If one sector of the market takes a downturn, its price decline will be offset by your other holdings. *¡Andale! ¡Con coraje!*

 Develop the right asset allocation—it's the most important part of investing.

INVESTING WEB SITES

These sites are in English-only except C.Com/Warner Financial Network, which is available in English and Spanish:

Alliance for Investor Education	www.investoreducation.org/
American Association of Individual Investors	www.aaii.org
American Express Financial Advisors	www.americanexpress.com
American Stock Exchange	www.amex.com
Association of Mutual Fund Investors	www.amfi.com
Bloomberg	www.bloomberg.com
C.Com/Warner Financial Network, or WFNet	http://ntweb.telescan.com/Warner/home1.html
Charles Schwab	www.schwab.com
Emerging Markets Companion	www.emgmkts.com
Fidelity Investments	www.fidelity.com
Investor Protection Trust	www.investorprotect.com
Merrill Lynch	www.plan.ml.com/zine
Mutual Fund Education Alliance	www.mfea.com
Nasdaq	www.nasdaq.com
New York Stock Exchange	www.nyse.com
100% No-Load Mutual Fund Council	www.100noloadfunds.com
Vanguard Group	www.vanguard.com

Asset allocation *(asignación de inversiones)*—or the proportion of stocks, bonds, international securities, and cash in your portfolio—is the single most important aspect of investing. Finding the best allocation depends on many factors, including your age, financial goals, and the state of the economy.

Many mutual fund companies and brokerage firms offer worksheets you can use to allocate your assets. Financial planners can help. And you can use a computer to decide on your allocation by using one of the programs available for free on some Internet sites. (Web sites are listed at left.)

One factor that all these formulas take into account is how long you think it might be before you will need your money. The younger you are, or the longer you can wait before needing to touch your investments, the more risk you can probably tolerate. (For asset allocation examples, see pages 102–103.)

 Regularly analyze your portfolio to determine if your assets are properly balanced between different classes of investments.

Whatever you do, don't make the mistake of figuring out your risk tolerance and asset allocation, then assuming you're done. You need to regularly evaluate your personal and professional situation and make adjustments to your portfolio when major changes take place place, such as the purchase of a home, the birth of a child, the loss of a job, the death of a spouse, retirement, or a big swing in the market.

 Use the bulk of your investing dollars to buy mutual funds.

For most investors, especially beginners, mutual funds are the best investment choice because they let you easily and instantly diversify your portfolio, give you access to securities that would otherwise be too expensive to buy, and are professionally managed.

There are funds to serve every investment goal. If you're very risk averse, start with a money market fund. Braver investors may want to invest in stock funds, but limit themselves to income, growth and income, or balanced funds. The lion-hearted Latino investor may feel perfectly comfortable with growth, aggressive growth, or international stock funds.

ASSET ALLOCATION

The following three examples assume a $30,000 portfolio and a five-year time frame:

1. THE CONSERVATIVE INVESTOR

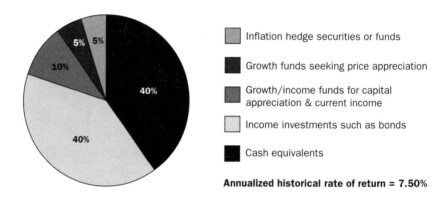

Inflation hedge securities or funds

Growth funds seeking price appreciation

Growth/income funds for capital appreciation & current income

Income investments such as bonds

Cash equivalents

Annualized historical rate of return = 7.50%

2. THE MODERATE INVESTOR

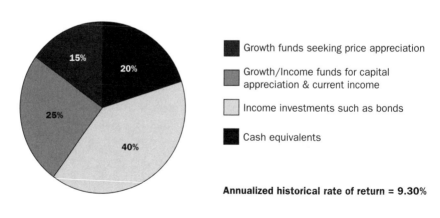

Growth funds seeking price appreciation

Growth/Income funds for capital appreciation & current income

Income investments such as bonds

Cash equivalents

Annualized historical rate of return = 9.30%

1. THE CONSERVATIVE INVESTOR

40% or $12,000 in cash equivalents.
40% or $12,000 in income investments such as bonds.
10% or $3,000 in growth/income funds for capital appreciation and current income.
5% or $1,500 in growth funds seeking price appreciation.
5% or $1,500 in inflation hedge securities or funds.
Annualized historical rate of return = 7.50%

2. THE MODERATE INVESTOR

20% or $6,000 in cash equivalents.
40% or $12,000 in income investments such as bonds.
25% or $7,500 in growth/income funds for capital appreciation and current income.
15% or $4,500 in growth funds seeking price appreciation.
Annualized historical rate of return = 9.30%

3. THE AGGRESSIVE INVESTOR

0% or $0 in cash equivalents.
10% or $3,000 in income investments such as bonds.
50% or $15,000 in growth/income funds for capital appreciation and current income.
40% or $12,000 in growth funds seeking price appreciation.
Annualized historical rate of return = 11.70%

3. THE AGGRESSIVE INVESTOR

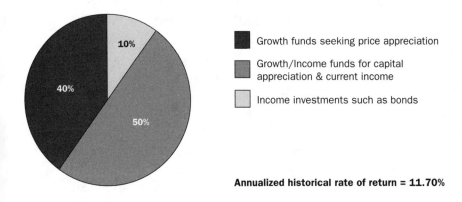

Growth funds seeking price appreciation

Growth/Income funds for capital appreciation & current income

Income investments such as bonds

Annualized historical rate of return = 11.70%

Learn how to evaluate mutual funds.

Once you've identified the types of funds that interest you, it's time to find and compare several funds in these categories. Say you want a growth fund. Start by calling several different fund companies or brokerages and asking for the names of some of their top performers in that category. IBC's Web site at www.ibcdata.com also posts the top-performing funds. Then, take the following steps:

Prospectus. Have the fund company send you each fund's prospectus, a free report detailing its objectives, fees and charges, and performance. (See the sidebar at right to learn how to read a prospectus.) While reading the prospectus, make sure the fund's objectives match yours, and that it invests in the types of securities you want. Look at the major holdings of the fund. For example, the investment objective for the Fidelity Blue Chip Growth fund is stated as "Long-term capital appreciation; invests primarily in diversified portfolio of common stocks of well-known companies."

Fund manager and company. Check into the record of the fund manager and the fund company. The best way to do this is to read about the manager's experience and philosophy for investing and analyzing economic trends in newspapers, magazines, and Web sites. The fund company should be financially healthy and have a good reputation.

Investment style. You should also feel comfortable with the manager's investment style in the specific fund you are considering, since he or she will be deciding which investments the fund should buy and sell.

Performance. Compare the fund's total return to that of other funds in its class, along with the market indices, such as the S&P 500 for large-company U.S. stocks, or the Russell 2000 for small-company stocks. A Wall Street mantra is that past performance is no indication of how an investment may perform in the future. Nonetheless, you should look at how a fund has performed over the last three, five, and ten years, if those data are available. Don't buy a fund only for its performance in the last quarter! *Nunca.* You can find the fund's total return in your newspaper's financial tables, and in the fund's prospectus. Fund performance can also be affected by the turnover ratio (how often the manager buys and sells).

SEVEN STEPS TO UNDERSTANDING A MUTUAL FUND PROSPECTUS

1. Look up the fund's investment goal as the first step to deter-mining whether it belongs in your portfolio. You can usually find the investment goal under a "goals" or "objectives" heading.

2. If the goal matches yours, turn to the list of fees and expenses. Typically, a prospectus will include a hypothetical example show-ing you the impact of these expenses on an investment held for a specified period of time.

3. Next, review the fund's "turnover ratio." This number tells what portion of the fund's securities are replaced within a year, with 90 percent being the average ratio for a stock fund. The higher the ratio, the higher the expenses. Consistent ratios over time may be a sign of stable management, while fluctuations may set off warning bells.

4. Also, take a look at the fund's discussion of "risk" to see what type of instruments the fund manager can employ, or is restricted from using, in trying to meet his or her objectives.

5. The prospectus also will chart historical financial data for the past ten years (or the entire life of the fund, if it is less than ten years).

6. Read the biographical information about managers of the fund and their histories in the prospectus as well.

7. Finally, read the prospectus from beginning to end to learn about the services provided by a fund, including IRAs, automatic invest-ment of dividends, capital gains distributions, check writing, infor-mation and help by telephone, and how to buy and sell shares.

Expenses. Finally, be sure you know how much the fund charges for its operating expenses. These include advisory fees paid to the fund manager and administrative costs such as trading, toll-free numbers, statements, and analyst fees. They often also include "12b-1" fees, which are used to cover sales and marketing costs.

Operating expenses are usually expressed as an annual percentage of the fund's average net assets. These "expense ratios" can range from 0.25 percent to more than 2 percent. While you don't have to pay operating expenses directly, you pay them indirectly because you're a shareholder of the fund. Operating expenses affect the value of your investment in a fund because they reduce the fund's return.

Keep your eye on a one-time cost known as a load *(carga)*, or mutual fund sales charge. A "front-end load" is a sales fee you pay when you first buy shares in a mutual fund. They typically range from 3 percent to 5 percent of the amount you initially invest. "Low-load" funds charge only 1 percent to 3 percent. A "rear load" or "back-end load" is a fee sometimes charged when you sell your shares depending on how long you have held the shares.

You've probably seen and heard a lot of advertisements about "no-load" funds that have no initial sales charges because you buy them directly from a fund family. But even they aren't free. Like all mutual funds, no-load funds have operating expense ratios. (More about load versus no-load funds a bit later.)

A good place to get objective information about mutual funds is from Morningstar Inc. in Chicago, an independent financial publisher. Morningstar produces one-page reports on individual mutual funds that include brief fund manager biographies, performance information, and descriptions of the types of securities held by the fund.

Morningstar reports also give each fund a rating of between one and five stars that's based on its three-year performance and risk level, as well as a numerical rating of between one and five, with five being best, that compares the fund to similar funds in its category. (Las Lauras recommend that you try to stick with funds that have at least three stars and numerical ratings of three.) One of the most useful features is an objective capsule report from a Morningstar analyst. Other resources are newsletters, newspapers, magazines, and the Internet.

Up to three free *Charles Schwab Mutual Fund Report Cards* (up to five for Schwab customers) are also available every year to investors. These report cards are one-page snapshots of mutual funds that include comparisons to other funds, Morningstar ratings, and information about long-term growth, performance, and expenses. Extra reports can be purchased for $3 each.

ACCIÓN To order a *Morningstar Report* for $5 each, call 800-735-0700. They can also be found at the library for free. To order *Charles Schwab Mutual Fund Report Cards*, call 800-4-NO-LOAD, stop into any Schwab office, or check the Web site at www.schwab.com.

 Consider money market funds as a key component of your cash reserves.

Money market funds are investments that offer safety, liquidity, and a yield, or interest rate, that's typically one to two percentage points higher than what you'd get from bank money market accounts (which are discussed in Chapter 1). The cost is almost always $1 per share.

Money market funds aren't federally insured, and some are riskier than others. But overall, they're considered very safe—almost as safe as insured bank accounts—because they usually invest in large, financially stable institutions that promise to repay their debts quickly. In fact, these securities typically carry an average maturity of less than 120 days.

With a money market fund, the interest paid to you by governments and big corporations in exchange for your investment dollars gets passed on to you in the form of dividends. These dividends can be wired into your bank account or mailed to you, usually once a month, or automatically reinvested to buy more shares.

Many investors use money market funds to temporarily park large sums of cash, or keep cash reserves. Money market funds usually require that you maintain a minimum balance. Some offer check-writing capabilities, but the number of checks you can write is often restricted.

While dividends paid by most money market funds are taxable, some money market funds invest only in tax-exempt securities, making the dividends that you receive exempt from federal taxes, and perhaps state and local taxes as well. But the yields paid by tax-exempt funds are lower than the yields on taxable funds, which can offset the tax advantage. Bottom line: Unless you're at or above the 31 percent tax bracket, you're better off in a taxable money market fund.

Consider index funds to start with—and maybe stay with.

To simplify the process of choosing from among the thousands of mutual funds on the market, consider getting started with index funds. Index funds are considered "passively managed" because all they seek to do is replicate the performance of a certain stock index such as the S&P 500 by owning the same stocks as those from which the index is calculated. Index funds are attractive for several reasons, including strong performance, low fees, and low taxes.

Since 1993, index funds that mirror the S&P 500 have posted higher returns than 80 percent of all "actively managed" funds that have managers who regularly buy and sell securities. And over seventy years, actively managed funds have lagged the S&P 500 index by 1 to 2 percentage points annually. S&P 500 index funds, on the other hand, tend to lag the actual index by less than one percentage point.

One reason is that the average index fund has an annual expense ratio of 0.2 percent, or just $2 per year on a $1,000 investment. The average actively managed mutual fund charges 1.3 percent per year, or $13 per year on a $1,000 investment. Today you can choose from more than 370 index funds.

 Consider international funds when you're diversifying your portfolio.

If you're a conservative investor, limit your international holdings to about 10 percent of your portfolio. If you're comfortable taking on more risk, you may want to increase your international holdings to as much as 25 percent.

The easiest way to start is with international index funds. As with U.S. index funds, the cost of international index funds is lower than actively managed international funds. They also minimize the stress of trying to choose from among various countries or regions of the world.

The most well-known index is the Morgan Stanley Europe, Australia, Asia, Far East Index, or EAFE Index, which contains more than 1,000 stocks. But there are many others including the International Pacific Index, the Southeast Asia Index, the Emerging Markets Index, and last, but certainly not least, the Latin American Index.

There are also many different types of international funds. Some invest in the securities of established markets in Europe and Asia. Regional funds invest in a specific geographic region. Single-country funds invest in a single foreign nation. Emerging markets funds invest in securities of developing countries. Global funds invest in both U.S. and non-U.S. stocks.

As Latinos, we have a natural inclination to invest in specific Latin American countries or companies because we've lived or traveled in the

LATIN AMERICAN MUTUAL FUNDS

ABN AMRO LATIN AMERICAN EQUITY COMMON SHARES	800-443-4725
AIM LATIN AMERICAN GROWTH FUND	800-959-4246
BANKERS TRUST INVESTMENT LATIN AMERICAN EQUITY	800-730-1313
EVERGREEN LATIN AMERICA FUND CLASS A	800-235-0064
EXCELSIOR LATIN AMERICA	800-446-1012
FEDERATED LATIN AMERICAN GROWTH	800-245-5000
FIDELITY LATIN AMERICA	800-544-8888
GOVETT LATIN AMERICA FUND	800-821-0803
INVESCO LATIN AMERICAN GROWTH FUND	800-525-8085
IVY SOUTH AMERICA CLASS A	800-777-6472
KEMPER LATIN AMERICA FUND A	800-621-1048
MERRILL LYNCH LATIN AMERICAN FUND CLASS B	800-637-3863
MONTGOMERY LATIN AMERICA FUND (R)	800-572-3863
PRUDENTIAL LATIN AMERICA EQUITY	800-225-1852
SCUDDER LATIN AMERICA	800-225-2470
T. ROWE PRICE LATIN AMERICA FUND	800-638-5660
TCW GALILEO LATIN AMERICA EQUITIES FUND	800-386-3829
TCW/DW LATIN AMERICAN GROWTH FUND	800-869-6397
TEMPLETON LATIN AMERICA CLASS ONE FUND	800-292-9293
VAN KAMPEN LATIN AMERICA FUND	800-282-4404
WEBS INDEX MEXICO (FREE)	800-810-9327
WRIGHT EQUIFUND-MEXICO	800-888-9471

region. *Fantástico.* Common investment wisdom is to invest in what you know. More Latin American funds are being introduced every day. Just don't ignore the rest of the world. (See page 109 for a list of Latin American funds.)

International funds have risks that aren't usually a factor with U.S. funds. Compared with U.S. funds, international funds often have much more political risk due to the impact that political events have on a country's economy. In addition, a decline in the value of a country's currency will reduce the value of your investment in U.S. dollar terms. And there's the risk that the information you get about a country's politics, economics, markets, or companies is incomplete. Of course, that risk of "imperfect" information exists in the United States, too, but in this country corporations usually adhere to higher standards and information is more widely distributed.

Choosing an international fund is similar to choosing a U.S. fund. First, decide what type of fund you want and what your investment objective is, and whether you want active or passive management. Then look at the fund manager's experience, the fund's past performance, how much risk is involved, and the costs.

 Clearly understand the difference between load and no-load mutual funds.

Remember, a load is simply a sales fee. If you're comfortable choosing funds on your own and love to track performance and returns, then you have an abundance of excellent no-load funds to choose from. The only time you may be tempted to buy a load fund is when you run across one that's especially worthy, based on its management, past performance, or objectives. After all, the "load" alone isn't what determines how good a fund is; it only sets the price of admission.

If you don't want to fly solo with your investments, you'll more than likely end up owning load funds as the trade-off for the advice and service from a commission-based financial planner or broker at a full-service firm. These financial professionals are paid in full or in part by commissions they earn on the products they sell. Planners or brokers should provide you with specific information about how they're paid. And you should expect and receive high-quality and comprehensive service regarding your investments and planning needs.

There is, however, a middle ground. If you're uncomfortable taking advice from someone who will receive a commission for an investment he or she recommends and sells to you, hire a fee-only financial planner. Fee-only planners provide advice, but since they don't sell any financial products they'll usually steer you to low-load or no-load funds. (More on financial planners in Chapter 10.)

¿Cuál es mejor?—a load or a no-load fund? Most studies show that load funds perform no better on average than no-load funds. Just take a look at any list of the year's top-performing mutual funds by total return with the cost of loads, if any, factored in. At any given time, the list will have both load funds and no-load funds.

What's most important is to know what kind of return you need over a specified period of time to meet your objectives, and whether a particular fund has historically produced that type of return. If you can get that information on your own and are willing to be a "student of the business," then find a good no-load fund. *Pero sea honesto consigo mismo:* Are you disciplined enough to study the markets and stay with your investment program even if it means riding out the inevitable roller coaster dips of the market? *Si no, busque ayuda.*

 Use dollar-cost averaging.

A good way to ease into investing is with dollar cost averaging. It makes so much sense that even seasoned investors do it. With dollar cost averaging *(compra de acciones en intervalos fijos y con desembolsos de cantidad constante)*, you invest a fixed dollar amount at fixed intervals over a period of time instead of one lump sum. This strategy lets you take advantage of any price decreases.

Say you invest $100 each month. If a mutual fund's shares sold for $20 last month, but drop to $10 this month, you'll be able to buy more shares for the same amount of money. Of course, prices can move in the other direction. So if shares sold for $10 last month, but rise to $20 this month, you'll be getting fewer shares for the same amount of money.

But overall, by regularly buying shares of a fund whether the market is up or down, you can reduce the average cost of your shares below what you would have paid if you'd invested in one lump sum.

Automatic investment plans can easily be set up so that money is automatically deducted from your paycheck or bank account and invested in mutual fund shares. *Recuerde, páguese si mismo primero.*

 Reinvest your dividends to reap the benefits of compounding.

Automatically reinvest your dividends in order to buy more shares of the fund. Reinvested dividends let you take advantage of compounding, or earning interest on the interest you've already earned as well as on the original principal amount.

Here's how it works: Say you invested $10,000 in an S&P index fund for the last twenty years. During that time, your principal would have grown by $38,000, and you would have received $16,000 in dividends, giving you a total of about $64,000 at the end. But if you had reinvested all your dividends, the total value of your investment would have grown to more than $110,000. *¡Eso es buen negocio!* Las Lauras love this strategy.

 Join an investment club.

We recommend that you funnel most of your investment dollars into mutual funds. There is one exception: Buying and selling individual stocks through an investment club is a great way to learn about investing in a fun, supportive, and inexpensive manner. *Y es perfecto para nosotros: otra excusa para reunirnos.*

There are about 32,000 investment clubs in the United States today, and the average portfolio size is $82,000, according to the National Association of Investors Corp. (NAIC), a nonprofit group that promotes investment clubs as a way to educate consumers about investing.

The NAIC has built its investment philosophy around four tried and true principles. First, invest regularly, whether the market is up or down (dollar-cost averaging). Second, reinvest all your earnings (compounding). Third, invest in growth companies (be somewhat aggressive). And fourth, diversify (to reduce risk).

Learning how to research and pick stocks takes some effort. But the NAIC makes things easier by providing a twelve-lesson study program to teach club members how to study stocks. The group also provides a check-list to help you complete a basic stock analysis, and a stock selection guide to help you decide whether to buy a particular stock.

ACCIÓN For a free "Investing Kit" from the NAIC, write to 711 West 13 Mile Rd., Madison Heights, MI 48071.

 When you join an investment club, use dividend reinvestment plans (DRIPs) or other stock purchase plans to buy your stocks.

When buying individual stocks for your investment club, you may be able to save money by buying shares directly from the company that issues the stock instead of through a broker by enrolling in a dividend reinvestment plan (DRIP) or other stock purchase plans.

You can choose from two types of DRIPs: traditional or super. With a traditional DRIP you can use a broker to buy the first share of a stock, then buy additional shares directly from the company. You can also purchase shares through the NAIC or another company called Temper of the Times by enrolling in their direct stock purchase plans. Either way, you'll have to pay some fees every time you buy a stock, but these fees are usually less expensive than brokerage commissions.

With a Super DRIP (also referred to as no-load stocks), you can buy the initial share of stock directly from the issuing company without having to use a broker or enroll in a direct stock purchase plan. You won't have the enrollment fees associated with traditional DRIPs, but you'll have to pay enrollment, additional purchase, and annual account fees.

ACCIÓN For a free list of companies that offer Super DRIPs, write to the *DRIP Investor* at 7412 Calumet Ave., Suite 200, Hammond, IN 46324. For more information about the NAIC Stock Service plan, call 888-780-8400. For more information about Temper's direct stock purchase plan, call 800-388-9993.

Consider Socially Responsible Investing.

Your money can be used to support companies that reflect your political, ethical, social and/or religious beliefs through socially responsible investing.

Critics of socially responsible investing say that you limit your returns, make diversification difficult, and increase the risk of losing money by excluding traditionally lucrative segments such as tobacco and alcohol. An argument can be made that it is more financially and socially effective to seek out the highest returns, wherever they come from, then donate some of the profits directly to charitable organizations.

But the idea that you can't "do well" financially if you try to "do good" with socially responsible investing isn't necessarily true. If you're careful, investing with a conscience can pay off with healthy returns and support for causes that are important to you and our community. Indeed, many financial experts argue that socially responsible filters also weed out bad management practices. *Al fin*, arguments against socially responsible investing don't address how many of us feel about our investments. And emotions are integral to anyone's sense of identity, regardless of background or heritage.

Look at the Domini 400 Social stock index. Modeled after the Standard & Poor's 500 index, it includes 400 companies that have been subjected to a variety of screens. Since inception in 1991, the Domini index has returned 302.78 percent versus 261.61 percent for the S&P 500. The Domini Social Equity Fund, which contains stock from all the companies in the Domini index, has posted a five-year average annual return of 20.77 percent, compared with 20.24 percent for the S&P 500. These returns support the argument that socially responsibly screens help "weed out" bad management.

Socially responsible investing is booming. Total assets in socially responsible mutual funds jumped from $64 billion in 1985 to $639 billion in 1996, according to the Social Investment Forum in Washington, D.C. Despite that growth, there's still no "Latino Fund" on the market that invests in Latino-owned businesses or in companies that promote Latinos. But you'll probably be able to find something that reflects your values, if not your ethnicity.

Many funds invest in companies with progressive policies toward the hiring and promotion of all people of color. Others stress "family values" such as the Aquinas Fund and the Catholic Values Investment Trust, both of which invest in companies whose activities are consistent with the teachings of the Roman Catholic Church. At the other end of the spectrum, the Meyers Pride Value Fund picks gay-friendly companies.

The only socially responsible mutual funds with significant foreign holdings are the Calvert World Values International Equity Fund, the Calvert New Africa Fund, the Citizens Global Equity Portfolio, and the MMA Praxis International Fund. Although foreign stocks are an excellent way to diversify a portfolio, the reason there aren't more socially responsible international funds is that it's very hard to screen foreign firms. For more information, check out Hal Brill, Jack A. Brill, and Cliff Feigenbaum's *Investing with Your Values: Making Money and Making a Difference* (Bloomberg Press), which discusses socially responsible investing in depth and provides up-to-date lists of recommended funds.

ACCIÓN For a free copy of *The Socially Responsible Financial Planning Handbook,* call Co-Op America at 800-58-GREEN, or write to 1612 K St. NW, No. 600, Washington, DC 20006. For a copy of the *Directory of Socially Responsible Investment Services,* send $2 to the Social Investment Forum, P.O. Box 57216, Washington, DC 20037, or call 202-872-5319. For more information on Community Development Loan Funds, call the National Association of Community Development Loan funds at 215-923-4754, or write to the association at 924 Cherry Street, 2nd Floor, Philadelphia, PA 19107.

 Understand the difference between a full-service brokerage and a discount brokerage.

We recommend mutual funds for most investors. But if you want to buy or sell stocks you'll probably need to open an account with a brokerage firm, which will charge you a fee for any service it performs. Full-service brokerages offer proprietary reports by their analysts on stocks and mutual funds, may actively manage your account, and make specific buy and sell recommendations. Fees, also called commissions, can be as high as 3 percent or more for every transaction.

Discount brokerages can save you more than 50 percent on commissions—and even more if you do it over the Internet. Discount brokerages won't actively manage your account or make specific buy and sell recommendations. But most offer investment information, and some will give you a range of investments that fit your criteria.

If you're comfortable picking your own stocks, then a discounter is the way to go. Otherwise, consider a full-service brokerage. There's one caveat: There have been instances where brokers have recommended unsuitable trades to investors just to garner more commissions.

To protect yourself, check the background of your broker. Establish a relationship. Don't blindly follow any broker's recommendation without asking questions and feeling satisfied with the rationale for why the investment is right for you. You may also want to do some independent research before buying.

ACCIÓN To reach full-service brokerages, call Merrill Lynch at 800-MERRILL or American Express Financial Advisors at 800-GET ADVICE. To reach National Discount Brokers, call 800-888-3999. To reach Schwab in English, call 800-435-4000. To reach Schwab's Centro Latinoamericano, call 800-362-1774. To reach Fidelity in English, call 800-544-8888. To reach Fidelity in Spanish, call 800-544-5670.

 Beware of investor scams.

Never, ever, buy an investment from someone who has called you on the telephone. *¡Por nada del mundo! ¡Jamás!* When you do finally decide to make an investment, check into the disciplinary history of the broker or brokerage before making a purchase by calling the National Association of Securities Dealers (NASD). Also check with your state's securities regulators, which often have more information than the NASD.

If you have a problem that you can't resolve with your broker or brokerage, file a complaint with the U.S. Securities and Exchange Commission's (SEC) Office of Investor Education and Assistance. The SEC also provides lots of free educational brochures such as *Ask Questions: Questions You Should Ask About Your Investment.* (For more about brokers see Chapter 10.)

ACCIÓN To reach the NASD for a background check on your broker or brokerage, call 800-289-9999. To get the number of your state's security regulator, call the National Fraud Information Center at 800-876-7060. To contact the SEC, call 800-SEC-0330.

❑ Never buy any investment unless you understand exactly how it works.

❑ Determine your financial goals, and when you want to achieve them.

❑ Figure out how much risk you're willing to take to achieve these goals.

❑ Develop a diversified asset allocation plan.

❑ Never totally abdicate the responsibility for your finances to others, even if you hire a financial adviser.

❑ Remember that past performance is no guarantee of how an investment may perform. Nobody can predict what will happen in the future.

❑ Focus on the long term. Don't get too nervous about the stock market's daily, or even yearly, ups and downs.

❑ Don't try to time the market. It's impossible.

❑ Take advantage of dollar cost averaging.

❑ Reinvest your dividends to reap the rewards of compounding.

ADDITIONAL RESOURCES

Recommended Magazines and Newspapers

Bloomberg Personal Finance: Targets the more sophisticated investor.

Consumer Reports: This magazine covers everything a consumer can possibly spend money on, from mutual funds to refrigerators. Lots of free information is also available from its Web site at www.consumerreports.org/.

Family Money: This magazine is perfect for the novice investor, with easy to understand articles from some of the nation's leading business journalists. The Web address is www.familymoney.com/.

Kiplinger's Personal Finance Magazine: Down-to-earth advice on a variety of investing and consumer topics. The Web site address is http://kiplinger.com/.

SmartMoney: One of the best overall personal finance magazines around, with plenty of information for novices and sophisticated investors. It has one of the best Web sites around, but the site is only available to subscribers of *The Wall Street Journal* Interactive Edition.

Money: Much good advice for serious investors. The Web site address is http://money.com/.

The Wall Street Journal: The world's Bible of business news. Access to the *Journal*'s excellent Web site at www.wsj.com/ is available by subscription only. Also available on the Web is *The Wall Street Journal Americas*, the daily business report published in Spanish and Portuguese, at http://wsj.com/americas.

Recommended Books

10 Minute Guide to Mutual Funds, by Werner Renberg (New York: MacMillan General References, 1996).

10 Minute Guide to the Stock Market, by Dain Vujovich (New York: Alpha Books, 1998).

Investing with Your Values: Making Money and Making a Difference, by Hal Brill, Jack A. Brill, and Cliff Feigenbaum (Princeton, New Jersey: Bloomberg Press, 1999).

Investing in Latin America: Best Stocks, Best Funds, by Michael Molinski (Princeton, New Jersey: Bloomberg Press, September 1999).

Keys to Investing in Government Securities, by Jay Goldinger (Hauppage, New York: Barron's Business Keys, 1995).

Starting and Running a Profitable Investment Club: the Official Guide from the National Association of Investment Clubs, by Kenneth S. Janke and Thomas E. O'Hara (New York: Times Books, 1998).

The New Commonsense Guide to Mutual Funds, by Mary Rowland (Princeton, New Jersey: Bloomberg Press, 1998).

The Only Investment Guide You'll Ever Need, by Andrew P. Tobias (New York: Harvest Books, 1999). A Spanish-language version is also available called *La único guía de inversión que usted necesitará* (New York: Harvest Books, 1998).

The Wall Street Journal Book of International Investing: Everything You Need to Know about Investing in Foreign Markets, by John A. Prestbo and Douglas R. Sease (New York: Hyperion, 1998).

◎

CHAPTER 5

Buying a Home

"THE BREAD OF YOUR OWN HOME IS ALWAYS GOOD"   —CUBA

W HEN HUMBERTO FIRST TRIED TO BUY A HOME IN 1992, HE approached several lenders to ask about loans *(préstamos)*. But he was repeatedly told he didn't have enough money for a down payment, even though he had $10,000 in savings. One bank loan officer never even bothered to return his calls. "I gave up and went to Hawaii," says the thirty-one-year-old Mexican-born restaurant manager.

In 1996 he tried again—and succeeded. *¿Cómo lo logró?* Humberto and his wife, along with his brother and sister-in-law, together managed to buy a $131,000 four-bedroom, two-bathroom home in Renton, Washington, with a down payment of just $5,000. They worked with Seattle-based Bedford Falls Funding, one of the growing number of lenders that are targeting Latinos.

Bedford Falls Funding has bilingual loan officers that provide large amounts of counseling and information to Latinos. "It was all done in Spanish," says Humberto. "I was confident that I understood everything." The mortgage company also accepts nontraditional credit records, and considers income from several sources and seasonal jobs when approving loans.

The American dream of homeownership is becoming a reality for more

Latinos like Humberto, thanks to a strong economy, low home loan interest rates, stricter enforcement of fair housing laws, and greater outreach by lenders to first-time and low- to moderate-income home buyers.

Between 1993 and 1996, Latino homeownership jumped 16 percent, according to a study by Harvard University's Joint Center for Housing Studies. *Estas son las buenas noticias.* The bad news is that despite the gains, just 43 percent of all Latinos owned their own homes in 1997, compared with 72.3 percent for non-Latino whites, U.S. Census figures show. And the denial rate for home loans, or mortgages, was 34.4 percent for Latinos in 1996, compared to 24.1 percent for non-Latino whites, says the Federal Financial Institutions Examinations Council.

Many of us never consider home ownership at all due to exaggerated perceptions of how much of a down payment is needed, an aversion to taking on so much debt, concerns about having to spend thirty years paying off a mortgage, and fears of being rejected for a loan, according to a 1996 report called *Focus Group Research on Barriers to Minority Homeownership* by the Freddie Mac Corp. and the Research Triangle Institute.

Latinos who apply for mortgages are sometimes denied because of credit scoring *(puntuación de crédito)*, a mathematical calculation that determines creditworthiness based on traditional credit history. Credit scoring ignores the fact that many of us have strong nontraditional credit records and additional income from extended family members who may live under the same roof.

Latinos need to know that there are many affordable housing and first-time homebuyer programs that provide free education about home buying as well as discounts on homes in economically distressed areas, mortgage tax credits, and home loans that require down payments of just 3 percent or less.

 Understand the benefits and disadvantages of owning a home.

Owning your own *casita* provides a sense of achievement, security, and privacy. It can give you more space to raise a family, access to better schools, and the means to become a permanent member of your community.

Ownership also helps keep housing costs stable. Mortgage interest, local property taxes, and certain moving expenses are tax deductible. And if you sell a home after living in it for at least two years, up to $500,000 profit is exempt from federal income taxes if you're married ($250,000 if you're single).

Owning property helps you build equity *(equidad)*, which is the differ-ence between the fair market value of a home and the amount still owed on the mortgage. For example, say you buy a house for $126,500—the median price for a U.S. home—with a $20,000 down payment, and a $106,500 loan. Your equity is $20,000. That's why buying a home is sometimes referred to as "forced savings" *(ahorros a la fuerza)*.

Your equity grows as the mortgage gets paid down, and as the home's market value rises, or appreciates *(apreciar)*. You can use this equity without selling the house by taking out a second mortgage *(hipoteca subordinada)* or a home equity line of credit *(crédito garantizado por la equidad del hogar)* to pay for expenses such as college tuition. In both cases, the loans are secured by the property.

But buying a home will probably be the biggest purchase you ever make, and you need to be aware of the possible drawbacks. For the first few years, you should expect to pay more for your monthly mortgage than you did for your monthly rent. You may need to cut back on other expenses.

Even if your mortgage is the same or less than what you paid in rent, you'll have other expenses such as property taxes, homeowners insurance, utilities, repairs, maintenance, even appliances and furniture. There's always a chance that property values will decline.

And you can lose your *casita*, your investment, and your good credit rat-ing if you default on a home loan or fail to make mortgage payments on a timely basis. If this happens the lender can foreclose *(ejecutar una hipoteca)* on your home, which means they can take it back, and sell it to someone else.

 Determine whether you're better off renting or buying.

Conventional wisdom says it's always better to buy a home than to rent, primarily because of the potential tax breaks. One of the biggest benefits of home ownership is the fact that you can deduct the annual interest you pay on your mortgage if it and other deductions exceed your standard deduction, which in 1999 is $4,300 if you're single, and $7,200 if you're married and fil-ing jointly.

But if you move around a lot, have a great deal on a rental property, can't take more than the standard deduction, or have low property taxes, renting may be better. Owning a home makes it harder and more expensive to pick up and move. Unless you plan to stay put for at least a few years it may be impossible for you to recoup the investment you've made in a home when you sell it, especially if the value of the property drops, or depreciates *(depreciar)*.

Rent typically eats up about 25 percent of our gross monthly pay. If you're paying a lot less than that, it may be better to take the extra cash you're saving every month and funnel it into an investment that will give you a good rate of return, such as a mutual fund or an investment vehicle such as an Individual Retirement Account (IRA).

 If you're interested in buying, educate yourself about the home buying process.

Read your newspaper's real estate section, books on home buying, Web sites for homebuyers, or the many free brochures offered by various agencies. *No puede leer demasiado.*

Try to attend a free home buying workshop. These seminars walk you through the home buying process step-by-step. They can also help you figure out if you're financially prepared to buy a home, how to obtain and check your credit report, and where to find affordable housing and first-time homebuyer programs. Many will send you certificates proving you've completed the workshop, which carry weight with some lenders.

The Consumer Credit Counseling Service (CCCS), a nonprofit financial counseling agency affiliated with the National Foundation for Consumer Credit, runs a Housing Education Program in some cities. Home buying fairs are also sponsored by the U.S. Department of Housing and Urban Affairs (HUD), and the Federal National Mortgage Association, or Fannie Mae, a private company chartered by the U.S. government to provide funds to mortgage lenders. All of these seminars are offered free of charge, and some are conducted *en español.*

ACCIÓN To find out if your local CCCS office has a Housing Education Program, call 800-388-2227. For home buying assistance from Fannie Mae, call 800-7FANNIE. For information about HUD's housing counseling, call 800-569-4287.

 Understand all the costs associated with buying a home.

The costs associated with buying a home are usually divided into two groups: the up-front costs, which is what you'll pay before you actually move into a home, and the ongoing costs, which is what you'll pay while you're living in the home.

UPFRONT COSTS

Down payment. With some exceptions, lenders usually expect buyers to come up with a portion of the home's price up front, known as the down payment *(pronto pago)*. The standard down payment used to be 20 percent of the home's purchase price. This is often the biggest obstacle for most people. For example, a 20 percent down payment for a home that costs $126,500 is $25,300, which means you'd need to borrow $101,200 to make up the difference.

Increasingly, however, lenders are beginning to require just 3 percent to 5 percent for a down payment, and some programs we describe later in this chapter don't require any down payment at all. A lower down payment can make a huge difference. A 5 percent down payment on the same $126,500 home is just $6,325. Of course, that means you'd have to borrow more money—$120,175—to close the deal.

Closing costs. Buyers and sellers can negotiate payment of closing costs *(gastos de cierre)*, which are the fees associated with settling the loan (we'll describe these costs in more depth later in this chapter). Total closing costs typically amount to between 3 percent and 6 percent of the total loan.

Settling-in costs. Don't forget about settling-in costs *(gastos de mudanza y muebles)*. The home may also need some repairs before it's in any shape for you to move in. And you'll usually have to buy major appliances such as a stove, refrigerator, and washer and dryer.

ONGOING COSTS

Principal. The monthly mortgage payment consists of a portion of the "principal, interest, property taxes, and insurance", or PITI. The principal is the amount of money you borrowed. When you make your monthly mortgage payment you're paying back a portion of the principal. In the early years the bulk of your payment goes toward the interest rather than the principal. This is known as amortization.

Interest. This is the fee for using the lender's funds and is usually expressed as a percentage of the loan amount. Interest is deductible on your federal tax returns if you itemize. The actual P&I (principal and interest) depends on how much you borrow, the interest rate, the repayment period or term, and whether you have a fixed-rate or adjustable-rate mortgage.

Taxes. Property taxes are paid to local governments. The amount varies depending on where you live, and they're deductible on your federal tax returns if you itemize.

Insurance. Homeowners insurance, which is required by lenders, protects you from any financial losses on your property due to hazards such as fire or wind. Private mortgage insurance (PMI) repays the lender if you default on a loan and may be required if you have a down payment of less than 20 percent.

Homeowners association dues. If you own a condominium or co-operative you'll have to pay a homeowners association fee, which is also called a maintenance fee or carrying charge. With a condo you own the unit you live in and a portion of the building's shared areas. With a co-op, you own shares of stock in a corporation that owns the land, building, and other facilities.

Miscellaneous costs. You'll be responsible for many other monthly expenses such as utilities (oil, gas, water, electricity, telephone) and maintenance costs.

ACCIÓN Fannie Mae offers the following two free brochures in both English and Spanish: *Opening the Door to a Home of Your Own: A Step-by-Step Home Buying Guide/Abriendo la Puerta de su Propio Hogar.* Call 800-611-9566 for an English version, and 800-690-7557 for a Spanish version. *The National New Americans Guide: How to Become a Citizen; How to*

Become a Homeowner. Call 800-544-9213 for an English version and 800-693-7557 for a Spanish version. HUD offers the following free brochure in English and Spanish: *The HUD Home Buying Guide.* Call 800-767-7468 for a copy.

 Assess your financial health.

Now it's time to figure out whether you've got the financial *agallas* to become a homeowner. Start by reviewing your credit record, cash reserves, job history, income, and debt.

Credit record. Your credit report contains a list of your credit accounts, when they were opened, whether you've paid your accounts on time, how much money you still owe on the accounts, and whether the accounts are held jointly with another person. If several people plan to live in the home and contribute to the monthly mortgage payment, everyone will need to obtain copies of their traditional or nontraditional credit records. (For more on credit see Chapter 2.)

Cash reserves. Some lenders want to see some cash reserves equal to at least two monthly mortgage payments over and above the down payment. These reserves should be in the bank for at least two months before you buy a house. However, some lenders will let you use gift funds from a relative for part of your down payment or closing costs.

Job history. One measurement of financial stability is the length of time you've held the same job or been in the same line of work. Ideally, it should be at least two years.

Income. Lenders will look at your gross monthly income, which is the amount of money you'd bring home if you didn't have to pay taxes. To see if you've got enough income after your expenses to pay for your home, they'll compare this amount to your future monthly housing costs (PITI plus utilities and maintenance). (Refer back to the budget you created in Chapter 1 to contrast your income with your expenses.)

Net worth. Lenders want to be sure you aren't carrying too many liabilities in such forms as student loan payments, auto loan payments, and credit card payments. As a first step with any lender, you will need to present documentation of all your assets and liabilities. (To compute your net worth, by

FIGURING YOUR NET WORTH

PERSONAL ASSETS:

Primary residence	$____	Automobiles and/or	
Vacation home	$____	motorcycles	$____
Furnishings (furniture &		Other property assets	
electronics)	$____	(musical instruments)	$____
Jewelry & art	$____	**Total Personal Assets**	**$____**

LIQUID AND INVESTMENT ASSETS:

Cash/Checking accounts	$____	Tax-free municipal bonds/	
Money Market accounts	$____	funds	$____
CD, Credit Unions, other		Stocks and stock mutual	
savings	$____	funds	$____
Bonds and bonds mutual		Stock options	$____
funds	$____	Limited partnerships	$____
U.S. Government obligations	$____	**Total Liquid and**	
		Investment Assets	**$____**

BUSINESS AND INVESTMENT REAL ESTATE ASSETS:

Notes Receivable	$____	**Total Business and Investment**	
Investment Real Estate	$____	**Real Estate Assets**	**$____**
Business(es)	$____		

subtracting your liabilities from your assets, see the worksheet above.)

Qualifying ratios. In addition, most lenders want your monthly PITI (principal, interest, taxes, and insurance) to be no more than 28 percent of your gross monthly income. Next, they look for your monthly debt burden to be no more than 36 percent of your gross monthly income. These two so-called qualifying ratios (*razones de calificación*) are referred to by lenders as the borrower's "28/36."

The qualifying ratios can change, however, if you can come up with a bigger down payment or have a spotless credit record. Some affordable hous-

RETIREMENT ASSETS:

IRAs	$____	Annuities	$____
Keogh or SEP IRA	$____	After-tax 401(k)	$____
Qualified Retirement Plans		**Total Retirement Assets**	**$____**
[e.g., 401(k), 403(b)]	$____		

NET WORTH = ASSETS – LIABILITIES

TOTAL ASSETS: $____

LIABILITIES:

Mortgage on primary		Charge accounts	$____
residence	$____	Personal or school loans	$____
Mortgage on vacation		Investment real estate	
residence	$____	loans	$____
Home equity loan	$____	Business loans	$____
Auto loans	$____	**TOTAL LIABILITIES**	**$____**

NET WORTH:

Total assets	$____	**SUBTRACT ASSETS FROM**	
Total liabilities	$____	**LIABILITIES FOR NET WORTH**	**$____**

ing programs also have more lenient qualifying ratios. For example, the qualifying ratio for Fannie Mae's Community Home Buyer's Program is 33/38.

 **Figure out what you can afford to buy.**

A general rule says you can afford a home that costs two-and-a-half times your gross annual salary. So if you earn $50,400 a year, the home loan you may be eligible for is $126,000. However, this formula doesn't include

INTEREST PAID FOR 30-YEAR MORTGAGE			
	INTEREST RATES		
LOAN AMOUNT	7%	7.5%	8%
$120,000	$789	$839	$844
$160,000	$1,064	$1,119	$1,174
$200,000	$1,331	$1,398	$1,468
$240,000	$1,587	$1,680	$1,761
$280,000	$1,863	$1,958	$2,055
$320,000	$2,129	$2,237	$2,348

factors such as debts, down payment, interest rate, term or type of mortgage (fixed-rate or adjustable-rate).

Another way is to figure out what you can afford is to use a loan payment handbook or chart, which can be obtained from bookstores or lenders. These charts tell you what the monthly mortgage payments would be at various interest rates based on the home cost and the size of the down payment. Unfortunately, property taxes and insurance aren't included. (See the chart above for an example.)

A more detailed way to figure out how big a mortgage you may be eligible for is to use the 28/36 qualifying ratio. First, divide your gross annual income by 12 to get your gross monthly income. Second, multiply your gross monthly income by 28 percent. Third, multiply your gross monthly income by 36 percent, and subtract your monthly debt payments. The difference—which must be a positive number—will be your maximum monthly mortgage payment. (See the exercise at right for the 28/36 equation.)

To determine the amount of the loan you may qualify for, multiply your maximum monthly mortgage payment by 80 percent (this estimates the principal and interest portion of the PITI). Divide the answer you get by the factor below that most closely represents today's interest rate environment. The solution will be the maximum loan amount you qualify for.

Interest Rate 30-Year P&I Factor

5.5 percent	.00568
6.0 percent	.00600
6.5 percent	.00632

CALCULATING YOUR MAXIMUM LOAN AMOUNT

To compute your maximum mortgage amount, you must use the lower of two numbers—the Housing Expense Ratio (1) and the Total Debt Ratio (2). For the purpose of our example, we'll assume a total gross monthly income of $4,200, total monthly debt payments of $400, a total housing expense ratio of 28 percent, and a total debt ratio of 36 percent.

Housing Expense Ratio (1)

Total Gross Monthly Income	$ 4,200	
Times 28 percent	x .28	
Maximum allowable for mortgage payment (PITI)	$1,176	(1)

Total Debt Ratio (2)

Total Gross Monthly Income	$4,200	
Times 36 percent	x .36	
Minus Total Monthly Debt Payments	- $400	
Maximum allowable for mortgage payment (PITI)	$1,112	(2)

Choose the lower of (1) or (2) $1,112   (3)

This figure estimates your maximum allowable mortgage payment (PITI), given your current gross monthly income and debts.

Multiply (3) by 80 percent to estimate the portion Of PITI that represents P&I payment only	$1,112	(3)
	x .80	
Maximum Allowable for P&I	$889.60	(4)
Divide (4) by the factor that most closely Represents today's interest rate (7.5%)	divided by .00699	

This is the maximum loan amount you qualify for: $127,267

SOURCE: FANNIE MAE

7.0 percent	.00665
7.5 percent	.00699
8.0 percent	.00734
8.5 percent	.00769
9.0 percent	.00805
9.5 percent	.00841

10.0 percent	.00878
10.5 percent	.00915
11 percent	.00953

It sounds confusing, but it becomes much clearer if you plug in real numbers. Say your gross annual income is $50,400, and your monthly debts are $400. First, divide $50,400 by 12 to get your gross monthly income of $4,200. Second, multiply $4,200 by 28 percent to get $1,176. Third, multiply $4,200 by your allowable debt-to-income ratio of 36 percent, and subtract your monthly debts of $400, to get $1,112. This solution is the maximum monthly mortgage you will be able to afford.

Now, multiply $1,112 by 80 percent. Divide the answer you get, $889.60, by the factor that most closely represents today's interest rate. We'll use 7 percent, or a factor of .00699. The maximum loan amount you qualify for is about $127,267.

 Set your housing priorities.

Try to narrow down the types of homes to look at. Among the things to consider in a home are size, new versus old, type of neighborhood, school district, type (single-family detached unit, condo, row house, or co-op), location (proximity to public transportation or work), and special features such as a garage.

Try to be flexible, especially if you're buying your first home. After building up some equity, you can trade up to your dream home. At the same time, there are certain things you should not be flexible about, such as number of bedrooms or location. Keep looking until you find something that feels right. Don't get caught up in the excitement and buy something just because a realtor tells you it's a good deal.

 Get prequalified for a home loan.

Before you actually start looking for a home you should go to a lender and get prequalified for a home loan. Prequalification isn't a guarantee that the lender will give you a mortgage. It simply tells you whether you qualify for a mortgage, and how large a home loan you qualify for, in principle.

The data you'll need to provide in order to get prequalified include your income, assets, credit report, debts, and expenses, as well as general information such as your name, age, marital status, number of children, address, and telephone number. Prequalification is generally valid for sixty days.

You shouldn't have to pay any fee to get prequalified. If a lender tries to sock you with a bill for the service, take your business elsewhere.

 Obtain the services of a real estate professional to help you find a home.

You can usually obtain the services of a real estate agent for free. That's because agents typically represent the interests of the sellers, and get paid a commission based on the home's sale price.

Agents can help you figure out what you can afford, show you houses that meet your requirements, provide prices and property tax rates, present your offer to the seller, and help you find financing and other services. They can give you the location of schools and tell you about other community services. And agents have computerized listings that can help you find homes that meet your requirements.

But since agents typically work for sellers, there could be a conflict of interest. They might tell the seller anything that could be beneficial to them, such as the highest price you're willing to pay for a home. However, they're also obligated to answer your questions honestly and tell you about any serious defects in a home that aren't visible to the naked eye.

What can you do to protect yourself from a dishonest agent? Never reveal the highest price you're willing to pay for a home to an agent working for the seller. *Mejor*, find a buyer's agent to work on your behalf. The buyer's agent will split the fee with the seller's agent so you shouldn't have to pay a *centaro* for this service.

One of the best ways to find a good agent is to ask for recommendations from family and friends who've recently bought homes. Drive through neighborhoods you're interested in and get the names and telephone numbers of agents listed on "For Sale" signs. And talk to agents hosting open houses.

If you're more comfortable using Spanish, check your local newspaper and telephone directory for ads from bilingual real estate agents. In addition, Century 21, the world's largest residential real estate company, has a toll-free number you can call at 888-988-2272 to find a Spanish-speaking agent in your area.

When looking at houses, takes notes and pictures so you can compare the features and prices later on. Check the house's interior and exterior, landscaping, and closet and storage space. Find out if there are any built-in appliances, and whether the plumbing, electrical, cooling, and heating systems are in working order.

When you find a home you really love, *mírala bien*. Look at it again during the morning and afternoon rush hours, and at night. Visit it during the week and again on weekends. This will give you a sense of how busy, noisy, and dangerous the neighborhood becomes.

 Get preapproved for a loan before making an offer on a house.

Prequalification tells you if you quality for a loan, and how large that loan may be. Preapproval actually approves that loan. Be sure you've been preapproved for a loan before you make an offer on a home, especially if you find a lender offering a good deal. A seller may be more willing to negotiate if they know you'll be able to get financing. And preapproval, which is generally valid for sixty days, can help reduce the time it takes to finalize a deal.

 Learn how to make an offer and negotiate a purchase.

How much you offer depends on the market value of the house, its condition, the circumstances surrounding the sale, how much you can afford, and the financing terms.

Ask your agent for a comparative market analysis, or CMA, of the home. This is a written report that includes the prices of comparable homes currently on the market or that have been sold in recent months.

Before making an offer, carefully inspect the home as best you can, and ask the agent and owner whether the house has any major problems. If it does, but you still want the house, estimate how much it may cost to make the repairs and ask the seller to reduce the asking price by the same amount.

When determining how much to offer, find out how long the home has been on the market, whether the price has dropped, how much the seller paid for it and when, and how much equity the seller has. If the sellers are in a hurry to sell, you may have more leverage. Your agent should have this information.

To make an offer, you give your agent a written and signed purchase and sale agreement that states your willingness to purchase the house for a given price under specified terms. The agent then presents your offer to the seller. You can write the agreement yourself, but we recommend using a broker or lawyer.

You also have to submit a good-faith payment known as earnest money with the agreement to show that you're serious about buying the house. The amount differs by location, but the check should be made out to the agent's brokerage firm, not the seller.

The earnest money is deposited into an escrow *(plica)*, or trust account. If the seller accepts your offer, the funds will be credited toward the down payment and other costs. If the seller rejects your offer you'll get the money back. But if the seller accepts your offer, then you back out of the deal, you may forfeit the money.

The purchase and sale agreement should include a legal description of the property, the amount of earnest money, your offering price, the size of your down payment and how you plan to finance the remainder, items of personal property that are to stay in the house, a proposed closing date and occupancy date, the length of time your offer is good for, and a list of contingencies.

Contingencies *(contingencias)* are terms that must be met for the contract to take effect. They typically include a financing contingency, which states that the deal will be called off and you'll get your earnest money back if you can't get the financing at the terms you've specified.

The inspection contingency gives you the right to back out of the deal or renegotiate the terms of the purchase if an inspection uncovers major problems with the structure or systems in the house. Most home inspections cost between $200 and $350.

After an agent presents your offer to the seller, the seller will either accept, reject, or make a counteroffer. If the seller accepts the offer, it becomes a legally binding contract. If the seller rejects the offer, you'll get back your earnest money. If the seller makes a counteroffer, it should be made in writing and presented to you by the agent.

The ping-pong game can go back and forth for a while. *Tenga paciencia.* Eventually you'll reach a point where either you or the seller refuses to negotiate any further. When that happens you can walk away or take the seller's final offer. Before doing so, however, you may want to ask the seller to provide other financing perks, such as paying for the title search, inspection, or other settlement costs.

ACCIÓN To find local members of the American Society of Home Inspectors, call 800-743-2744. Freddie Mac offers a brochure in English and Spanish: *Consumer Home Inspection Kit.* To obtain a copy call 800-FREDDIE.

 Check with at least six different lenders when shopping around for a mortgage.

After you sign the sales contract you'll have between thirty and sixty days to obtain a mortgage. Go to at least six different lenders when shopping around, including banks, savings and loans, credit unions, mortgage companies, and even on-line companies, if possible. (For home buying Web sites, see the list at right.)

You can use a mortgage broker if you prefer dealing with a real person. Brokers don't make loans. They act as middlemen and bring borrowers and lenders together for a fee that's paid by either the borrower, seller, or lender. They can be particularly helpful if you've got a special situation or needs, such as a bad credit record or small down payment.

ACCIÓN For a list of mortgage brokers in your area, write to the National Association of Mortgage Brokers at 8201 Greensboro Drive, Street 300, McLean, VA 22102. Fannie Mae also offers a free brochure, *Choosing the Mortgage That's Right for You/Cómo Escoger el Mejor Préstamo Hipotecario.* Call 800-611-9566 for an English version and 800-782-2729 to speak to a Spanish-speaking operator.

Decide on the type of mortgage you want.

You need to decide whether you want a fixed-rate mortgage, which is the most common, or an adjustable-rate mortgage.

Fixed-rate mortgage. A fixed-rate mortgage *(hipoteca de tasa de interés fija)* carries the same interest rate for its entire term, which is typically 30 years. Your total monthly principal and interest payments stay the same for the life of the loan, although the proportion of interest to principal changes with each monthly payment, and your taxes and insurance payments go up.

A big advantage of fixed-rate mortgages is the peace of mind that comes with knowing your monthly payments won't change. Another is that if interest rates drop, you may have an opportunity to refinance *(refinanciar)*, or pay off your old home loan with another one at a better rate.

Adjustable-rate mortgage. With an adjustable-rate mortgage *(hipote-*

HOME-BUYING WEB SITES

BANK RATE MONITOR	www.bankrate.com/
BANX QUOTE	www.banxquote.com/
CYBERHOMES	www.cyberhomes.com/
E-LOAN	www.eloan.com/
FANNIE MAE	www.fanniemae.com/
FREDDIE MAC	www.freddiemac.com/
HOMEBYNET	www.homebynet.com/
HOMESEEKERS	www.homeseekers.com/
HOMESHART	www.homeshark.com/
HUD	www.hud.gov/
INTUIT	www.quickenmortgage.com/
KEYSTROKE FINANCIAL	www.keystrokenet.com/
LOANGUIDE	www.loanguide.com/
MOVEQUEST	www.movequest.com/
REALTOR.COM	www. realtor.com/
REALTY LOCATOR	www.realtylocator.com/
U.S. DEPARTMENT OF VETERAN AFFAIRS	www.va.gov/

ca de tasa de interés ajustable), lenders adjust the interest rate of your home loan, usually no more than once a year. The rates are pegged to an economic index, such as one-year Treasury securities, plus a fixed number of percentage points.

Because you're taking the risk that interest rates will rise, initial rates tend to be lower than those of fixed-rate mortgages. This reduces your monthly mortgage payments early on, but if interest rates shoot up you could end up paying much more than you would have with a fixed-rate mortgage.

Home owners do get some protection. Federal law requires a cap on all adjustable-rate mortgages that limit annual rate changes between adjustment periods and limit the total the rate can increase over the life of the loan. These caps are usually 2 percent and 6 percent, respectively.

With any mortgage, you'll need to compare the following factors:

Down payment. In some cases you may have to buy private mortgage insurance (PMI) if you put down less than 20 percent. Ask lenders what the lowest allowable down payment is, both with and without PMI.

Private mortgage insurance. How much you pay for private mortgage insurance *(seguro hipotecario privado)* depends on many factors including the size of the down payment, type of mortgage, and amount of insurance coverage. Typically, the lower your down payment, the higher the PMI premiums, which range from .005 percent to .0085 percent of the loan. Premiums are usually folded into your monthly mortgage payment. But lender-paid policies are also available, although you'll probably have to pay a higher interest rate for your mortgage.

Interest rates. The interest rate *(tasa de interés)* determines what size home loan you qualify for, as well as your monthly mortgage payments. Seemingly small differences in interest rates can make a big impact in what you pay. Your monthly mortgage payment for a thirty-year fixed-rate loan of $120,000 at 7.5 percent would be $839 (this doesn't include the taxes and insurance). But it drops to $798 with an interest rate of 7 percent.

Points. Some lenders charge extra up-front, one-time loan origination fees *(cargo por originación de préstamos)* that are described in terms of points *(puntos)*. Each point is equal to one percent of the loan amount. One point on a loan of $120,000, for instance, would be $1,200. The more points you pay, the lower your interest rate should be. Points can be paid by either the buyer or seller, but either way they're tax deductible by the buyer.

Annual percentage rate. The annual percentage rate, or APR, takes into account the actual interest rate, monthly compound interest, points, and some closing costs. That's why the APR is usually a few tenths of a percentage higher than the stated interest rate.

Prepayment penalties. Some lenders will charge you a fee if you pay your mortgage off before a specified period of time. Look for a loan with no prepayment penalties *(penalidades por prepago)* if you think you may sell your house and pay off the mortgage early, or refinance your mortgage if interest rates drop.

Rate lock-in. The interest rate a lender quotes when you apply for a loan may not be the same interest rate that's in effect when you close the loan. To protect against fluctuations, ask the lender to hold, or "lock in" *(fijación de tasa)*, the interest rate that was originally stated to you. There may or may not be a charge for this. (For a checklist showing how to compare mortgages, see page 138.)

 Stay away from "creative financing," and don't speed up your monthly mortgage payments unless you're sure you can afford to do so.

Bobo alert: Avoid balloon mortgages, graduated payment mortgages, graduated equity mortgages, and shared appreciation mortgages. And check with a trusted financial adviser before going with a fifteen-year mortgage, or a biweekly mortgage.

A fixed-rate fifteen-year loan will have a lower interest rate than a thirty-year fixed-rate loan. You'll also build equity a lot faster. However, your monthly mortgage payments will be higher. For many people it might be better to pay less per month with a thirty-year mortgage and use the extra money for other investments.

With a biweekly mortgage, half of your monthly mortgage payment is automatically deducted from your checking or savings account every two weeks. This plan adds up to thirteen payments per year instead of twelve, which can cut a thirty-year fixed-rate mortgage to twenty-two years. (With an adjustable-rate mortgage the term won't change but each new

---

MORTGAGE CHECKLIST

Compare the following when shopping for a mortgage:
- ❏ What is the interest rate?
- ❏ Is the interest rate fixed or adjustable?
- ❏ What is the term of the loan?
- ❏ What is the lowest down payment allowed—with and without private mortgage insurance?
- ❏ If private mortgage insurance is required, how much does it cost, and how long is it required?
- ❏ Is the lender charging "points" and how do they affect the interest rate?
- ❏ What is the annual percentage rate?
- ❏ Are there prepayment penalties?
- ❏ How and when can you lock in the rate, and is there a charge to lock it in?
- ❏ Is escrow required?
- ❏ What is the loan processing time?
- ❏ What are the estimated closing costs?

---

monthly payment will be lower because you'll be paying off extra principal.) Again, it may be better to pay less with a monthly mortgage and invest the extra money elsewhere.

ACCIÓN HSH Associates provides a Homebuyer's Mortgage Kit for $20 that includes mortgage rates on most lenders in your area, and a mortgage shopping primer. Call 800-UPDATES for more information. Check your local newspaper and Web sites. Prerecorded information about the latest mortgage rates is also available by calling the Federal Home Loan Mortgage Association, or "Freddie Mac," a private company created by the federal government to provide funds to mortgage lenders, at 888-780-2060. Fannie Mae offers a free brochure called *Choosing the Mortgage That's Right for You*. Call 800-611-9566 for an English version and 800-690-7557 for a Spanish version.

Prepare for the loan application and interview.

Once you've decided on a lender you should get a copy of the loan application, schedule an interview with a loan officer, and find out what documents you'll need to bring with you for the meeting.

Dale gas. You can speed up the loan process by bringing the home's purchase contract; bank account numbers, your bank's address, and your latest statement; pay stubs, W-2 forms for the past two years, or other proof of employment or salary; debt information including loan and credit card numbers and names and addresses of your creditors; and proof of mortgage or rental payments you've made in the past.

In processing your loan, the lender is primarily interested in the property, your financial health, and your credit history. You'll probably have to pay for a professional appraiser to estimate the home's value. The lender will order your credit report and will verify all the financial information on your application.

After the loan application is signed, you may have to pay a nonrefundable application fee to cover the cost of the home's appraisal and your credit report. You may also have to accept the loan if it's offered, or pay the lender's processing costs if it's rejected.

Federal law requires that the lender send you a truth-in-lending statement *(informe de veracidad en contratos de préstamo)* within three days after getting your initial loan application. It discloses the APR and other loan terms such as the finance charge, the amount financed, and the total payments required. You'll also find a "good faith estimate" of the closing costs.

When the loan is approved you'll get a commitment letter *(carta de compromiso)*, or formal loan offer. You'll also be given a set amount of time to accept the offer and close the loan. The letter will state the loan amount, the term, the loan origination fee, points, and PITI (principal, interest, taxes, and insurance).

 Understand how to close the deal.

The closing date—the meeting at which your loan is finalized, your mortgage is issued, and you get the keys to your new house—is scheduled after you accept the commitment letter. The agent often coordinates this date with the buyer, the seller, the lender, and the closing agent.

Depending on where you live, the closing agent can be the lender, a real estate broker, an attorney for the buyer or seller, an escrow company, the third-party that holds the earnest money, or a title insurance company.

A title search *(estudio de título)*, which the buyer typically pays for, is required before the closing. A title search ensures that the seller really owns the property. It also determines whether any creditors or the Internal Revenue Service (IRS) has filed any liens *(gravámenes)*, or legal claims, against the property for unpaid bills or taxes. The seller must pay any outstanding claims before or at closing.

The lender will often require title insurance, which protects against defects in the title. There are two types of policies. A lender's policy protects the lender if a problem with the title is found after the property has been purchased. An owner's policy protects you against the same thing.

Some lenders also require a survey, paid for by the buyer, to confirm a property's boundaries. In many areas, a certificate is required from a termite inspection firm stating that the property is free of visible termite infestation and termite damage. The seller usually pays for this.

The closing itself is usually a formal meeting attended by the buyer and seller, the agent, the lender's representatives, and the title company. In some cases, however, there's no meeting. Instead, an escrow agent processes all the paperwork and collects and disburses the funds.

The lender is required by law to give you a brochure called *Buying Your Home: Settlement Costs and Helpful Information.* If the lender fails to do so you can get a copy by contacting your real estate agent's office or a HUD regional office.

Although an attorney may not be required, it's probably a good idea to hire your own to review the contract. Ask the agent and lender for recommendations, and contact your local bar association for referrals to attorneys who specialize in real estate.

During the closing, many documents will be explained and signed. They include:

HUD-1 Settlement Statement. This form is required by federal law and is filled out by the settlement agent conducting the closing. It itemizes the services provided and lists the charges to the buyer and seller, and must be signed by the buyer and seller. It must be presented to the buyer at least twenty-four hours before closing.

The note. The note (*nota*) is a legal IOU that represents your promise to pay the lender according to the terms agreed upon. The note includes the date on which payments must be made, where they must be sent, and the penalties that will be assessed if you default.

The mortgage. The mortgage is a legal document that secures the note and gives the lender legal claim to your house if you default on the loan. In some states a deed of trust is used instead of a mortgage (see below). In this case, the buyer receives title to the property, but signs a deed of trust that conveys title to a third party called a trustee. The trustee holds the title until the loan is paid in full.

The deed. The deed (*título de propiedad*) transfers ownership from the seller to the buyer. The seller must bring the deed to the closing, and it must be properly signed and notarized.

Closing costs. Closing costs—both the amount and who pays—can be negotiated between the buyer and the seller. But they usually include: the loan origination fee covering the administrative costs of processing the loan; points; appraisal fee; credit report fee; assumption fee if you take over the payments on the seller's existing loan; advance payments of interest, private mortgage insurance, hazard insurance, escrow accounts, or reserves; title charges; recording and transfer fees; additional charges such as surveyor's fees or termite inspections; and adjustments.

The closing agent usually won't release the checks to the seller or the agent until the mortgage or deed of trust is signed and the deed is recorded at the registry of deeds or the county clerk's office.

 Know where to go if you believe your loan application has been unfairly denied.

The lender is required to explain its decision in writing if your application for a home loan is denied. If the explanation is unsatisfactory or unclear, go to the loan officer in person and ask for an explanation, and for suggestions as to what you can do to get approval in the future. If you believe you're being discriminated against, file a complaint with the lender, the lender's regulatory agency, and HUD's Office of Fair Housing and Equal Opportunity at 800-669-9777.

 Learn when and how to refinance your mortgage.

Most experts recommend refinancing your mortgage when the market rate is at least two percentage points below the rate on your loan. *Pero tenga cuidado.* The fees associated with refinancing your mortgage could exceed the two-point savings unless you plan to remain in the home for at least another three years.

When you refinance, you should count on paying between 3 percent and 6 percent of the outstanding principal of your loan in closing costs, plus any prepayment penalties.

You may, however, be able to trim costs in other ways. If you refinance with the same lender that holds your original loan, the lender will sometimes waive appraisal fees or prepayment penalties, and negotiate interest rates and points.

ACCIÓN A brochure called *A Consumer's Guide to Mortgage Refinancings* describes the costs of refinancing and helps you determine if refinancing is right for you. For a copy send $0.50 to the Consumer Information Center, Pueblo, CO 81009. Be sure to specify the name of the brochure and ID #331E. It's also available free on the Web at www.pueblo.gsa.gov/.

 Investigate affordable homeownership and first-time homebuyer programs.

Eligibility for first-time or low- to moderate-income home buyer programs offered on the local, state, and federal level is usually based on income and household size. Loan amounts are also capped.

But the term "first-time homebuyer" isn't as strict as it sounds. In most cases you're considered eligible for a first-time homebuyer program as long as you haven't owned a home within the past three years. Here's a sample of some of these programs:

Private. Ask lenders if they have programs for first-time or low- to moderate- income homebuyers. Some of these programs require a down payment of just 3 percent, of which 1 or 2 percent can come in the form of a gift (these are called 3/1 or 3/2 mortgages). Others offer personal loans to help cover the down payment and closing costs.

Local. Many cities and counties each year offer a limited number of Mortgage Credit Certificates that provide tax credits of up to 20 percent on a homeowner's annual mortgage interest deduction. Low-interest "silent second mortgages" (*hipotecas subordinadas y ocultas*), which don't have to be paid back for years, are also available for help with down payments.

In addition, entire housing developments or individual units in housing developments are set aside for first-time and low- to moderate-income homebuyers. For more information call your city and county housing agencies (the numbers are listed in the government pages of your telephone directory).

State. Most states have affordable-housing programs. In California, for example, the California Housing Finance Administration has a program that requires a down payment of just 3 percent. (For a list of state housing agencies and phone numbers, see pages 144–45.)

Federal. The U.S. Department of Veterans' Affairs offers home loans to eligible veterans that don't require any down payment at all (some states also offer their own home loan programs for veterans). Loans generally can't exceed $203,000, and buyers can negotiate the interest rate with the lenders. No private mortgage insurance is required.

ACCIÓN To reach the U.S. Department of Veterans Affairs, or to get the number of your state veteran's affairs office, call 800-827-1000.

Freddie Mac programs for low- to moderate-income homebuyers require a down payment of just 3 percent or provide assistance with closing costs. Homes can also be purchased through Freddie Mac's HomeSteps program with a down payment of 5 percent. The maximum loan in 1998 was $227,150. No appraisal, application fee, or private mortgage insurance is required.

STATE HELP FOR HOMEBUYERS

State, District of Columbia, and Puerto Rican housing agencies. Calls to an 800 or 888 number are free when made within the respective states:

ALABAMA	334-244-9200 / 800-325-2432
ALASKA	907-338-6100 / 800-478-AHFC
ARIZONA	602-280-1365
ARKANSAS	501-682-5900
CALIFORNIA	800-789-CHFA
COLORADO	303-297-2432 / 800-877-2432
CONNECTICUT	860-721-9501 / 800-533-9208
DELAWARE	302-577-3720
DISTRICT OF COLUMBIA	202-408-0415
FLORIDA	904-488-4197
GEORGIA	404-679-4840 / 800-359-4663
HAWAII	808-587-0640
IDAHO	208-331-4882 / 800-526-7145
ILLINOIS	312-836-5200 / 800-942-8439
INDIANA	317-232-7777 / 800-872-0371
IOWA	515-242-4990 / 800-432-7230
	/ 800-432-7230
KANSAS	785-296-5865 / 800-752-4422
KENTUCKY	502-564-7630 / 800-633-8896
LOUISIANA	504-342-1320
MAINE	207-626-4600 / 800-452-4668
MARYLAND	410-514-7007 / 800-638-7781
MASSACHUSETTS	617-854-1000 / 800-882-1154
MICHIGAN	517-373-8370 / 800-327-9158
MINNESOTA	612-296-7608 / 800-710-8871
MISSISSIPPI	601-354-6062 / 800-544-6960

MISSOURI	816-759-6600
MONTANA	406-444-3040 / 800-761-6264
NEBRASKA	402-434-3900 / 800-204-6432
NEVADA	702-687-4258 / 800-227-4960
NEW HAMPSHIRE	603-472-8623 / 800-649-0470
NEW JERSEY	609-278-7400 / 800-654-6873
NEW MEXICO	505-843-6880 / 800-444-6880
NEW YORK	212-688-4000 / 800-382-4663
NORTH CAROLINA	919-781-6115
NORTH DAKOTA	701-328-8080 / 800-292-8621
OHIO	614-466-7970 / 888-643-2636
OKLAHOMA	405-848-1144 / 800-256-1489
	/ 800-256-1489
OREGON	503-986-2000
PENNSYLVANIA	717-780-3800 / 800-822-1174
PUERTO RICO	787-765-7577
RHODE ISLAND	401-751-5566 / 800-427-5560
SOUTH CAROLINA	803-734-2000
SOUTH DAKOTA	605-773-3181 / 800-540-4251
TENNESSEE	615-741-2400 / 800-228-8432
TEXAS	512-475-3800 / 800-792-2119
UTAH	801-521-6950 / 800-284-6950
	/ 800-284-6950
VERMONT	802-864-5743
VIRGINIA	804-782-1986 / 800-968-7837
WASHINGTON	206-464-7139 / 800-67-HOME
WEST VIRGINIA	304-345-6475 / 800-933-9843
WISCONSIN	608-266-7884 / 800-33-HOUSE
WYOMING	307-265-0603 / 800-273-4635

ACCIÓN For information about Freddie Mac's HomeSteps program, call 800-972-7555.

The Rural Housing Service of the Farmers Home Administration has a single-family housing program that provides loans, grants, and loan guarantees for very low- to moderate-income rural residents. Interest rates are low, no down payment is required, and the maximum loan amounts vary by location.

ACCIÓN For information about programs for rural residents, contact your state's Rural Housing Service office or call 202-720-4323.

Fannie Mae offers at least ten affordable housing programs through a network of lenders. Down payments can be as low as 3 percent. Qualifying income is lower. Gifts, grants, or loans are available for closing costs. Cash reserve requirements are lower or non-existent.

In addition, "silent second mortgages" are available. So are lease-purchase agreements (*arrendamientos con opción de compra*), where a portion of your rent payments is placed in a savings so it can accumulate and be used for a down payment later on. And nontraditional credit is accepted. The maximum loan amount in 1998 was $227,150, and no private mortgage insurance is required.

ACCIÓN For information about Fannie Mae programs, call 800-688-HOME or 800-732-6643.

The Officer Next Door program makes HUD-owned properties available to law enforcement officers at a 50 percent discount. They also need a down payment of just $100 if they use a mortgage insured by HUD's Federal Housing Administration (FHA). These homes are located in areas that have been targeted for revitalization.

FHA-insured loans, which are also available to the general public, are usually limited to $67,500, but the amount rises to $160,950 in high-cost areas such as San Francisco or New York. They usually require a down payment of 5 percent or less.

ACCIÓN For information about the Officer Next Door
program call 800-217-6970. For information about FHA-insured
mortgage loans call 800-CALL-FHA. The Mortgage Insurance
Companies of America also offer a free brochure in English and
Spanish: *How to Buy a Home With a Low Down Payment/Como
Comprar Una Vivienda con Un Pago Inicial Reducido.* For a free
copy, write to MICA, 727 15th St., NW, 12th Floor, Washington,
DC 20542.

❏ Determine whether you're better off renting or buying.

❏ Educate yourself about the home buying process by reading your
   newspaper's real estate section and attending free home buying
   seminars.

❏ Assess your financial health, and figure out what you can afford
   to buy.

❏ Understand all the up-front and ongoing costs of buying and maintaining a home.

❏ Define your housing priorities, including the type of house (new or
   existing), size, and location.

❏ Get prequalified for a home loan before you start looking, and get
   preapproval for a home loan before you make an offer on a house.

❏ Obtain the services of a qualified real estate professional to help you
   find the right home.

❏ Check with at least six different lenders when shopping around for a
   mortgage.

❏ Investigate affordable housing and first-time home buyer programs.

ADDITIONAL RESOURCES

Recommended Books
*How to Buy the Home You Want For the Best Price in Any Market: From a Real Estate
Insider Who Knows All the Tricks,* by Terry Eilers (New York: Hyperion, 1997).

CHAPTER 6

Paying for College

"INSTRUCTION IN YOUTH IS LIKE ENGRAVING IN STONES"   —COLOMBIA

WHY SHOULD LATINOS GO TO COLLEGE? AS ABUELITA USED TO SAY, "*La educación es la base del progreso.*" And we aren't just referring to money, although that's a major part of the equation. We're also talking about finding stimulating, fulfilling, and meaningful work.

That's the message Manuel, 18, and his two older sisters got from their Salvadoran parents while they struggled to make ends meet as a maid and plumber in Los Angeles. Manuel is now attending the University of Southern California and plans to become a broadcast journalist. One sister is an elementary school teacher, and another is working as a paralegal while attending college part-time. "Where I grew up, a lot of people have the view that you go to high school, then get a job," he says. "But college is my chance to do what I really want to do."

The effect that higher education can have on a paycheck is hard to ignore. Average annual starting salaries for graduates with Bachelor's degrees in 1997 was $24,448 for special education majors, $30,154 for accounting majors, and $40,093 for computer engineering majors, according to the National Association of Colleges and Employers.

Latinos understand the difference an education can make. When asked about the ingredients necessary for getting ahead in life, 96 percent of Latinos in a survey by Miami-based Strategy Research Corp. cited "education," compared to 88 percent of non-Latino whites. Latinos rated education higher than "working hard," "knowing the right people," "being talented," and "having successful parents or family."

Yet the number of Latinos earning college degrees, although rising, remains alarmingly low. In 1994, 4.3 percent of all Bachelor's degrees awarded in the United States went to Latinos, compared to 80.3 percent for non-Latino whites, according to the most recent figures available from the U.S. Department of Education.

The reasons behind the dismal Latino college graduate rates are too varied and complicated to adequately cover here. However, we can discuss one of the biggest hurdles facing all families who want to send their children to college—the high price tag. For many Latinos, the struggle to pay for school begins even sooner than college if they send their children to private or parochial elementary, junior high, and high school.

College costs have risen an average of 6 percent every year since 1992. During the 1998-99 academic year, annual tuition, fees, and room and board averaged $22,533 at a four-year private institution, $10,458 at a four-year public institution, $7,333 at a private two-year institution, and $1,633 at a public two-year institution, according to the College Board's Annual Survey of Colleges.

Hay muchas opciones. If you can, save and invest money for future education expenses. Government financial aid is available in the form of grants (free money that's given based on financial need), loans (money that must be paid back with interest), and work-study (campus-based jobs). There are also hundreds of private scholarships (free money that's given based on either financial need or merit).

 Look for scholarships to pay for private elementary, junior high, and high school.

While no government financial aid is available to help defray pre-college school costs, many schools provide scholarships, tuition remission, or discounts, especially if more than one child from the same *familia* is attending.

Some scholarships are need-based and determined by household income and size. Others are merit-based and awarded to students with academic, athletic, or artistic talents, although these are becoming less common.

Con más frecuencia, families are also obtaining loans to pay private elementary, junior high, and high school expenses, or using special plans that allow them to pay for tuition and other expenses by installment, usually monthly or quarterly.

To find out whether you're eligible for financial aid, you'll have to fill out the school's financial aid application form. Several factors will be weighed to determine how much, if any, money you'll get: income, assets, cost of living, household size, age of the parents, and number of children in private elementary and secondary schools and college.

Many private schools use the School and Student Service for Financial Aid Form (SSS), which costs $16 to process. Catholic schools usually use the Private School Aid Service (PSAS) application, which costs $12 to process. These forms can be obtained directly from schools.

The forms can be pretty daunting and require large amounts of data, all of which must be substantiated with copies of your tax returns. In fact, the process is even more complicated than college financial aid application forms because elementary and secondary schools have a lot less aid to offer than colleges. Some schools offer free seminars to explain the process.

The average annual tuition for a private K through 12 school is $3,116, according to the Council for American Private Education (CAPE). But tuition varies greatly and depends on which organization runs the school, whether it's a day school or boarding school, and where it is located.

For example, the most expensive schools are those belonging to the National Association of Independent Schools (NAIS). For these schools, median annual tuition in the Eastern United States ranges from $3,800 for preschool to $14,745 for 12th grade; in the Western United States it's $7,335 for preschool and $11,550 for 12th grade.

However, almost 17 percent of NAIS students receive need-based financial aid that averaged $6,540 per year, while merit-based scholarships averaged about $2,228 per year in 1997. Check with each individual school about the type of financial aid it offers.

Catholic schools tend to be among the least expensive private schools, and the cost depends on how many children attend the same school, whether the family is a member of the parish, whether the student is Catholic, what grade the student is in, whether tuition is paid yearly or monthly, and a family's financial need.

The average annual tuition for the first Catholic elementary school child of a family in the parish in grade one to grade eight was $1,303 in 1994–95, the most recent figures available, according to the National Catholic Educational Association (NCEA). For high school students, median fresh-man annual tuition in 1993 was $3,100.

About 82 percent of Catholic elementary schools offer some type of tuition assistance, says the NCEA. And 97 percent of all Catholic high schools grant financial aid, with each grant averaging $1,098. As with inde-pendent schools, check with each Catholic school to find out about finan-cial aid possibilities. (For a list of other private school organizations, see pages 154–55.)

It may be tempting to borrow money to pay for elementary, junior high, and high school. *Tenga cuidado.* You should only do it as a last resort. Remember, you've still got to pay for college. Instead, it may be better to budget for private school expenses, or get a second job. (See Chapter 1 for more information about budgeting.)

While you may be able to pay for at least some private school costs by saving and investing, you'll have to start long before you have children. Otherwise, you won't have enough time to invest aggressively enough to see any significant returns. (See the box at right for a list of companies offering K–12 loans or payment plans.)

ACCIÓN The NAIS has three free brochures: *Financing a Private School Education, Family Guide to Financial Aid and Choosing the Right School,* and *The Boarding School Directory.* Write to the NAIS Office of Financial Aid Services, 1620 L Street NW, Washington, DC 20036-5605. The NAIS also offers a hotline for families of color seeking information about inde-pendent schools at 800-343-9138.

 Save or invest for your children's college educa-tion if you can.

As with any investment, the more time you have until you need the money, the more aggressive you should be (mutual funds). The closer your child gets to leaving for college, the more conservative you should be (bonds, CDs, money market accounts).

These rules are pretty fundamental. *¿Pero cuánto?* How much money should you save each month? The answer depends on what you can afford, how much time you have, whether you expect your child to go to a public or private school, and how much of the total bill you intend to pay.

Say you've got a five-year old son. You need to get an estimate of how much four years at a private or public university will cost thirteen years down the road. First, take the current average annual cost of a public and private university ($19,213 and $7,472, respectively) and add 6 percent to each.

Second, take the new sums ($20,366 and $7,920) and again add 6 percent to each. You have to repeat this calculation sixteen times (thirteen years until he starts school, plus the extra four years it will take him to finish). You can be more precise by using the current price of a specific school instead of the average prices for public and private schools. (The box found on page 156 shows cost increases for public and private colleges assuming 6 percent inflation over the next 21 years.)

COMPANIES OFFERING LOANS, PAYMENT PLANS

Here's a list of companies that offer loans and payment plans to pay for private K–12 schools (some also offer college loans):

ACADEMIC MANAGEMENT RESOURCES	800-531-4300
EDUCATION RESOURCES INSTITUTE	800-255-TERI
FACTS TUITION MANAGEMENT	800-624-7092
FIRST MARBLEHEAD	800-895-4283
HIGHER EDUCATION SERVICES, INC.	800-422-0010
KEY EDUCATION RESOURCES	800-540-1855
P.L.A.T.O. JUNIOR EDUCATION LOAN	800-263-3527
TUITION MANAGEMENT SYSTEMS	800-722-4867
USA GROUP TUITION PAYMENT PLANS	800-348-4605
WYNWOOD, INC.	800-270-9098

SOURCE: NATIONAL ASSOCIATION OF INDEPENDENT SCHOOLS

PRIVATE SCHOOL ORGANIZATIONS IN THE UNITED STATES

These organizations provide directories of their member schools (most for free, but some for a price). Financial aid information must be obtained from each individual school:

AMERICAN MONTESSORI SOCIETY
281 Park Avenue South
New York, NY 10010
212-358-1250
Free directory.

ASSOCIATION OF MILITARY COLLEGES AND SCHOOLS OF THE U.S.
9115 McNair Drive
Alexandria, VA 22309
703-360-1678
Free directory.

CHRISTIAN SCHOOLS INTERNATIONAL
3350 East Paris Avenue SE
Grand Rapids, MI 49512
616-957-1570
Free directory.

EVANGELICAL LUTHERAN CHURCH IN AMERICA
8765 West Higgans Road
Chicago, IL 60361
773-380-2845, ext. 2857
Free directory

FRIENDS COUNCIL ON EDUCATION
1507 Cherry Street
Philadelphia, PA 19102
215-241-7289
Free directory.

LUTHERAN CHURCH-MISSOURI SYNOD
1333 South Kirkwood Road

St. Louis, MO 63122
314-965-9917, ext. 1293
Directory called "The Lutheran Annual" available for $12.50 by call-
ing 800-325-3040.

NORTH AMERICAN DIVISION, SEVENTH-DAY ADVENTISTS
12501 Old Columbia Pike
Silver Spring, MD 20901
301-680-6441
Call to find schools in your area.

NATIONAL ASSOCIATION OF EPISCOPAL SCHOOLS
815 Second Avenue
New York, NY 10017
800-334-7626
Directory available for $14.95 by calling (800) number.

NATIONAL CATHOLIC EDUCATIONAL ASSOCIATION
1077 30th Street NW
Washington, DC 20007
202-337-6232
Directory called "Catholic Schools in America" is available for $47
by calling 800-468-0813. Copies are also available in most
Diocesan libraries.

NATIONAL SOCIETY FOR HEBREW DAY SCHOOLS
160 Broadway
New York, NY 10038
212-227-1000, ext. 113
Directory available for $18 by calling 718-259-1223.

SOLOMON SCHECHTER DAY SCHOOL ASSOCIATION
155 Fifth Avenue
New York, NY 10010
212-533-7800
Free directory.

TUITION COSTS

Here's how much state and private college tuition, fees, and room and board will increase every year over the next 21 years, assuming an annual inflation rate of 6 percent:

YEAR	STATE	PRIVATE
1998–99	$10,458	$22,533
1999–2000	$11,085	$23,885
2000–2001	$11,751	$25,318
2001–2002	$12,456	$26,837
2002–2003	$13,203	$28,447
2003–2004	$13,995	$30,154
2004–2005	$14,835	$31,936
2005–2006	$15,725	$33,881
2006–2007	$16,668	$35,914
2007–2008	$17,669	$38,069
2008–2009	$18,729	$40,353
2009–2010	$19,852	$42,774
2010–2011	$21,044	$45,341
2011–2012	$22,306	$48,061
2012–2013	$23,645	$50,945
2013–2014	$25,063	$54,002
2014–2015	$26,567	$57,242
2015–2016	$28,161	$60,676
2016–2017	$29,851	$64,317
2017–2018	$31,642	$68,176
2018–2019	$33,540	$72,266
2019–2020	$35,553	$76,602

When you add up the four years that *el niño* will spend in college (2011 to 2014), you'll get a total of $190,028 for a private school, or $73,894 for a public school. Assuming an average annual return of 10 percent, that means you'll have to invest $7,749 per year, or $645.75 per month, over the next 13 years to pay for private school, and $3,013, or $251 per month, to pay for public school. *¡Ay!* And that's just one *niño!* You'll need even more money if you plan to send more than one child to college.

Cálmense. Remember, these are rough estimates only. In reality, college costs may be higher or lower depending on inflation and whether your child commutes or lives on campus, among other things.

ACCIÓN Many different types of on-line calculators can help you figure out how much college will cost, and how much money you need to save to pay for it. Go to The Financial Aid Information Page at www.finaid.org/finaid.html; the Mutual Fund Education Alliance's College Worksheet at www.mfea.com; or The College Board's worksheet at www.collegeboard.com. If you don't have Internet access, go to the library or a school guidance counselor's office and ask for a book by The College Board called *Meeting College Costs: What You Need to Know Before Your Child and Your Money Leave Home.* This book contains several worksheets.

 If your child is heading to college, apply for financial aid, no matter how high your income.

Even if your child doesn't qualify for grants, he or she may be eligible for low-interest student loans or work-study programs. You'll never know unless you try.

The first step is to fill out the Free Application for Federal Student Aid (FAFSA). The information you provide on this form will be plugged into a formula that determines your expected family contribution (EFC), or the amount of money you and your child are expected to contribute toward education expenses.

The EFC is then subtracted from the total cost of one year of college. The amount left over, if any, is the financial need. The EFC remains the same no matter how much a school costs. For example, if your EFC is $5,000, and the school costs $10,000, financial need is $5,000. If the school costs $20,000, financial need jumps to $15,000.

The EFC is based on the available income and assets of the parents and the student. That means there's a certain amount of income and assets that parents and students are allowed to keep.

For example, the amount accumulated in retirement accounts such as

IRAs and 401(k)s won't be considered assets for financial aid purposes. But the annual contributions made to these retirement plans will be considered as income if they were tax deductible.

There's also an income protection allowance, which is based on the number of family members living in the household and the number of family members in college, and an asset protection allowance, which is based on the age of the older parent.

After subtracting the income and asset protection allowances, parents are expected to contribute up to 47 percent of their remaining income and 5.6 percent of their remaining savings toward education expenses, while dependent students are expected to contribute 50 percent of their income and 35 percent of their savings over $2,200.

The EFC formula changes depending on whether the person seeking financial aid is a dependent student or an independent student. (The EFC Formula Book from the U.S. Department of Education walks you through different scenarios.)

The FAFSA should be completed and sent in as soon as you can after January 1, but no later than May 1, of your child's senior year in high school. The sooner you can send in the FAFSA, the better. If you wait, you might get more loans than grants. The form must be filled out every year that your child needs financial aid.

You'll need a draft version of your income tax return to meet early application requirements and deadlines. Many schools will also require a copy of your actual return sometime after it's been filed on April 15 to verify the information you've provided.

About four weeks after submitting your FAFSA, you'll get a Student Aid Report (SAR), which will tell you your expected family contribution. Make sure the SAR is correct. If not, corrections can be made on Part 2 of the SAR and sent to the address on the report.

The financial aid administrators at the colleges will verify the information on your FAFSA where your child has been accepted. They'll determine your financial aid eligibility and send you a financial aid award letter that describes the grants, loans, and work-study in the package.

Some schools may also require you to fill out their own financial aid forms as well as a College Scholarship Services (CSS) Financial Aid Profile, which is more detailed and often determines a higher expected family contribution. Find out what's required from the school's financial aid office.

Some expensive private schools, such as Princeton, Harvard, Yale, Stanford, and the Massachusetts Institute of Technology are so concerned about competition for middle- and lower-income students that they're liberalizing their financial aid policies to woo candidates who might otherwise attend state schools.

Among the changes, loans for students whose families earn less than $40,000 a year are turned into grants. The share of grants over loans for students from families earning between $40,000 and $75,000 a year is increased. And home equity is no longer included when calculating family assets if annual household income is $90,000 or less.

Financial need is typically met with a package of grants, loans, and work-study, as well as state, school, and private scholarships. Here's a rundown of the federal programs, the eligibility requirements, and the amount of money each can provide:

Pell Grants. Pell grants are awarded only to undergraduate students, and are based on financial need, although students are allowed to earn up to $2,200 without losing their eligibility for the grants. The maximum award for 1999 was $4,500, but will rise to a maximum of $5,800 over the next five years. How much a student gets depends on the estimated family contribution, and the cost to attend the specific school.

Perkins Loans. Some schools get money from the federal government to offer Perkins loans. The amount of each award depend on the availability of government funds, and a student's financial need.

Federal Supplemental Educational Opportunity Grant Program. Some schools also get money from the federal government to offer grants. The amount of each award depends on the availability of government funds, financial need, and the amount of other aid the student has already received.

Federal Parent Loans for Undergraduate Students (FPLUS). FPLUS loans allow parents with good credit records to borrow money to pay for the educational expenses of an undergraduate child. (If parents don't have a good credit history, they can still get these loans if they get someone to co-sign for it.)

The maximum amount parents can borrow is equal to the cost of attendance minus any other financial aid. For example, if the cost of attendance is $8,000, and your child gets $4,000 in financial aid, the maximum amount you could borrow would be $4,000.

The interest rate is variable, but it's capped at 9 percent, and adjusted once a year. There's also a fee equal to 4 percent of the total amount of the loan. Parents must begin repaying both interest and principal while a student is still in school.

Federal Direct Student Loan and Federal Stafford Loan Programs. These two loans are either subsidized or unsubsidized. Subsidized loans are based on financial need. A student won't be charged any interest until he or she starts repaying the loan.

Unsubsidized loans are not need based. A student will be charged interest from the time the loan is disbursed until it's paid in full. If a student can't pay the interest while still in school, it will be added to the principal amount of the loan, increasing the total amount that has to be repaid.

Dependent undergraduates can borrow up to $2,635 the first year, $3,500 the second year, and $5,500 after that. Dependent students whose parents can't get a FPLUS loan, and independent undergraduates can borrow up to $6,625 the first year, $7,500 the second year, and $10,500 after that.

Graduate students can generally borrow up to $18,500 each academic year. The interest rate on these loans is variable and is pegged to the federal Treasury bill interest rate plus 1.7 percentage points while the student is in school, and 2.3 percent after the student graduates. But it will never exceed 8.25 percent. The interest is adjusted once a year. You may be charged fees of up to 4 percent of the total amount of each loan.

Federal Work-Study. Some schools also get money from the federal government to offer jobs, which are usually on campus and pay at least the minimum wage.

Interest payments made on student loans for the first 60 months can be deducted if you meet certain income requirements. The maximum annual deduction is $1,500 in 1999; $2,000 in 2000; and $2,500 from 2001 and on. If you're a single taxpayer, you can claim the full deduction if your annual adjusted gross income, or AGI, is $40,000 or less ($60,000 or less if you're married filing jointly). The deduction is phased out for single filers with an annual AGI of $40,000 to $55,000 ($60,000 to $75,000 if you're married filing jointly). (Taxes and deductions are covered in Chapter 9.)

ACCIÓN To obtain a copy of the FAFSA and The EFC Formula Book call 800-4FED-AID. You can also file your FAFSA application on-line at www.ed.gov/. For more information about federal student aid programs get a free copy of *The Student Aid Guide* from the U.S. Department of Education by calling 800-433-3243.

 Consider shifting or reducing some of your assets to improve your child's financial aid eligibility.

There are many creative and perfectly legal steps you can take to increase your child's financial aid eligibility. This includes shifting or reducing your assets to slash your expected family contribution and boost your financial need.

Freshman financial aid awards are based in part on income for the year ending December 31 of your child's senior year in high school. This is called the base year. Some steps can be taken during the base year, while others should only be taken the year before the base year.

The year before the base year is the time to cash in your investments and fatten your savings account, which is considered an asset for financial aid purposes. During the base year you should reduce your savings account by buying big ticket items with extra cash and by paying off outstanding debts.

This is how it works: Say you've got $60,000 in savings, and $30,000 in debt. If you pay off your debt, you're left with $30,000 in savings. Counting the asset protection allowance, your assets are reduced significantly, which may qualify you for more financial aid.

If you sell a stock, bond, or other investment for more than what you paid for it, the difference is called a capital gain. But if you sell it for less than what you originally paid for it, it's called a capital loss. Since capital gains are considered income for financial aid purposes, you should try to avoid them during the base year, or at least offset them with capital losses.

 **Apply for private scholarships.**

HISPANIC SERVING INSTITUTIONS

These schools have at least 25 percent Latino enrollment:

California State University, Bakersfield
California State University, Los Angeles
The College of Santa Fe (New Mexico)
Del Mar College (Corpus Christi, Texas)
East Los Angeles College (California)
El Paso Community College (Texas)
Florida International University (Miami)
Hostos Community College (Bronx, New York)
Lehman College (Bronx, New York)
Mercy College (Dobbs Ferry, New York)
Miami-Dade Community College (Florida)
Mount Saint Mary's College (Los Angeles, California)
New Mexico Highlands University (Las Vegas, New Mexico)
New Mexico State University (Albuquerque)
Northern New Mexico Community College (Española and El Rito)
Our Lady of the Lake University (San Antonio, Texas)
Palo Alto College (San Antonio, Texas)
Pueblo Community College (Colorado)
Rio Hondo College (Whittier, California)
San Antonio College (Texas)

Billions of dollars in private scholarships are awarded every year based on a student's ethnic background, religious affiliation, athletic, artistic or community achievements, or parental affiliation with labor unions or fraternal organizations.

It's true that schools will reduce a student's financial aid if private scholarship money is awarded. But finding free money is still worth the effort. ¿Por qué? You may be able to convince the school to reduce the loan portion of your child's financial aid package instead of the grant portion.

The first place to look is close to home. Many companies provide scholarships to their employees' children. Charitable organizations often give scholarships to volunteers. Civic groups, such as the Boy Scouts, Rotary Club, American Legion, and the Elks Club also give awards.

San Bernardino Valley College (California)
Santa Fe Community College (Gainesville, Florida)
St. Mary's University of San Antonio (Texas)
St. Thomas University (Miami, Florida)
Sul Ross State University (Alpine, Texas)
Texas A&M International University (Laredo)
Texas A&M University, Corpus Christi
Texas A&M University, Kingsville
The University of The Incarnate Word (San Antonio, Texas)
The University of New Mexico (Albuquerque)
University of Puerto Rico, Arecibo Technological University
University of Puerto Rico, Bayamon Technological University College
University of Puerto Rico, Humacao University College
University of Puerto Rico, Medical Science Campus
University of Puerto Rico, Ponce Technological University
University of Puerto Rico, Rio Piedras Campus
University of Puerto Rico, Mayaguez
University of Puerto Rico, Central Administration
University of Texas-Pan American (Edinburg)
University of Texas, San Antonio
University of Texas, El Paso
Western New Mexico University (Silver City)

SOURCE: HISPANIC ASSOCIATION OF COLLEGES AND UNIVERSITIES (HACU)

Ask your child's high school's guidance counselor and the financial aid office at the schools your child applies to about private or school-specific scholarships. Lists of these scholarships can also be found in dozens of books, most of which you can find in libraries.

Be sure to apply to Hispanic-serving institutions, which are defined by the Hispanic Association of Colleges and Universities (HACU) as having student populations that are at least 25 percent Latino. Many of these schools provide financial aid to Latinos and have good Latino retention and graduation rates. (See the box above for a HACU listing of such institutions.)

One of the easiest and fastest ways to find scholarships is to use the Internet. Most schools have their own Web sites that include financial aid information. But there are also many free scholarship search services on the

FREE WEB-BASED SCHOLARSHIP SEARCH SERVICES

College Board's ex-Pan Scholarship Search at www.collegeboard.org/fundfinder/bin/fundfind01.pl offers access to its database with more than 3,300 scholarships.

CollegeNet at www.collegenet.com offers access to its MACH25 scholarship database listing more than 500,000 private scholarships.

FastWeb at www.fastweb.com/ offers access to its database of more than 275,000 scholarships. Two added bonuses: You can apply for some scholarships directly on-line, and FastWeb will e-mail potential scholarship matches directly to you.

Minority On-Line Information Service at http://web.fie.com/molis/ provides information and links to minority-serving institutions, scholarships, and fellowships.

Sallie Mae at www.salliemae.com/ offers access to its College Aid Sources for Higher Education, or CASHE, database.

The Financial Aid Information Page at www.finaid.org/ offers the most comprehensive information about college financial aid, including a Financial Aid for Minority Students section with links to databases, fellowships, and scholarships.

The Scholarship Resource Network's SRN Express at www.rams.com/srn/index.htm offers access to an abbreviated version of its SRN database with more than 8,000 scholarships.

Web. (For a list of free scholarship search services, see the box above.)

Students with stellar academic records and sky-high Scholastic Aptitude Test (SAT) scores won't have any problem finding the money to go to school. There are also many grants set aside specifically for Latinos or minorities. But even average students can find scholarships. (See the box at right for a list of key Latino scholarships.)

ACCIÓN The Congressional Hispanic Caucus Institute at 800-EXCEL-DC provides access to more than 200,000 Latino-

ORGANIZATIONS OFFERING SCHOLARSHIPS TO LATINOS

American GI Forum's Hispanic Educational
   Foundation of the United States
3301 Mountain Rd., NW
Alburquerque, NM 87104
To find your local AGIF chapter: 505-243-7551

Hispanic Association of Colleges and Universities
Student Support Systems
4204 Gardendale Street, #216
San Antonio, TX 78299   210-692-3805

League of United Latin American Citizens
   (LULAC)
National Educational Service Centers Inc.
777 N. Capitol Street NE #305
Washington, DC 20002   202-408-0060

Mexican American Legal Defense and
   Educational Fund (MALDEF)
634 S. Spring Street, 11th Floor
Los Angeles, CA 90014   213-629-2512

National Hispanic Scholarship Fund
One Sansome Street, Suite 1000
San Francisco, CA 94104   415-445-9930

U.S. Hispanic Chamber of Commerce
   Scholarship
1030 Fifteenth Street, NW #206
Washington, DC 20005   202-842-1212

specific financial aid resources (call during business hours
Monday through Friday). It will also assemble a comprehensive
college financial aid strategy based on a student's field of interest. There is no charge for the service, and bilingual help is
available. Another great resource is *Hispanic* magazine's annu-

al bilingual guide to the top twenty-five colleges for Hispanics, which is distributed free every Fall.

 Beware of scholarship search scams.

¡Cuidado! There are many legitimate scholarship search services. Unfortunately, there are just as many fraudulent ones that offer to find students scholarships for a fee. And there is no centralized source that can provide a list of legitimate services. But you can protect yourself by following a few basic rules:

- ❏ Stay away from any company that "guarantees" scholarships. Many of these services simply provide lists of scholarships. They don't actually award the money.
- ❏ Never give a credit card or bank account number over the telephone without first getting information from the company in writing.
- ❏ Stay away from a company that says it is "holding" your scholarship, and the only way to get it is to pay a fee.

 Bargain with schools for a better financial aid package for your child.

Some schools will tell you up front, usually in the acceptance or financial aid award letter, whether or not they'll negotiate for a better financial aid package. If you're unsure, anonymously call the financial aid office and ask.

You're on solid bargaining ground if your financial situation changes (there's a job loss, the size of your family increases, or you have unexpected medical bills), or if your child has offers from other schools. And let's face it—many schools desperately want to increase the number of minority students.

You can either talk to a school's financial aid counselor in person, or write a letter, then follow up with a telephone call. Always be polite. State the facts clearly. Try to provide supporting materials whenever possible (copies of financial aid award offers from other schools, for instance).

Consider special programs that can help defray college costs.

When most parents think about paying for college, the first things that come to mind are personal savings, followed by grants, loans, scholarships, and work-study. But there are many other ways to trim the cost of an education. Here's a sample:

Cooperative education. Cooperative education, which combines class studies with work experience, is one of the best-kept secrets around. More than 200,000 students at about 900 two-year and four-year schools participate in co-op programs every year.

At some schools, students work full-time for a semester, then go to school full-time for a semester. Others have parallel programs where students work part-time and go to school part-time. A grade point average of at least 2.0 and completion of a certain number of courses is often required to participate.

One drawback is that the money a student earns is factored into the financial aid equation, which can lower the financial aid package. But the costs of participating in a cooperative education program, such as travel and living expenses, are also considered. That can push the cost of attendance higher, increasing a student's financial need.

Even if some financial aid is lost, the benefits of working may outweigh the disadvantages. Students can gain valuable work experience and contacts in their chosen field. And some students can earn up to $14,000 a year, which can trim the amount of loans they need.

ACCIÓN For a free copy of *A College Guide to Cooperative Education,* write to the National Commission for Cooperative Education at 360 Huntington Ave., Boston, MA 02115, or check the Web site at www.co-op.edu/. The commission also publishes a more comprehensive book called *The Directory of College Cooperative Education Programs,* which can be found in most libraries. The Cooperative Education Association also offers a free listing of schools that offer co-op programs. To obtain a copy, write to CEA, 8640 Guilford Rd., Suite 215, Columbia, MD 21046, or check the Web site at www.ceainc.org/.

Military service. The federal government offers several Reserve Officer's Training Corps (ROTC) scholarships to students who are willing to serve in the Air Force, Army, Navy, or Marines after they graduate from college. The National Guard also offers financial aid in many states.

Financial aid is available to veterans of the U.S. armed forces as well. The Montgomery GI-Bill, for example, provides up to $427.87 a month for thirty-six months, with inflation adjustments, to qualified veterans. And some states provide free or reduced tuition at state schools to veterans, or children of veterans who were disabled or killed while in service.

ACCIÓN For more information, call the Air Force ROTC at 334-953-2019; the Army ROTC at 800-USA-ROTC; the Marines ROTC at 708-784-9448, ext. 1356; and the Navy ROTC at 800-327-NAVY. For a copy of *Need a Lift?,* the American Legion's financial aid guide for veterans and their families, send $3 to P.O. Box 1050, Indianapolis, IN 46206.

Pre-paid tuition plans. Many states (and a growing number of private colleges) have programs that allow you to pay today's prices for your child's future college education. But there are drawbacks. Your child may not want to go to a state school or any college at all. And essentially, your return on investment will be equal to the rate of college cost inflation. That's great if college costs rise rapidly. But if they don't, you can probably get a better return by investing elsewhere. (For a list of states offering pre-paid tuition plans, see the box at right.)

Installment plans. Installment plans allow you to pay your expected family contribution as you go, usually by the month, instead of having to come up with one big sum all at once. Colleges often contract with outside firms to collect the payments. An administrative fee may be levied once a year to set up the plan. But since no interest is charged, paying by installment could be cheaper than taking out a loan. For more information contact the financial aid offices of the colleges your child is applying to.

ACCIÓN To obtain a free list of schools that offer tuition reductions, freezes or special pricing programs call the

PRE-PAID TUITION PLANS

For an updated list call the College Savings Plan Network at 877-277-6496 or go to www.collegesavings.org).

ALABAMA	800-252-7228
ALASKA	800-478-0003
(*in-state ONLY)	
COLORADO	800-478-5651
FLORIDA	800-552-4723
ILLINOIS	877-877-3724
MARYLAND	888-463-4723
MASSACHUSETTS	800-449-6332
MICHIGAN	800-638-4543
MISSISSIPPI	800-987-4450
NEVADA	888-477-2667
OHIO	800-233-6734
PENNSYLVANIA	800-440-4000
SOUTH CAROLINA	888-772-4723
TENNESSEE	888-486-2378
TEXAS	800-445-4723
VIRGINIA	888-567-0540
WASHINGTON	877-438-8848
WEST VIRGINIA	800-307-4701
WYOMING	307-766-5766

* Program suspended, but honoring contracts

American Council on Education (ACE) at 202-939-9365, or check the Web site at www.acenet.edu/.

 Consider other investment strategies to help pay for college.

College savings plans. Many states have savings plans that allow you to defer state taxes on the earnings until the money is withdrawn to pay for college expenses. Once the funds are withdrawn, they'll be taxed at the student's rate, which is usually lower than the parent's rate.

These savings plans are essentially mutual funds, with each state decid-

COLLEGE SAVINGS PLANS

For an updated list, call the College Savings Plan Network at 877-277-6496 or go to www.collegesavings.org).

Arizona	602-229-2592
Connecticut	888-799-2438
Delaware	800-292-7935
Indiana	888-814-6800
Iowa	888-446-6696
Kentucky	800-338-0318
Louisiana	800-259-5626,ext. 0523
Montana	800-888-2723
New Hampshire	603-271-2621
New Jersey	877-465-2378
New York	877-697-2837
North Carolina	800-600-3453
Rhode Island	877-474-4378
Utah	800-418-2551
Wisconsin	888-338-3789

SAVINGS PLANS TO BE OPERATIONAL IN 1999

California	916-526-3027
District of Columbia	202-727-6055
Maine	207-623-3263
Minnesota	800-657-3866, ext. 3377
Missouri	573-751-2411
New Mexico	505-827-7383
Oklahoma	405-521-3191
Vermont	802-642-3177

SOURCE: COLLEGE SAVINGS PLAN NETWORK OF THE NATIONAL ASSOCIATION OF STATE TREASURERS

ing for itself how to invest the funds. The minimum and maximum amounts that can be invested in these savings plans every year varies from state to state. (See the box above for a list of states with college savings plans.)

Education bonds. Fourteen states can issue education savings bonds, also known as college savings bonds or baccaulareate bonds. However, only Illinois, Massachusetts, Michigan, and New Hampshire plan to issue any in the next three years, according to the College Savings Plan Network. These are zero-coupon municipal bonds, which like Series EE bonds are sold at a discount at a price much lower than their value at maturity.

Although they're marketed as college savings bonds, they can be used for any purpose. They're sold in denominations of $1,000, are exempt from state and local taxes, and can be purchased through any retail broker. In some states, education bonds are not factored into the financial aid equation.

Series EE savings bonds. Series EE bonds can be purchased in banks, savings and loans, and from many employers through an automatic payroll savings plan. The amount printed on a Series EE bond is its denomination, or face amount. Series EE bonds are sold at half of their face amount. For example, a $100 Series EE bond will cost you $50. Series EE bonds can be bought in denominations of $50, $75, $100, $200, $500, $1,000, $5,000, and $10,000. The amount of Series EE bonds that you can buy is limited to $30,000 per person per calendar year, and the Series EE bonds stop paying interest after thirty years.

The interest earned on Series EE bonds is always based on your initial investment (half of the face amount), and accumulates at 90 percent of the average yield on 5-year Treasury securities for the previous six months. Interest is adjusted twice a year, added to the Series EE bonds monthly, and compounded semi-annually. So when you redeem Series EE bonds, you get back your original investment (half of the face amount), plus interest, as long as you've held it for at least five years.

You can cash the Series EE bonds anytime after six months, but you'll have to pay a penalty equal to three months worth of interest if you redeem them in less than five years. For example, if you pay $2,500 for a bond with a face amount of $5,000, and cash it in nine months, you'll forfeit three months' worth of interest earned on your original $2,500 investment.

You can also choose to hold your Series EE bonds until the value reaches the full-face amount. How long that takes depends on interest rates. However, the U.S. Department of Treasury will make a one-time adjustment after seventeen years to bring your Series EE bonds to their full face amount.

Interest earned on Series EE bonds are exempt from state and local income taxes, and you can defer Federal income tax until you redeem the bonds or they stop earning interest after thirty years.

If Series EE bonds are used to pay for college education expenses, all of the interest can be excluded if income is $50,850 or less for single filers, and $76,250 or less for joint filers. Interest can be partially excluded if income is between $50,850 and $65,850 for single filers, and between $76,250 and $106,250 for joint filers.

Series EE bonds are solid conservative investments. They're a good place to park your money if your child has only a few years left until it's time to start college. But remember, even with the tax breaks, you're better off investing more aggressively if you've got more than five years before college.

With inflation-indexed savings bonds, payments are adjusted semi-annually to reflect the ongoing inflation rate. Interest is compounded twice a year. They can be purchased in increments of as little as $50, but no more than $30,000 of the savings bonds can be purchased in any calendar year.

Federal taxes can be deferred until the savings bonds are cashed in or they mature. But as with Series EE savings bonds, some or all of the taxes can be avoided if you use the inflation-indexed savings bonds to pay for your children's college educations. To qualify, your income must not exceed $67,250 for single parents, and $108,350 for married couples filing jointly.

Like Series EE bonds, inflation-indexed savings bonds can be redeemed anytime after six months, but you'll have to pay a penalty equal to three-month's worth of interest if you redeem them in less than five years. The interest earned on inflation-indexed savings bonds is divided into two parts. The first is a permanent 3.4 percent fixed rate that will be paid over the life of the bond. The second is a payment based on the rate of inflation. The payment adjustment will be revised every six months according to movements in the Consumer Price Index.

CollegeSure CDs. This is a certificate of deposit with a variable interest rate that's guaranteed to keep pace with the rising cost of college. The minimum deposit is $1,000, and the Federal Deposit Insurance Corp. (FDIC) insures amounts for up to $100,000.

The CD works well if tuition costs rise dramatically. But if tuition inflation is low, you might get a better interest rate with another type of CD. In addition, interest earned on the CollegeSure CD is taxable.

ACCIÓN For more information about CollegeSure CDs, call 800-888-2723. A brochure, *A Great Way to Save—U.S. Savings Bonds Investor Information,* is available in English and Spanish by writing to Savings Bonds Operations Office, Bureau of Public Debt, U.S. Department of the Treasury, Parkersburg, WV 26106-1328. More information in English and Spanish is also available from the Bureau of Public Debt's Web site at www.savingsbonds.gov/.

UTMA and UGMA accounts. The Uniform Transfer to Minors Act (UTMA) and the Uniform Gift to Minors Act (UGMA) allows you to set up custodial accounts to keep funds in your child's name. (The one you use depends on where you live.)

Money in the account won't be taxed as long as less than $650 is generated in interest or dividend income per year. If a child is aged 13 or younger, interest or dividend income that's more than $650 per year, but less than $1,300, will be taxed at the child's tax rate (15 percent federal). Anything above $1,300 will be taxed at the parents' tax rate (up to 39.6 percent). This is called the "kiddie tax." All the money in the account will be taxed at the child's rate once a child turns 14.

Since the account is in the child's name, the entire pot becomes the child's at the "age of majority," which is either eighteen or twenty-one depending on where you live. And that's one of the biggest potential drawbacks. Your child may not want to go to college at all. Or worse, he or she may blow the money on a sports car or Caribbean cruise.

Another problem is that these accounts could shrink the amount of financial aid your child gets. Under the current formula, after subtracting certain allowances, parents are expected to contribute up to 5.6 percent of their savings, and children are expected to contribute 35 percent of their savings over $2,200, before they can qualify for financial aid.

So if you have $20,000 in savings held in your name, you may be expected to pay up to 5.6 percent of that amount, or $1,120, toward college expenses. But if your child has $20,000 in an UTMA or UGMA account, he or she will definitely be expected to pay 35 percent over $2,200, or $6,230, toward college expenses.

 Don't use UTMA or UGMA accounts if you want financial aid.

If you've already got an UTMA or UGMA account, and want to liquidate it because you're worried about the financial aid ramifications, you can do it, but the IRS can disallow the gift, charge you with back taxes and interest, and tax the money at the parents' tax rate.

Giftrusts/Giftshares. Giftrusts and Giftshares are trusts that invest in mutual funds. Like UTMAs and UGMAs, they're designed to let you give money to a child by establishing an irrevocable trust, which can't be canceled or changed in any way by you or the child before its specified termination date.

But unlike UTMAs and UGMAs, where children get the money at the age of majority (either eighteen or twenty-one) no matter what, giftrusts and giftshares give you more flexibility in determining when your child will get access to the funds.

There are currently two such trusts on the market, the Royce Giftshares Fund and American Century's Twentieth Century Giftrust Fund. Royce offers a withdrawal and accumulation option. Twentieth Century only has an accumulation option.

With the accumulation option, the trust is set up for a child for a minimum of ten years, or until the child's age of majority, whichever is later. With the withdrawal option, the funds can be withdrawn before the trust terminates, but only to pay for college expenses.

One benefit of giftrusts and giftshares is that they force you to keep the money invested in the market via a mutual fund for an extended period of time. However, this can also be a drawback if the fund performs badly, or if the fund manager leaves.

And as with UTMA and UGMA accounts, the money your child has in the trust will be considered an asset for financial aid purposes. So don't set up a giftrust or giftshare if you plan to apply for financial aid. Instead, invest your money in traditional mutual funds, and keep them in your name.

ACCIÓN For more information about the Royce Giftshares Fund, call 800-221-4268. For more information about Twentieth Century Giftrust Fund, call 800-345-2021.

Home equity loans and lines of credit. You can obtain a home equity loan or home equity line of credit on the difference between the fair market value of your home and the amount still owed on the mortgage.

With a loan you pay a fixed or variable interest rate on the entire amount, and repay the loan within a specified period of time. For example, if you borrow $80,000, you'll pay interest on the entire amount even though you only use $20,000 to pay for the first year of college.

With a line of credit, you withdraw only what you need, and you pay interest only when you withdraw the money. For this reason, a line of credit may be less expensive.

The interest you pay on either a equity home loan or home equity line of credit is tax deductible if you itemize. However, your home will be used as collateral so you may lose it and ruin your credit record if you have trouble paying back the amount you borrow.

Cash value life insurance loans. With a cash value policy, a portion of your premium goes to pay for the insurance portion of the plan, and the rest goes to an investment portion. The cash value in the investment portion builds tax-deferred, and can be used as collateral for a loan.

As we mentioned in Chapter 3, cash value life insurance policies should ideally be purchased by people who can afford the higher premiums, have maxed out of other retirement savings plans, such as IRAs and 401(k)s, or expect to have to pay large estate taxes.

But if you've got a cash value policy, you can borrow up to 90 percent of its value from the insurance company. You can't shop around for an interest rate on a cash value loan. You must pay the rate that's stated in your policy. Generally, the interest you pay on this type of loan is not tax deductible.

Traditional IRAs. With traditional IRAs, individuals can deposit up to $2,000 of their annual earnings every year ($4,000 a year for married couples with one nonworking spouse). The tax-deductibility of the contributions depends on income and the existence of other retirement coverage, such as pensions or 401(k)s.

Parents can withdraw money from their traditional IRAs to pay for college expenses without paying the usual 10 percent penalty for withdrawals made before age 59$\frac{1}{2}$. However, these withdrawals are considered income, which means they'll be taxed and will reduce financial aid eligibility.

Education IRAs. Education IRAs are offered through banks and mutual fund companies. In addition to contributions to traditional IRAs, Education IRAs allow you to invest up to $500 a year in the name of a child under the age of 18 to pay for tuition fees, books, and supplies (but not room and board).

The money that's withdrawn to pay for college is exempt from federal taxes if a single filer earns $95,000 a year or less, and if joint filers earn $150,000 a year or less. The money is partially exempt if a single filer earns between $95,000 and $110,000, and if joint filers earn between $150,000 and $160,000.

Contributions aren't tax deductible. If a child doesn't use the money in the account, it can be rolled over into another child's account. If there's any money left in the account after the child turns thirty, it is subject to taxes and a 10 percent withdrawal penalty.

Education IRAs have three big drawbacks. First, they prohibit you from setting up a pre-paid tuition plan (which we describe earlier in this chapter). Second, any withdrawal from an education IRA will prevent you from claiming a Hope Credit or Lifetime Earning credit (described later in this chapter) for the same year. Third, the money will be considered among a student's assets, not the parents' assets, when determining financial aid.

A better option may be a Roth IRA. With a Roth IRA, each parent can contribute $2,000 every year. The earnings can be left in the account for retirement, when they can be withdrawn tax-free. But money can also be withdrawn at any time without penalty, tax, or restrictions, as long as you adhere to specific rules. (For more on Roth IRAs go to Chapter 7.)

401(k) loans. With a 401(k) plan, you can funnel pre-tax income from your paycheck into a variety of investment vehicles (stocks, mutual funds, and money market accounts). This lowers your annual tax bill. And you don't pay any taxes on your contributions or earnings until you withdraw the money.

You can usually borrow up to 50 percent of the balance in your 401(k) account or $50,000, whichever is less, to pay for medical expenses, a house down payment, or college tuition. As with a cash value loan, you can't shop around for a good interest rate. You have to use the rate that's in your employer's written policy.

You have five years to pay back the loan on your 401(k). If you don't, the Internal Revenue Service (IRS) will consider it a withdrawal, tax the amount as income, and levy a 10 percent penalty. And if you quit or lose your job before you pay back the loan, it becomes due immediately.

Borrowing from your 401(k) should be used as a last resort. After all, why pay anything to use money that technically belongs to you? Even though you're paying yourself back with interest, you're really just breaking even at best because the money probably would have earned a higher rate of return if you had left it invested.

Another thing to consider is the fact that you'll be paying taxes twice on the money you borrow. That's because the money you use to repay the loan is made with after-tax dollars. When you withdraw the money in retirement, the money will be taxed again.

 Consider other ways to cut the cost of higher education.

Education costs can be reduced if your child takes Advanced Placement (AP) classes while still in high school. Many colleges accept a score of 3.0 or better on an AP Achievement Test for first-year course credit.

Classes taken at a community college during high school can also be transferred to a college. Another option is to complete two years at a community college, then transfer to a four-year college.

Some colleges offer combination undergraduate and graduate degrees that could trim the total time needed to complete school. Your child may also be able to commute to a nearby school and save on room and board.

Encourage your child to apply to schools where he or she will stand out, schools with large endowments, which indicate they have a lot of aid to offer, and schools that promise to match any private scholarship money. Any college guide such as *Barron's* or *Peterson's* should provide this information.

An employer may be willing to pay for college classes. Tuition assistance isn't considered taxable income if it's used for undergraduate courses, but it's taxable if it's used for graduate courses.

The Hope Scholarship is a tax credit that amounts to $1,500 for the first two years of college. Lifetime Learning can be used for your child's subsequent years in college. It can be worth up to $1,000 a year through 2002, and $2,000 a year thereafter. You can't claim either credit in a year when you withdraw money from an Education IRA. And the impact the credits will have on financial aid eligibility are unclear.

With both programs you're eligible for the entire credit if you earn

$40,000 or less as a single filer, or $80,000 as a joint filer. You can take a partial credit if you earn between $40,000 and $50,000 as a single filer, and between $80,000 and $100,000 as a joint filer. For more information, contact an accountant or the Internal Revenue Service. (See Chapter 9.)

Under current law, individuals can give up to $10,000 a year tax-free to any individual (a married couple can give $20,000). But there's no limit to the tax-exempt amount if the money is paid directly to a school to pay for tuition. This is one great way for affluent grandparents to reduce the size of their estates, thereby lowering their estate tax bill.

 Investigate trade schools.

Not everyone is destined to go to a four-year college. Your child can do very well by attending a two-year community college or a trade school that prepares workers for jobs in industries such as computer technology, health care, cosmetology, auto repair, and massage therapy. *Lo más importante es la preparación para trabajar.*

While there are many excellent trade schools that provide worthwhile training, most states are also peppered with diploma mills. These fly-by-night schools hand out virtually worthless degrees to anyone who can afford to pay the tuition.

When trying to decide on a program, first be sure you understand the difference between junior colleges, four-year universities and graduate programs that bestow academic degrees, and trade schools that award occupational certificates.

You also have to decide between a training program offered by a junior college and one offered by a trade school. The advantage of a community college is that it's inexpensive. It can costs hundreds of dollars a year, compared to thousands of dollars a year, for a trade school.

Another thing to consider is the reputation of the programs. The best way to size up a program is to visit a school and talk to students and teachers. This will also give you a chance to check out the facilities. Get a list of alumni and employers that hire graduates of the school as well.

You may also want to find out what percentage of a school's graduates have defaulted on their student loans. These figures are available from the school and the U.S. Department of Education. A low default rate may indicate that graduates are getting decent-paying jobs.

Most schools will claim to be accredited by one organization or another. Determining the value of this accreditation can be pretty difficult because there are dozens of private organizations that evaluate programs. And some very good schools aren't accredited at all.

You're probably pretty safe if you check a school's accreditation with the U.S. Department of Education (two- and four-year colleges); the Distance Education and Training Council (training offered via the Internet or by correspondence); the Accrediting Commission of Career Schools/Colleges of Technology (occupational, trade, and technical education); and the appropriate regional accrediting agency. (For a list of accreditation agencies, see the box on page 180.)

Anyone who's considering a trade school or any type of nontraditional education should read the following three books written by Dr. John Bear and Mariah Bear, and published by Ten Speed Press in Berkeley, California: *Bears' Guide to Finding Money for College; Bears' Guide to Earning College Degrees Nontraditionally;* and *College Degrees by Mail and Modem.*

There's also a counseling-by-mail service called Degree Consulting Services that specializes in nontraditional education. Degree Consulting will research programs, outline your options, make specific recommendations, and answer your questions within 14 days. You also get a year of follow-up advice and updates. The total cost is $75.

ACCIÓN To reach Degree Consulting Services, call 707-539-6466; send e-mail to degrees@sonic.net, or write to P.O. Box 3533, Santa Rosa, CA 95402.

 **Pay your student loans.**

The average four-year college graduate ends up $12,343 in debt, according to 1997 figures from the U.S. Department of Education. Graduate students can easily end up owing three times that amount or more by the time they finish school.

If you start having trouble repaying your student loans, don't panic. There

KEY ACCREDITING AGENCIES

NATIONAL

Accrediting Commission of Career Schools/Colleges of Technology (occupational, trade and technical education): 202-336-6850

Distance Education and Training Council (training offered via the Internet or by correspondence): 202-234-5100

U.S. Department of Education (two- and four-year colleges): 202-708-7417

REGIONAL

Middle States Association of Colleges and Schools (Delaware, District of Columbia, Maryland, New Jersey, New York, Pennsylvania, Puerto Rico): 215-662-5606

New England Association of Colleges and Schools (Connecticut, Maine, Massachusetts, New Hampshire, Rhode Island, Vermont): 617-271-0022

North Central Association of Colleges and Schools (Arizona, Arkansas, Colorado, Illinois, Indiana, Iowa, Kansas, Michigan, Minnesota, Missouri, Nebraska, New Mexico, North Dakota, Ohio, Oklahoma, South Dakota, West Virginia, Wisconsin, Wyoming): 800-621-7440

Northwest Association of Colleges and Schools (Alaska, Idaho, Montana, Nevada, Oregon, Utah, Washington): 425-827-2005

Southern Association of Colleges and Schools (Alabama, Florida, Georgia, Kentucky, Louisiana, Mississippi, North Carolina, South Carolina, Tennessee, Texas, Virginia): 800-248-7701

Western Association of Colleges and Schools (California, Hawaii): 510-632-5000.

are many programs available that can help you defer payments for a while, or reduce the size of your payments by consolidating your loans or stretching out the terms of your loans. You may even be able to erase some of the loans.

Defaulting on a loan can have serious consequences. Your wages may be garnished or your tax refunds confiscated. In addition, your credit rating could be ruined (which will make it harder to get credit cards, car loans, or home loans), and you won't be able to get any more student loans.

Deferral. A deferral *(aplazamiento)* is probably your best option because it will delay student loan repayment for a specified period, usually between six months and three years. But you must meet certain criteria such as economic hardship, temporary disability, unemployment, or a return to school.

You may also be eligible for a deferment if you're a working parent with small children, belong to a uniformed U.S. government service, teach needy populations, perform community service, or work in a health care profession.

For certain loans, the government will pay your interest during deferment, which means your balance remains the same. But with others, the interest will be added to the principal if you can't pay it during the deferral. The type of deferral you get depends on the kind of loans you have and when you got them.

Forbearance. Forbearance *(tolerancia)* is the next best thing after deferment because the borrower has the option to reduce or stop student loan payments for a specific period of time. It's less attractive than a deferment because interest on the loans will always accrue and be added to the principal.

Forbearance is granted at the discretion of the lender, and doesn't depend on the type of loans you have or when you got them. It can last from six months to three years.

Consolidation. If your deferment or forbearance runs out, or you couldn't get either one, you may be able to lower your total monthly student loan payments with a loan consolidation, which combines all of your loans into a single loan with a lower interest rate. Most government loans can be consolidated, although some private loans can only be consolidated through third-party lenders.

Extended repayment *(reembolso)* options let you lower your monthly payment options by stretching out the time over which your loan is due— usually between twelve and thirty years. Graduated repayment plans have payments that start out low and rise every few years. "Income contingent" or "income sensitive" plans base your monthly loan payments on your annual income, the size of your household, and the amount of the loan.

Default. Technically, you're in default *(incumplimiento de pago)* if your loan payments are at least 180 days past due. But you can "rehabilitate" defaulted loans by making twelve consecutive monthly payments. At that time your

STUDENT LOAN CONSOLIDATION OR REPAYMENT OPTIONS

Chela Financial: 800-AT-CHELA.

Citibank: 800-967-2400.

Federal Direct Loan Program Servicing Center: 800-848-0979.

Sallie Mae: For deferment or forbearance for loans call 888-272-5543. For student loan repayment options call 800-643-0040.

U.S. Department of Education: If you've defaulted on a student loan or need information about student loan repayment options, call 800-4FED-AID.

USA Group: 800-382-4506.

negative credit reports will be deleted, and you'll be given a nine-year repayment schedule. (See the box above for a list of where to go for help with student loans.)

Loan forgiveness. About 300 nonprofit organizations and government agencies will reward graduates for service with loan forgiveness *(perdón de préstamo)*, through which all or part of student loans are forgiven.

There are many well-known programs. Volunteers who work with Americorp meet community needs ranging from housing renovation to child immunization. Members of Volunteers in Service to America (VISTA), a program within Americorp, help nonprofit organizations expand their services in low-income communities. Volunteers for the Peace Corps, a separate program, work in agriculture, education, forestry, health, engineering, skilled trades, business, urban planning, and environmental science in more than ninety countries.

ACCIÓN To contact Americorp, call 800-942-2677. To contact the Peace Corp, call 800-424-8580. For more information about loan forgiveness programs, call the National College Scholarship Foundation at 301-548-9423, or write to 16728 Frontenak Terrace, Rockville, MD 20855.

- ❏ Look for financial aid if you want to send your child to private or parochial school for grades K through 12.
- ❏ Save and invest for your children's college education if you can. Use aggressive investments when they're young, and more conservative investments as they get to high school.
- ❏ Apply for government financial aid—even if you've got a high income—by completing the FAFSA and any other forms a school may require.
- ❏ Consider shifting or reducing some of your assets to improve your child's financial aid eligibility.
- ❏ Find and apply for private scholarships, which can be tracked down in the library or on the Web.
- ❏ Be aware of deadlines to submit financial aid and private scholarship applications—and meet them.
- ❏ Bargain with schools to get a better financial aid package for your child.
- ❏ Consider special programs that can help reduce education expenses, such as cooperative education, and loan forgiveness programs.
- ❏ If you plan to attend a trade school, first check a school's credentials and talk to students, instructors, and employers.
- ❏ Pay your student loans, and learn what your options are if you start to struggle.

ADDITIONAL RESOURCES

Recommended Books

College Financial Aid for Dummies, by Dr. Herm Davis and Joyce Lain Kennedy (Foster City, California: IDG Books Worldwide, 1997).

Take Control of Your Student Loans, by Robin Leonard and Shae Irving (Berkeley: Nolo Press, 1997).

The Hispanic Scholarship Directory: Over 500 Ways to Finance Your Education, ed. Andres Tobar (Carlsbad, California: WPR Publishing, 1997).

The Minority and Women's Complete Scholarship Book, by Student Services L.L.C. (Naperville, Illinois: SourceBooks, 1998).

The Scholarship Book 1998/1999: The Complete Guide to Private-Sector Scholarships, Grants, and Loans for Undergraduates, by Daniel Cassidy (Englewood Hills, New Jersey: Prentice-Hall, 1998).

CHAPTER 7

Retirement

"ONE WHO DOES NOT LOOK AHEAD, REMAINS BEHIND" —MEXICO

L ATINOS DO A WONDERFUL JOB OF TAKING CARE OF *FAMILIA*—CHILDREN, parents, brothers, sisters, nieces, nephews, extended family, and close friends. We can stretch a *peso* pretty far. But we often do so at the expense of our own future needs, especially retirement. Latinos have such a strong work ethic that retirement may seem selfish, or lazy, or something someone does only when sick or near death.

When we do think about *el retiro*, many Latinos assume that Social Security will cover most, if not all, expenses. And if there happens to be any shortfall, we figure that our children will take care of us. After all, that's what Latino families have done for generations.

The figures prove it. About 32 percent of all Latinos in the workplace participate in pension plans, compared to 51 percent of non-Latino whites, according to the most recent figures available from the U.S. Department of Labor. Just 32 percent of Latinos aged fifty-five or older receive a pension, compared to 52 percent of non-Latino whites, says the U.S. Census Bureau. And about 12 percent of Latinos set money aside in 401(k)s, compared to 28 percent of all white workers, says Gerontology Professor Yung-Ping Chen of the University of Massachusetts, Boston.

"The 1998 Retirement Confidence Survey" by the American Savings and Education Council and the Employee Benefit Research Institute found that 48 percent of Latinos aren't confident that they're doing a good job of preparing financially for retirement, compared to 26 percent of whites, 33 percent of African Americans, and 24 percent of Asian Americans. A whopping 62 percent of Latinos said they aren't currently saving any money for retirement.

An article by James Smith for the Rand Corporation, a public policy research group, that appeared in *The Journal of Human Resources* in 1995 found that there are also huge disparities between whites and Latinos when it comes to financial assets, home equity, and business holdings. The typical non-Latino white head of household between the ages of 51 and 61 has saved $300,000, for instance, while the typical Latino household has saved less than $500. Four of ten Latino heads of households have nothing.

We need to change our thinking about retirement. It can be a chance to start another career, travel, focus on hobbies, or *pasar más tiempo con nuestras familias y amigos.* We should have the option of working only if we want to, not because we have to.

On a practical level, retirement planning is important because there's no guarantee that Social Security, at least in its current form, will be around forever. Old-style pensions are also disappearing. And more workers are being forced to handle their own retirement savings through Individual Retirement Accounts or 401(k) plans.

Social Security is facing big potential changes. Eligibility may be pushed beyond age 67, and some privatization may permit people to invest a portion of their Social Security dollars. If that happens, knowing how to prepare for our own retirement will be more important than ever.

The Social Security trust is expected to run out of money in 2029 if there aren't any legislative changes. What does that mean? Right now, a huge number of younger Latinos are paying into a Social Security system that's providing benefits for a mostly non-Latino white, elderly population with higher incomes. When it comes time for Latinos to collect Social Security, there may not be much left.

Planning ahead gave Delia, a former San Francisco health care administrator, the resources to start her own consulting business, travel, and do charity work after she retired at age fifty-five. And when her mother had a stroke, Delia had the time to care for her. "I can do this because I'm not tied down with a job," she says.

Damian, a thirty-year-old Mexican-American law professor from Chicago, started contributing to an IRA at age twenty-three, then joined his company's 401(k) plan. His wants to retire at age fifty-five and write fiction. "I look at my dad. All he's getting is Social Security, which isn't enough. All of us kids have to give him money to help him get by," he says.

 Get a ballpark estimate of how much money you'll need in retirement.

Conventional wisdom has long maintained that you'll need up to 80 percent of your annual income to maintain the lifestyle in retirement that you have today. But you may need a lot less than 80 percent if you've managed to save some money, own a house, inherit some money, get help from your kids, or simply live a more moderate lifestyle. There's also a good chance your tax bracket will drop, and that you'll get some Social Security benefits.

You won't spend the same amount of money all through retirement, either. You may spend more in the early years traveling or visiting *los nietos*, less in the middle years when you start to slow down, and more in the later years if you have health problems. The advice from las Lauras: hope for the best, but prepare for the worst.

Calculate how much you'll need for retirement by tallying the money you'll likely get from Social Security, your employer's pension or profit-sharing plan, part-time jobs, and any money you've squirreled away in 401(k) accounts, Individual Retirement Accounts (*cuenta de retiro individual*), or IRAS, and other savings.

How much money you can expect from Social Security is based on your earnings record. To get an estimate, you'll need to contact the Social Security Administration and request a free Personal Earnings and Benefit Statement by calling 800-537-7005, or checking the Web site at www.ssa.gov/. You can request a similar statement from employers that will owe you a pension.

After you've gathered these estimates, you'll have to crunch some numbers to determine how much money you'll need during retirement. But don't let that scare you. There are lots of worksheets that can do it for you. (See the box on pages 190–91 for a retirement worksheet.)

If saving enough to provide 80 percent of your current annual income in retirement looks impossible, don't give up. Drop the figure to 60 percent, or even 40 percent, of your current annual income. The point is to establish a goal and do everything you possibly can to reach it.

ACCIÓN The American Savings and Education Council offers a retirement worksheet called "The Ballpark Estimate." To use it online, go to www.asec.org/. If you don't have access to the Net, you can obtain savings education brochures and worksheets, including the Ballpark Estimate, in English and Spanish by sending a self-addressed, stamped number 10 business-size envelope with $1.21 return postage to: ASEC Spanish & English Brochures, Suite 600, 2121 "K" Street NW, Washington, DC 20037-1896.

 Start saving even if it's just a small amount every month. And the earlier the better.

After you come up with a savings goal and determine how much you need to set aside every month to reach it, make a budget. Start by figuring out how much money you bring home, how much you spend, and what expenses you can cut and funnel into savings and investments. (*No se olvide* —more information on budgets is available in Chapter 1.)

A painless way to save is to set up an automatic payroll deposit plan (*plan de depósitos de nóminas*), which sends money straight out of your paycheck into a savings or investment account. And if you get a tax refund or bonus, use it to pay off high-interest credit card debt, pay down your mortgage, or stick it in a savings or investment account.

Most important, you should start participating in a defined contribution retirement plan (*plan de contribuciones definidas*) such as a 401(k) plan. As the name implies, these plans specify how much you can contribute. Depending on your income, many of the contributions are tax deductible, and most of the earnings grow tax-free until withdrawal.

Through the magic of tax-deferred compounding, saving just a few dollars every week can really grow. Remember, compounding is earning interest on the interest you've already earned, as well as on the original principal amount. The sooner you start taking advantage of compounding, the better.

For example, if you start making a $5 weekly contribution to a 401(k) plan when you're 25 years old, you'll end up with $75,639 at age 65, assuming an 8 percent average annual return. But if you wait until age 35, you'll have just $32,291. And if you wait until age 55, the amount plummets to just $3,964.

The main tax-deferred retirement plans to choose from are Individual Retirement Accounts (IRAs), 401(k)s, Simplified Employee Pensions (SEPs), a Savings Incentive Match Plan for Employees (SIMPLE), and qualified retirement plans, or Keoghs. Religious, charitable, educational, and other nonprofit groups use 403(b)s, while government institutions, local schools, and state university systems use 457 plans. Both are similar to 401(k)s.

ACCIÓN A brochure called *Top 10 Ways to Beat the Clock and Prepare for Retirement* is available in English and Spanish from the Department of Labor's Pension and Welfare Benefits Administration by calling 800-998-7542.

 Don't lose track of your defined-benefit pension plan if you have one.

A defined-benefit pension plan *(plan de pensión de beneficios definidos)* promises a specific amount of money for a specific amount of time when you retire. It's fully funded by your employer. How much money you get depends on your age, number of years of service, and salary. You're eligible for benefits after vesting *(adquisición)*, or working at the firm for a specific period of time.

Under current law, employees are usually partially vested after three years, and fully vested between five and seven years. However, government employees and people who work for religious groups must work for a company for ten years before getting vested. Many of these plans are partially insured by the Pension Benefit Guarantee Corporation, a federal agency.

Defined-benefit pension plans aren't as common now as they were a few years ago. But if you've got one, it's important to make sure your employer (or former employer if you've changed jobs) has your current address and telephone number in case you need to be notified about changes to the plan, or you need an earnings and benefits statement. *No se pierdan o perderán pesos.*

A RETIREMENT CALCULATOR

Below we offer you an example of a good basic retirement calculator, adapted from one designed by the American Savings Education Council. It is not meant to tell you exactly how much to save, but it will give you a helpful estimate.

If you have Internet access, you can find the ASEC's on-line calculator at www.asec.org/ under the heading "Ballpark Estimate."

1. **How much annual income will you want when you retire?** $_____
Figure 70 percent of your current annual income just to maintain your current standard of living. (Some financial planners, looking in detail at your particular situation, might propose a higher or lower percentage, but use 70 percent for now.)

2. **Subtract the income you expect to receive annually from:**
Social Securities Benefits .... $_____
If you make under $25,000, enter $8,000; between $25,000 and $40,000, enter $12000; over $40,000, enter $14,500
Traditional Employer Pension .... $_____
a plan that pays a set dollar amount for life, where the dollar amount depends on salary and years of service (in today's dollars)
Part-time Income .... $_____
Other .... $_____

SUBTOTAL .... $_____

3. **This is how much you need to make up for each retirement year:** $_____

Now you want a ballpark estimate of how much money you'll need to have saved by the day you retire. Assumptions: your investments earn a constant real rate of return of 3 percent after inflation; you live to age 87; and you'll begin to receive some income from Social Security at age 65.

4. To determine the amount you'll need to save, multiply the amount you need to make up (from line # 3, above) by the factor below. $_____

Age you expect to retire	Your factor is
55	21.0
60	18.9
65	16.4
70	13.6

5. If you expect to retire before age 65, multiply your Social Security
benefit (from line #2) by the factor below. $_____

Age you expect to retire	Your factor is
55	8.8
60	4.7

6. Multiply your savings to date by the factor below (include
money accumulated in all your 401(k) plans, IRAs, and
similar retirement plans): $_____

If you want to retire in	Your factor is
10 years	1.3
15 years	1.6
20 years	1.8
25 years	2.1
30 years	2.4
35 years	2.8
40 years	3.3

**7. Total additional savings needed at retirement (add lines #4
and 5, then subtract line 6 from that sum:):** $_____
Don't panic. To see how much to save each year in order to reach
your goal amount, factor in compounding over the years you have
until retirement. That's where your money not only earns interest,
your interest starts earning interest as well, creating a snowball effect.

**8. To determine the annual amount you'll need to save, multiply
the total amount from line #7 by the factor below:** $_____

If you want to retire in	Your factor is
10 years	.085
15 years	.052
20 years	.036
25 years	.027
30 years	.020
35 years	.016
40 years	.013

SEE? It's not impossible or even particularly painful. It just takes planning. And
the sooner you start, the better off you'll be.

THIS WORKSHEET SIMPLIFIES SEVERAL RETIREMENT PLANNING ISSUES SUCH AS PROJECTED SOCIAL SECURITY BENEFITS AND EARNINGS
ASSUMPTIONS ON SAVINGS. IT ALSO REFLECTS TODAY'S DOLLARS; THEREFORE YOU WILL NEED TO RE-CALCULATE YOUR RETIREMENT NEEDS
ANNUALLY AND AS YOUR SALARY AND CIRCUMSTANCES CHANGE. YOU MAY WANT TO CONSIDER DOING FURTHER ANALYSIS, EITHER YOURSELF
USING A MORE DETAILED WORKSHEET OR COMPUTER SOFTWARE, OR WITH THE ASSISTANCE OF A FINANCIAL PROFESSIONAL.

SOURCE: THE AMERICAN SAVINGS AND EDUCATION COUNCIL

When it's time to collect your pension, you can take it in one lump sum (*suma global*), or in one of three types of annuities (*anualidades*), which make monthly payments for a specific period of time.

A single-life annuity is the most generous, but stops payment when you die. A joint-option annuity pays less, but keeps paying your spouse or beneficiaries after you die and until they die. A term-certain annuity guarantees to pay you for a limited period, after which you're on your own. If you die during that period, your survivors will get payment.

With a lump sum distribution, you get one big check up front. The benefit of a lump sum over an annuity is that you can invest the money yourself and perhaps outpace inflation. If you annuitize, the money you get over time isn't adjusted for inflation, which means it buys less.

If you take a lump sum, think about rolling (*transferencia*) the money over into an IRA. The money will continue to grow tax-free. You can control how to invest it, and when to make withdrawals. And money in an IRA gets some protection from creditors should you ever face bankruptcy.

If you decide to pocket the entire amount, it may push you into a higher tax bracket. But you can also use income averaging (*promedio de ingresos*) to calculate your taxes. To be eligible for five-year averaging, you must have been born before July 1, 1940 (five-year averaging will be eliminated after 1999). To be eligible for ten-year averaging, you must have been born before January 1, 1936.

ACCIÓN Two free brochures, *What You Should Know About Your Pension Rights,* and *Women and Pensions: What Women Need to Know and Do,* are available in English and Spanish by calling the Pension and Welfare Benefits Administration at 800-998-7542.

 Understand what your government benefits are and how to get them.

The Social Security System provides income to qualified retirees, but it also pays for Medicare, Medicaid, disability insurance, and Supplemental Security Income.

Medicare, the nation's largest health insurance program, provides bene-

fits to people aged 65 or older, the disabled, and people with permanent kidney failure. Medicaid provides medical assistance for the financially needy,
and is funded jointly by federal and state governments. Workers pay for disability insurance with their Social Security taxes. Eligibility is based on
work history, and the benefits are determined by earnings. Supplemental
Security Income is financed through general tax revenues. Benefits are paid
to people with low income and limited resources. (For more information see
Chapter 3.)

The primary function of Social Security is to provide old-age benefits to
retirees. However, it's not intended to meet 100 percent of your needs. At
best, you can view it as a modest foundation on which to build a retirement
plan with other savings and pensions.

For Social Security purposes, the usual retirement age is now 65. This is
called the "full retirement age." The benefit that's payable is known as the
"full retirement benefit." Because of longer life expectancies, however, the
full retirement age will gradually rise until it reaches age 67. (For a chart
showing ages and corresponding benefits, see page 194.)

You can start your Social Security benefits as early as age 62, but the
amount of money you receive will be less than the full retirement benefit.
Your benefits will be permanently reduced based on the number of months
you'll receive checks before you reach full retirement age. Check with the
SSA to find out how much they'll be reduced.

¿Le gusta trabajar? You can continue to work and get Social Security benefits, but how much you receive depends on your age and income. If you're
under age 65, you can earn up to $8,640 a year without affecting your bene-
fits. But your benefits will be reduced $1 for every $2 you earn above that
limit.

If you're between 65 and 69 years of age, you can earn up to $13,500 a
year with no effect on your benefits. But your benefits will be reduced $1 for
every $3 you earn above that limit. Once you hit age 70, you can earn any
amount and not affect your Social Security benefits.

When applying for Social Security benefits, you and your spouse will
need your Social Security numbers, original or certified copies of your birth
certificates or other proof of age and identification, your marriage certificate
or divorce documents, birth certificates or adoption orders if you're seeking
benefits for any children, and copies of your most recent tax return.

AGE TO RECEIVE FULL SOCIAL SECURITY BENEFITS	
IF THIS IS YOUR BIRTH YEAR . . .	THIS IS THE AGE YOU MUST BE TO GET FULL SOCIAL SECURITY BENEFITS.
Up to 1937	65 years
1938	65 years, two months
1939	65 years, four months
1940	65 years, six months
1941	65 years, eight months
1942	65 years, ten months
1943–54	66 years
1955	66 years, two months
1956	66 years, four months
1957	66 years, six months
1958	66 years, eight months
1959	66 years, ten months
1960 and on	67 years

SOURCE: SOCIAL SECURITY ADMINISTRATION.

ACCIÓN Free brochures are available in English and Spanish: *Social Security Retirement Benefits, Social Security: The Basic Facts,* and *Understanding the Benefits,* by calling SSA at 800-772-1213, or checking the Web site at www.ssa.gov/.

Participate in your company's 401(k) plan, and contribute the maximum amount.

If your employer offers a 401(k) plan, you should participate *todo lo que pueda y lo más pronto que pueda.* Contributions to 401(k)s reduce your taxable income on a dollar for dollar basis. The money in your 401(K) grows tax-free, although you pay taxes upon withdrawal. Matching contributions by some employers range from ten cents to one dollar for every dollar you contribute, up to between 3 percent and 6 percent of your total annual income.

You may have to wait as long as a year before you can begin participating in your company's 401(k) plan. You may have to be at least twenty-one years old. Some companies may let you start right away, but they'll make you wait a certain period of time before matching your contribution. Others let you join only on a specific date. Check with the plan administrator in your benefits department for details.

The most you can contribute to a 401(k) is $10,000 a year. But most employers limit your contribution to a certain percentage of your gross pay. The contributions will be deducted from your paycheck every pay period, and the amount will be noted on your paycheck.

Most 401(k) plans offer a variety of investment options including cash (money market funds and Treasury Bills), stocks (domestic and international, small-cap and large-cap), bonds (with varying maturities), and mutual funds. How you divide your assets depends on your risk tolerance and how soon you'll need the money. (For more information see Chapter 4.)

If you work at a religious, charitable, education, or other nonprofit group, you may be offered a 403(b), which is similar to a 401(k). 403(b) plans are also referred to as Tax-Deferred Annuities (anualidad de impuestos diferidos), or TDAs. If you work at a government institution, local school, or state university system, you may be offered a 457 plan.

The 403(b)s are trickier than 401(k)s. One type of 403(b) plan lets you set aside tax-deferred income in an annuity contract offered by an insurance company (more on annuities later in this chapter). The other, called a 403(b)7, can be set up with a mutual fund company and lets you choose between annuities and mutual funds.

You can contribute up to $10,000 a year to a 403(b), but in some cases you can contribute up to $12,500 a year through a "catch up" clause. There's one caveat: Not all 403(b) plans comply with the Employee Retirement Income Security Act of 1974, known as ERISA, which requires that employers be prudent and vigilant in selecting, maintaining and reviewing retirement plan investments.

A 457 plan can be just as confusing. It is a tax-deferred supplemental retirement program that allows public employees to contribute up to $8,000 or 25 percent of their pre-tax income, whichever is less, to a retirement account. Savings grow tax-deferred, and there's no penalty for withdrawal before age 59$\frac{1}{2}$.

No employer-matching contributions are required with 457 plans. They're simply salary deferrals. Worst of all, they're nonqualified plans, which means there's no guarantee that these funds will be there when you need them, because the money can be taken by the employer or the employer's creditors.

Almost everything about 401(k) plans are great—except the costs. Fees are charged for transactions, for managing and administering the plan, and for servicing members. Not only are these costs rising, but many employers don't adequately disclose what they are.

If you're thinking of participating in a 401(k), a 403(b) or a 457 plan, or already contribute to one, we urge you to read one of the few books we've seen that comprehensively describes all three plans: *A Commonsense Guide to Your 401(k)* by Mary Rowland (Bloomberg Press, 1998).

Your employer should provide information about offered plans, either through written materials or seminars. Many Web sites have basic information about 401(k)s. Personalized advice about 401(k)s is harder to come by, but you can always get help from a financial planner.

The Teachers Insurance and Annuity Association College Retirement Equities Fund (TIAA-CREF) provides Spanish-speaking counselors and Spanish-language brochures on 403(b) plans. The ICMA Retirement Corp. offers a brochure on 457 plans called *Tax Shelter for Your Future* in both English and Spanish.

ACCIÓN For a free brochure, *Life Advice About 401(k) Plans for Retirement,* write to the Consumer Information Center, Pueblo, CO 81009. Be sure to ask for pamphlet #655D. It's also available on the Web at www.pueblo.gsa.gov/. To reach TIAA-CREF for 403(b) information call 800-842-2733. To reach ICMA Retirement Corp. for 457 plan information, call 800-669-7400. For a free brochure called *A Look at 401(k) Plan Fees,* call the Pension and Welfare Benefits Administration at 800-998-7542, or check the Web site at www.dol.gov/dol/pwba.

 Be aware of the penalties if you make an early withdrawal from a 401(k).

You can get access to your 401(k) funds before age 59 1/2 if you qualify for a hardship withdrawal *(retiro de apuro).* A hardship is defined by the IRS as "an immediate and heavy financial need." These needs include medical expenses, tuition, a down payment on a principal residence, and money to prevent eviction from or foreclosure on a principal residence.

No es fácil calificar. Before giving you the money, your employer must be satisfied that you've exhausted every other means of paying for these needs, including borrowing from your 401(k). After you get the money, you'll be prohibited from contributing to your 401(k) for one year.

Pero eso no es todo. You'll still pay a stiff price for getting your hands on the money. There's a 10 percent federal penalty for early withdrawal, and perhaps a state penalty. And there are state and federal taxes due on the amount withdrawn. In fact, you could end up losing about half the amount to penalties and taxes. *¡Ay!*

 Only borrow money from your 401(k) as a last resort.

Some people say 401(k) loans are a great deal because the interest you pay is lower than that on credit card charges, and you pay the interest back to yourself. Others are dead-set against it. It's your money, they argue, so why pay a premium to borrow it?

The decision to borrow from a 401(k) is a very personal one. But we believe you should only do it as a last resort. *¿Por qué?* You may be able to get just as good a deal, or even better, by shopping around for a no-fee, low-interest credit card or even a home equity loan.

Borrowing from a 401(k) can also be expensive. You can borrow up to half of your 401(k) account balance, but no more than $50,000. The interest rate is typically the prime rate plus 1 percent. Many 401(k)s charge one-time fees of up to $75 to set up the loan, and fees of up to $50 a year to administer it.

The loan must be paid back within five years (unless it's being used to buy a home) and right away if you leave your job. If you don't pay it back, you'll owe federal and state income taxes on the outstanding balance, and you'll be charged a 10 percent penalty, and perhaps a state penalty.

Some 401(k)s limit the amount you can borrow. Others only let you borrow for specific "hardships." The two biggest reasons to avoid borrowing from your 401(k) are the cost and the double-taxation issue. Taking a loan from your 401(k)—and reducing or suspending contributions while you're paying it back—keeps your money from growing as fast as it could have if you left it in.

And your loan payments are essentially taxed twice. First, you borrow pre-tax money, but pay it back with after-tax money. Second, when you retire and start withdrawing money from your 401(k), you'll have to pay taxes again on those same dollars.

 Be careful with your 401(k) when you leave your company.

If you leave your company, the money that's accumulated in your 401(k) plan can be left where it is (if that's allowed), rolled over into an IRA or your new employer's 401(k) plan within sixty days, or withdrawn periodically for at least five years or until you turn 59 1/2, whichever is later.

Here's how the sixty-day deadline works: If the money is sent directly to you, 20 percent of the entire amount will be automatically withheld for federal taxes. You must come up with the 20 percent difference yourself and deposit the full amount into a new 401(k) or IRA within sixty days to avoid all penalties.

If you miss the sixty-day deadline, you'll get socked with federal, state, and local income taxes on whatever amount you kept, and a 10 percent early withdrawal penalty if you're under age 59 1/2. These penalties and taxes could whittle away almost half of the amount.

Leave it. If you have $5,000 or more in your 401(k), you can leave it where it is (less than $5,000 can only be left if your former employer lets you). You won't be able to make any more contributions to the plan or take any loans. Any outstanding loans must be paid off or they'll be taxed as distributions.

If your account has less than $5,000 and your former employer won't let you leave it, you must give instructions for depositing the money into another retirement account right away or they'll send you the money—and the sixty-day deadline starts ticking.

IRA/401(k) rollovers. With a regular rollover, the money is sent directly to you, and you have sixty days to transfer the money into another tax-deferred account. With a direct rollover your former employer's plan trustee sends the full amount directly to your new employer's 401(k) plan trustee or IRA sponsor. If the check is mailed to you, make sure it is made out to the new trustee or sponsor to avoid automatic deduction of taxes.

If you don't like your new company's 401(k) plan, or it doesn't allow rollovers, you can put the money into a separate IRA. If this so-called "conduit IRA" is kept separate from your other IRAs, and you don't make any more contributions to it, you can roll it into a new 401(k) plan in the future.

Annuitize. You can annuitize, or make periodic withdrawals from the plan based on your life expectancy. You'll avoid the 10 percent early withdrawal penalty, but you'll owe tax on the money when you get it. Withdrawals must be made for at least five years or until age 59½, whichever is later.

 Consider an IRA.

Anyone who has earned income can set up an IRA account at a bank, credit union, brokerage firm, insurance company, or mutual fund firm. The money in your IRA can be placed in several different types of investments including CDs, money market accounts, Treasuries, stocks, bonds, and mutual funds. In most cases, you'll pay taxes when you withdraw the money.

Your contribution may be fully or partially tax-deductible, depending on your income, the type of IRA you choose, and whether you or your spouse is participating in an employer-sponsored retirement plan such as a 401(k). There are three types of IRAs: traditional (deductible and nondeductible), Roth IRAs, and Education IRAs.

Traditional deductible IRAs. You can contribute up to $2,000 annually to an IRA ($4,000 annually if you're married). Your contribution is fully tax deductible if neither you nor your spouse participates in an employer-sponsored retirement plan, no matter how high your income.

If you're single and participate in an employer-sponsored retirement plan, the IRA deductibility begins phasing out when your adjusted gross income (AGI) reaches $30,000, and is completely eliminated when it exceeds $40,000. The phaseout ranges will rise to between $50,000 and $60,000 by 2005.

If you're married and you participate in an employer-sponsored retirement plan, the IRA deductibility begins phasing out when your combined AGI reaches $50,000, and is completely eliminated when it exceeds $60,000.

The phaseout ranges will rise to between $80,000 and $100,000 by 2007.

If you're married and you're not covered by an employer-sponsored retirement plan, but your spouse is, the IRA deductibility begins phasing out when your combined AGI reaches $150,000, and is completely eliminated when it exceeds $160,000. All distributions are treated as ordinary income and are subject to tax at the time of withdrawal.

Traditional nondeductible IRAs. You can still make an IRA contribution of up to $2,000 if you're single ($4,000 *si son casados*) if your income exceeds the phaseout range. You just won't get a tax deduction. Gains on contributions are taxable as ordinary income at the time of withdrawal.

With traditional deductible and nondeductible IRAs, mandatory withdrawals are required at age $70\frac{1}{2}$, or at death. If you make a withdrawal before age $59\frac{1}{2}$ you'll have to pay a 10 percent penalty unless you use the money for higher education expenses, to buy a first home (withdrawals are limited to $10,000), or to pay for unreimbursed medical expenses that exceed 7.5 percent of your AGI.

Roth IRAs. You can contribute up to $2,000 to a Roth IRA ($4,000 if you're married), depending on your AGI. The contribution isn't tax deductible, but withdrawals are completely tax-free as long as you adhere to some specific rules.

If you're single, you can contribute the full $2,000 to a Roth IRA if your AGI is $95,000 or less. The contribution begins phasing out when your AGI is between $95,000 and $110,000, and is completely eliminated when it exceeds $110,000.

If you're married, you can contribute the full $4,000 to a Roth IRA if your AGI is $150,000 or less. The contribution begins phasing out when your AGI is between $150,000 to $160,000, and is completely eliminated when it exceeds $160,000.

Unlike traditional IRAs, no mandatory withdrawals are required, and contributions can continue to be made to a Roth IRA after age $70\frac{1}{2}$ if you keep working. And if you die before depleting the money in the Roth IRA, the remaining funds will pass tax-free to your heirs.

Withdrawals are completely tax-free as long as you hold the account for at least five years, distributions are made after age $59\frac{1}{2}$ after death, or on account of disability, or the money is used to pay for higher education expenses or a first time home purchase (withdrawals are limited to $10,000).

Otherwise, early withdrawals are subject to a 10 percent penalty.

You can convert, or roll over, your traditional IRA to a Roth IRA as long as your individual or joint AGI doesn't exceed $100,000. (Married couples who file separately can't convert.) The conversion will be considered a taxable distribution from your current IRA, but it won't be subject to the 10 percent penalty tax on distributions made before age $59^{1}/_{2}$. The tax can be paid in four equal installments if the conversion was made in 1998. But conversions made in 1999 and thereafter must be paid all at once.

Because assets converted to a Roth IRA are taxed at regular income tax rates, converting when the market is down means a lower tax bill because the value of your IRA will also decline. But if you convert when the market is high, you can take advantage of an IRS rule that lets you undo the conversion, then reconvert to a Roth IRA, to reduce your tax bill. However, you can only reconvert once in 1999. New rules governing conversions after 1999 have not yet been announced.

If you're starting from scratch, las Lauras recommend a Roth IRA instead of a traditional IRA because it will likely produce more after-tax income. Figuring whether to convert from a traditional IRA to a Roth IRA, however, gets a lot more complicated.

Don't covert if you're a few years away from retirement and you think your income will drop enough to push you into a lower tax bracket, or if you plan to take money out of your traditional IRA to pay the taxes on the money you shift to a Roth IRA.

Why? If you convert to a Roth IRA and you're close to retirement, you'll wind up with a bigger tax bill up front while saving relatively little in taxes at withdrawal. And it's never a good idea to take money out of any IRA that would otherwise be compounding over time.

Consider converting to a Roth IRA if you can't deduct a traditional IRA, if you expect to be in the same tax bracket when you retire, or if you expect to be at a higher tax bracket when you retire. Remember, traditional IRAs are taxed as ordinary income upon withdrawal, while Roth IRAs are tax-free.

The bottom line is that you have to do the math. Most IRA sponsors provide worksheets, computer software, or on-line calculators to help you figure out whether to convert. But you should also talk to your financial planner or a tax professional if you have one.

While Roth IRAs are free from federal taxes, earnings from Roth IRAs may be treated as unearned income for state tax purposes in six states—Arkansas, Georgia, Hawaii, Massachusetts, New Jersey, and North Carolina, plus the District of Columbia—unless state tax laws are changed. Check with your IRA sponsor for details.

Education IRAs. With an education IRA, you or anyone else who's so inclined can contribute up to $500 a year per child to a tax-free investment account. The contributions aren't tax deductible, but the gains are tax-free as long as the money is used to pay for education. (For more information go to Chapter 6.)

Like 401(k)s, IRAs offer a variety of investment options, and your asset allocation depends on your risk tolerance and how soon you'll need the money. (For more information see Chapter 4.) When shopping around for a place to open an IRA, compare fees and be sure the plan offers you the types of investments you want.

Almost all mutual fund firms and banks can provide free brochures and kits about IRAs. Merrill Lynch, Schwab, Fidelity, and T. Rowe Price offer materials in both English and Spanish, or can connect you to a customer service representative who speaks Spanish.

ACCIÓN To reach Merrill Lynch, call 800-MERRILL. To reach Schwab in English, call 800-435-4000. To reach Schwab's Centro Latinoamericano, call 800-362-1774. To reach Fidelity in English, call 800-544-8888; in Spanish, call 800-544-5670. To reach T. Rowe Price, call 800-638-5660.

 Try to contribute to both a 401(k) and an IRA.

You should try to contribute the maximum amount possible to your 401(k) plan and an IRA. But if you have to choose, most people would be better off funding a 401(k) first because the contribution limits are higher (up to $10,000 a year) than they are for an IRA ($2,000 for individuals and $4,000 for couples).

There are other benefits as well. The money comes straight out of your paycheck, which makes saving easy and painless. Because this money goes into your investments on a regular basis, you get the advantage of dollar-cost averaging. And you can make a lump sum withdrawal from a 401(k) plan and use income averaging to calculate your taxes. Your employer may even match your 401(k) contribution, putting in anywhere from ten cents to one dollar for every dollar you put in.

You can always make an IRA contribution even if you participate in a 401(k). But the contribution will be tax-deductible only if you meet certain income requirements. Individuals get full IRA deductions if their income is $30,000 or less, partial deductions if their income is between $30,000 and $40,000, and no deductions if their income is above $40,000. The phaseout limits will rise to between $50,000 and $60,000 by 2005.

Married couples filing jointly get full IRA deductions if their income is $50,000 or less, partial deductions if their income is between $50,000 and $60,000, and no deductions if their income is above $60,000. The phaseout limits will rise to between $80,000 and $100,000 by 2007.

 Contribute to a SEP-IRA if you're eligible.

SEP-IRAs are a combination pension plan and IRA, and can be set up by any business owner or by the self-employed through a mutual fund company, bank or brokerage. Contributions to SEP-IRA accounts, which are made by employers, are fully deductible. But they're limited to 15 percent of annual compensation or $30,000, whichever is less.

 Contribute to a SIMPLE IRA or SIMPLE 401(k) if you're eligible.

SIMPLE IRAs and 401(k)s are limited to businesses with 100 employees or less who earned at least $5,000 during the previous calendar year and have no other retirement plan. These plans are easy and inexpensive to set up and maintain. With both, the maximum annual employee contribution is $6,000.

With a SIMPLE IRA, employers are required to make a dollar-for-dollar matching contribution for every participating employee, up to a maximum of 3 percent of the employee's pay. Or the employer can choose to make a flat

2 percent contribution for every employee, whether they participate or not.

No loans or hardship withdrawals are allowed with SIMPLE IRAs, and withdrawals taken before age 59 ½ are subject to a 10 percent federal penalty, and perhaps a state penalty. In addition, if you make a withdrawal within two years of opening a SIMPLE IRA, you'll have to pay a 25 percent penalty. Loans and hardship withdrawals may be allowed, but you should check with your plan's administrator for details.

> **ACCIÓN** A free brochure called *Savings Incentive Match Plans for Employees of Small Employers: A Small Business Retirement Savings Advantage,* is available from the Pension and Welfare Benefits Administration by calling 800-998-7542.

 Contribute to a Keogh plan if you're eligible.

Retirement plans known as Keoghs are for corporations and the self-employed. Contributions are deductible, regardless of income level or participation in an employer-sponsored retirement plan. But qualified plans are a lot more expensive to set up and harder to maintain than either SEPs or SIMPLEs.

There are three types of defined contribution Keoghs: a profit-sharing plan, a money purchase plan, or a combination of the two. There's also a defined benefit Keogh, but this type of plan is pretty rare.

With a profit-sharing Keogh, you can contribute up to 15 percent of your net annual earnings or $24,000, whichever is less. With a money purchase Keogh, you can contribute up to 25 percent of your annual net earnings, or $30,000, whichever is less.

With a combination Keogh, you choose a base level percentage that you can contribute to your money purchase plan every year, and you can contribute to your profit sharing plan on a fluctuating basis every year. But the combined annual contribution is a maximum of 25 percent of your annual net earnings, or $30,000, whichever is less.

With a defined benefit Keogh, you can contribute up to 100 percent of your net earnings to reach a pre-determined benefit of up to $130,000 a year when you retire. An actuary must review your account every year to determine what your contribution should be. If you contribute too much during the year, you must withdraw the excess or you'll have to pay a 10 percent penalty on the amount.

With most Keoghs, withdrawal of funds before age 59½ will result in a 10 percent federal penalty on the amount withdrawn, and perhaps a state penalty. You'll also have to pay ordinary income tax on the amount, and you must begin taking distributions after age 70½. Loans may be available, but you should refer to your summary plan description, or SPD, for details.

 How do you choose between a SEP, SIMPLE, Keogh, or traditional 401(k)?

If you're self-employed or run a small business and would like to set up a retirement plan for yourself or your employees, deciding what to do becomes more complicated. You need to ask yourself several *preguntas:*

- ❏ How much can you set aside for a plan?
- ❏ Do you want to make contributions for employees or do you want them to defer income?
- ❏ How much time and money do you want to spend on the plan?
- ❏ Is the primary purpose of the plan to benefit employees or to provide a tax break for you, the employer?

A good financial planner may be able to help you set up a SEP, SIMPLE, or Keogh for yourself. But if you're setting up a plan for your employees, consider getting advice from a retirement and employee benefit plan administrator who can help determine what's best for your company.

ACCIÓN Two free brochures, *Simplified Employee Pensions: What Small Businesses Need to Know* and *Simple Retirement Solutions for Small Businesses,* are available from the Pension and Welfare Benefits Administration by calling 800-998-7542.

 Don't forget about long-term care insurance.

Nothing will eat away at your retirement nest egg faster than a long-term disability. Long-term care insurance pays for all or part of nursing home or in-home care. Premiums for some long-term care insurance plans qualify as a tax deduction if these costs, plus other medical expenses, exceed 7.5 percent of adjusted gross income. Benefits from long-term care insurance payments are also excluded from taxable income. (For more information see Chapter 3.)

 Consider a reverse mortgage if you own a home and need cash.

If you're at least sixty-two years old, and either own your own home or have a very small mortgage to pay off, a good source of extra income might be borrowing against the equity in your home with a reverse mortgage. The loan doesn't have to be repaid until you sell the property, move, or die. You'll recall from Chapter 5 that with a traditional mortgage, you pay back your home loan every month. Lenders recover their principal and interest with a reverse mortgage when the home is sold. The remaining proceeds, if any, go to you or your beneficiaries.

If the proceeds from the sale don't cover the principal and interest owed, the lender can't come after you or your estate for the difference. In other words, you'll never owe more than the value of your home.

You can take the money from a reverse mortgage in one lump sum, receive regular monthly payments for a specific period of time or as long as you live in your home, use it as a line of credit, or combine all of the options.

There are no credit or income qualifications with reverse mortgages as there are with other types of loans. Most seniors live on fixed incomes, which makes it hard to qualify for anything but a reverse mortgage.

Reverse mortgages sound good, but there are drawbacks. Your debt gets bigger over time, which means the equity in your home gets smaller. This can leave your heirs empty-handed.

Even though the money you receive from a reverse mortgage is tax-free, it may affect your SSI or Medicaid benefits, which are intended for low-income consumers.

The amount of money you get from a reverse mortgage is often capped, depending on which program you choose. For example, both HUD's Home Equity Conversion Mortgage (HECM) and Fannie Mae's Home Keeper Reverse Mortgage are limited to $214,000. If you need to borrow more than that, you'll need to work with a private lender.

And the costs associated with reverse mortgages vary greatly and can be hard to figure out. You can compare reverse mortgages with the Total Annual Loan Cost (TALC) that lenders disclose under federal Truth-in-Lending laws. The TALC includes an appraisal, credit report, interest rate, and the loan origination fee.

The TALC must be given to you at least three days before closing on a reverse mortgage. You'll also have a three-day grace period after signing the contract to back out of the deal.

How do you determine whether a reverse mortgage is right for you? If you need a small amount of money, it may be better to borrow from family or friends, or get a personal loan if you can.

Many city and county agencies help cash-strapped seniors pay their heating bills during the winter. To find these agencies call the National Association for Agencies on Aging's Eldercare Locator at 800-677-1116.

If you know you'll need a large amount of money and aren't tied to remaining in your home, you may want to sell it, buy a smaller place, and pocket the extra cash.

In fact, Fannie Mae has a reverse mortgage product, called the Home Keeper for Home Purchase, designed to help you keep more money in your pocket when you buy a new home.

As with a traditional reverse mortgage, you must be at least sixty-two to qualify. The amount of equity available is based on your age and the value of the property.

Say you're seventy-six and want to buy a $100,000 condo. Since you probably don't have the income to qualify for a home loan, you'd typically have to pay for the condo in full.

But with a Home Keeper for Home Purchase reverse mortgage, you'd qualify for a loan of $52,000. That means you could take that amount and combine it with $48,000 from savings and buy the condo. That would eliminate your monthly mortgage payments and leave you with more cash in your pocket. And you don't have to repay the loan until you move, you sell the condo, or die.

If you're like many seniors, you may be unwilling to leave your longtime home—and you may need a large sum of money for an extended period of time. If so, a reverse mortgage may be for you.

The first thing to do if you think you want a reverse mortgage is to contact one of the free HUD-approved reverse mortgage counseling centers. In fact, you'll be required to go through counseling if you get a HUD reverse mortgage. Reverse mortgage counseling is strongly recommended for everyone. It doesn't matter how sophisticated you are or whether or not you're getting a HUD product.

ACCIÓN

❏ For more information about HUD reverse mortgages, and to get a list of HUD-approved reverse mortgage counselors, call 888-466-3487.

❏ For more information about Fannie Mae's Home Keeper, a list of participating lenders, and a free copy of *Money from Home: A Consumer's Guide to Reverse Mortgage Options,* call 800-732-6643.

❏ For more information about all types of reverse mortgages and a free guide on how to convert the equity in your home to cash, request *Home Made Money,* AARP Home Equity Information Center, 601 E St., NW, Washington, D.C. 20049.

❏ For a list of preferred mortgage lenders that will provide you with a comparison of various reverse mortgage products and their costs, send $1 and a self-addressed, stamped business-size envelope to NCHEC Preferred, 7373 147th St. West, Room 115, Apple Valley, MN 55124.

 Consider selling, or borrowing, from your life insurance policy.

If you are terminally ill or elderly, a viatical settlement company will typically pay you a lump sum of 60 percent to 90 percent of the face value of a life insurance policy, depending on your life expectancy. After you die, the viatical company receives all the benefits from your life insurance policy.

Accelerated death benefits, also known as living benefits, are available through some insurance companies on some policies. To qualify, you generally must have a short life expectancy—between six months and 12 months. The payment you get ranges from 25 percent to 95 percent of the policy's face value (most offer 50 percent). The remainder of the policy will be paid to your beneficiaries after you die.

You can also get cash for your whole and universal life insurance policy by borrowing against its cash value (this option is generally not available on a term or group insurance policy). The interest rate you'll owe on the loan can be fixed or variable. The death benefit will be restored to you if you repay the loan and interest. If you don't, the loan and interest will be subtracted from the death benefit, and your heirs will get the rest. (For more information see Chapter 3.)

 Stay away from variable annuities unless you've consulted with a trusted, objective financial planner.

Variable annuities—mutual funds with an insurance component that allows investment earnings to grow tax-deferred—are among the most complex, expensive, and controversial financial products on the market. Critics say greedy salespeople are pushing variable annuities to pocket hefty up-front commissions of up to 7 percent. Supporters argue that variable annuities let you save an unlimited amount of cash tax-free until retirement.

¿Y qué decimos? Because of the controversy, we recommend seeking advice from an objective financial planner. (For more on financial planners go to Chapter 10.) If you're still interested in a variable annuity after completing an in-depth financial analysis, take your time and shop around by looking at no-load variable annuities, which can save you a lot of money. (See the chart on page 210 for a list of no-load variable annuities.)

Even die-hard do-it-yourself investors can get quick free help from Fidelity Investments and T. Rowe Price, two mutual fund companies that also sell variable annuities. These companies offer worksheets, calculators, and software to help investors choose between a variable annuity or mutual fund.

Remember, the first rule of investing is never buy anything you don't understand. With that in mind, here's an explanation of how variable annuities work, who they're for, and what your alternatives are.

A variable annuity is a tax-deferred insurance product that invests in

NO-LOAD VARIABLE ANNUITIES

Ameritas No-Load Variable Annuity	800-255-9678
Anchor Advisor (SunAmerica)	800-445-7862
Galaxy Variable Annuity (American Skandia)	800-541-3087
Jack White Value Advantage Plus	800-622-3699
Janus Retirement Advantage	800-504-4440
John Hancock Marketplace Variable Annuity	888-742-6262
Providian Life Advisor's Edge	800-866-6007
Schwab Investment Advantage	800-838-0650
Schwab Variable Annuity	800-838-0650
Scudder Horizon Plan	800-225-2470
T.Rowe Price No-Load Variable Annuity	800-469-6587
Touchstone Advisor Variable Annuity	800-669-2796
USAA Life Variable Annuity	800-531-4440
Vanguard Variable Annuity Plan	800-523-9954

SOURCE: MORNINGSTAR, INC.

mutual fund-like accounts known as sub-accounts. There are no limits on how much you can contribute to a variable annuity. Your contributions aren't tax deductible, but your earnings grow tax-deferred.

These investments are meant to be held a long time so that the benefits of the tax-deferral offset the high fees. How long is open to debate, but Morningstar Inc. says the "break-even" point for most variable annuities is about twenty years.

Variable annuities carry two layers of big fees—one for money management, and the other for an insurance contract with a death benefit that essentially guarantees your principal is safe. That means if you die before you start withdrawing the money, your heirs will receive an amount at least equal to your initial investment.

The value of your annuity investment can fluctuate, which is why they're called variable. (Fixed annuities invest in bonds and provide a steady amount of income.) When you withdraw money from a variable annuity, you'll pay ordinary income tax rates of up to 39.6 percent. With a mutual fund, you'll pay a maximum of 20 percent on the capital gain as long as you've held it for at least 18 months.

You can't withdraw the money from a variable annuity before age $59\frac{1}{2}$

or you'll get socked with a 10 percent penalty. And if you cancel your variable annuity in the first year you may have to pay a surrender charge of as much as 7 percent. These surrender charges typically decrease to zero after seven years.

You can withdraw funds from variable annuities in three ways: in a lump sum; in fixed monthly amounts until the money runs out; or in fixed monthly amounts for the rest of your life, even if your account runs dry before you die. However, should you die before the money runs out, your heirs won't inherit what's left unless you buy a more expensive joint variable annuity.

In addition to the 20 percent capital gains tax rate, mutual funds have other advantages over variable annuities. If you lose money on a mutual fund, those losses are tax deductible. No so with a variable annuity. You can also bequeath your mutual fund shares to charity or leave them in your estate to escape the capital gains tax altogether. If you leave your variable annuity to anyone but your spouse, it will be taxed at ordinary income tax rates. Currently, you can reallocate money within a variable annuity, or exchange one variable annuity for another, tax-free.

In general, you should only consider a variable annuity if you've contributed the maximum amount to your 401(k) or IRA, you don't need the money until age $59\frac{1}{2}$, you can wait at least 20 years until you start withdrawing the funds, and you think your tax rate will be lower than 20 percent when you retire.

If you've already got a variable annuity, don't put any more money into it without a detailed financial analysis. You may even want to consider switching your variable annuity into a cheaper no-load version, depending on how much of a surrender fee you'll have to pay. The overall savings may be worth it in the long run.

ACCIÓN To use Fidelity's annuity calculator, call 800-544-2442 (you can use it over the telephone, or schedule an appointment with a specialist). To get a free copy of T. Rowe Price's No-Load Fixed and Variable Annuity Analyzer software, call 800-469-5304.

❑ Try to estimate how much money you'll need in retirement.

❑ Start saving and investing even if it's just a small amount every month. The earlier the better.

❑ Don't be too conservative with your investments as you get older—you could live a very long time after retirement.

❑ Don't lose track of your defined-benefit pension plan if you have one.

❑ Understand what your government benefits are and how to get them.

❑ Participate in your company's 401(k) plan or an IRA, and contribute the maximum amount you can afford.

❑ Be careful with your 401(k) when you leave your company.

❑ Consider a SEP, SIMPLE, or a Keogh if you're eligible.

❑ If you own a home and need cash, consider a reverse mortgage only after getting counseling from a HUD-approved agency.

❑ Stay away from variable annuities unless you understand exactly how they work and have consulted with a trusted financial planner.

ADDITIONAL RESOURCES

Recommended Books

A Commonsense Guide to Your 401(k), by Mary Rowland (Princeton, New Jersey: Bloomberg Press, 1997).

Get a Life: You Don't Need a Million to Retire Well, by Ralph Warner. (Berkeley: Nolo Press, 1998).

IRAs, 410(k)s and Other Retirement Plans: Taking Your Money Out, by Twila Slesnick and John Suttle (Berkeley: Nolo Press, 1998).

Social Security, Medicare and Pensions: Get the Most Out of Your Retirement and Medical Benefits, by Joseph Matthews and Dorothy Matthews Berman (Berkeley: Nolo Press, 6th edition, 1996; 7th edition, 1999).

CHAPTER 8

Estate Planning

"THERE IS A REMEDY FOR ALL THINGS EXCEPT DEATH" —PUERTO RICO

THE LATINO ATTITUDE TOWARD DEATH IS FILLED WITH CONTRADIC-
tions. Consider *El Día de los Muertos,* or the Day of the Dead. This fes-
tive and ironic Mexican holiday, celebrated all across the United States, wel-
comes the returning spirits of loved ones and acknowledges that death is an
inevitable part of life.

On the Day of the Dead we build altars, burn incense, and offer food and
drink to the dearly departed. We display paper mache skeletons dressed as
mariachis or newlyweds, skulls of sugar, and bread shaped like corpses. We
also decorate graves and hold picnics at cemeteries.

Despite the seemingly light-hearted attitude many Latinos have toward
death, however, most of us don't have wills. We don't pre-arrange funerals. We
don't specify what to do if we're on life support. And we don't designate anyone to make our financial or medical decisions if we become incapacitated.
Reconocemos que este es un tema desagradable. Too many of us take the lazy way
out and figure our families will deal with everything when the time comes.
La Laura who has worked as both a financial planner and a lawyer has witnessed all too often the sad result of Latino avoidance of estate planning.

Complicating matters is the fact that most Latin American countries don't have so-called death taxes. In Latin America, passing on our estate to our heirs is considered a right, not a privilege. It's the reverse in the United States.

Proper estate planning *(planificación del patrimonio)* can ensure that our assets will be distributed the way we want them to be. We can name a guardian for our minor children. We can also reduce estate taxes *(impuestos sucesorios)*, leaving more assets for our survivors.

Delia, a retired health care administrator from San Francisco, had an uncomfortable heart-to-heart talk with her mother about estate planning. Six months later, her mother suffered a massive stroke. Fortunately, Delia was able to make confident decisions about medical care because of their previous conversation. "It was informal, but it really helped," she says. "It's important to talk about these things out of consideration for those who have to make arrangements."

Our estate *(patrimonio)* is what we own, minus our debts, at the time of death. If the value of our estate exceeds a certain amount, $625,000 for individuals and $1.25 million for married couples, we'll owe death taxes to the federal government.

Some of us may assume our estates will easily fall under these limits. But that's not necessarily so, especially if we own a home or other real estate in a high-priced area such as California or New York, have a life insurance policy, or own a small business.

The backbone of estate planning is a will *(testamento)*, a legal document that outlines how to dispose of our assets and names an executor *(albacea)* to manage our estate, collect the assets, and distribute them according to the will. Most important, we can name a guardian for our children in a will.

With or without a will, some or all of our assets must go through probate *(verificación oficial de los testamentos)*, a court procedure during which our assets are identified, estate taxes and debts are paid, all lawyer, appraiser, accountant and court fees are paid, and assets are distributed to our designated beneficiaries. Depending on which state we live in, probate can take months, even years, to resolve. The average cost is about 5 percent of the total estate.

Many of us believe that if we die without a will, our spouse or partner will automatically inherit our estate. Or we think we can use a will to leave our assets to anyone we want. But how our assets are distributed depends on whether we live in a community property state or a common-law state.

In community property states—Arizona, California, Idaho, Louisiana, Nevada, New Mexico, Texas, Washington, Wisconsin, and Puerto Rico—all assets acquired during the marriage are presumed to be community property equally owned by the two spouses. The exceptions are assets acquired through gifts and inheritance. In common-law states—all other states plus Washington, D.C.—we're required to leave a minimum amount known as a "statutory share" to our spouse, usually one-half or one-third of our estate.

If we die without a will, or intestate (*intestado*), our money and possessions will be distributed according to the laws of our state. The court will appoint a guardian for our minor children, and an administrator to carry out the duties of an executor. If we wanted to leave something to a favorite niece, sibling, or charity, we'll be out of luck, because the state administrator will have no way of knowing that.

Probate can often be speeded or completely avoided, taxes slashed, eliminated or deferred, through coordinated financial, tax and legal planning. Las Lauras strongly recommend reading up on the subject and seeking advice from qualified financial planners, attorneys, and tax professionals.

 You can avoid probate with joint ownership of assets with rights of survivorship.

With this arrangement, also known as the "poor man's will," an asset is jointly owned by two or more people. When one person dies, ownership of the asset automatically passes to the survivor or survivors without probate.

Besides avoiding probate, the advantage of joint ownership is that the entire procedure is private. A will, on the other hand, is a matter of public record. That means anyone, even strangers, can find out what your estate is worth and what you gave to whom.

Joint ownership is most commonly used between spouses, or between parents and children, grandparents and grandchildren, gay couples, or friends. It can usually be set up for bank accounts (known as payable-on-death accounts or Totten Trusts), retirement accounts, stocks and bonds, cars, and real estate.

If you live in a community property state, your spouse most likely already owns half of whatever you own, with or without joint ownership. So even if you own an asset in your own name, get the written consent of your spouse if you want to leave that asset to someone else.

If you live in a common-law state, your spouse can claim his or her statutory share of your estate, with or without joint ownership. So here again, if you own an asset solely in your name, you can leave it to someone else as long as your spouse gives his or her consent.

Joint ownership is useful, but it has its limits. Both owners have the right to use the jointly held asset, which can create a problem if one decides to withdraw or sell assets without telling the other. Joint ownership is also hard to dissolve once it's established.

When one spouse dies, no estate taxes are due when assets pass to a surviving spouse. But estate taxes may be owed when the surviving spouse dies if the estate is large enough, unless gifts are made to reduce the size of the estate.

Another thing to remember is that payable-on-death accounts supercede wills. That means even if you name a different beneficiary for the bank account in your will, the person named as the beneficiary on a payable-on-death account would get the money.

 Consider using affidavits or simplified court procedures to avoid probate.

You can avoid probate if your estate meets certain size requirements (the exact amount depends on the state you're in) with affidavits or simplified court procedures. Some states allow both procedures, while others use just one.

With an affidavit (*afidavit*), your beneficiary prepares a short document signed under oath stating that he or she is entitled to certain property. Eligible estates range from one or two motor vehicles in Washington, D.C. to more than $100,000 in California and New Mexico. A simplified court procedure known as summary or informal probate, is a faster version of regular probate. Eligible estates range from $500 or less in Mississippi to $200,000 in Nevada.

The downside to an affidavit or a summary probate is that real estate transactions may be prohibited, depending on the state. There could be a waiting period of a month or two to obtain the property. And summary probate may be restricted to the surviving spouse or children.

For a comprehensive review of these two probate-avoidance strategies we recommend two books: *8 Ways to Avoid Probate: Quick & Easy Ways to Save Your Family Thousands of Dollars*, by Mary Randolph (Nolo Press), and *Plan Your Estate*, by Denis Clifford and Cora Jordan (Nolo Press).

 Consider using a living trust to avoid probate.

A trust *(fideicomiso)* is a legal arrangement that passes ownership of your assets to someone else (a trustee) for the benefit of another (a beneficiary). Revocable trusts can be canceled or changed. Irrevocable trusts are permanent.

There are essentially two types of trusts. A testamentary trust *(fideicomiso testamentario)* is irrevocable. It is created in your will, and only becomes effective after your death. A living trust *(fideicomiso durante la vida)* is revocable and is established while you're alive. This type of trust is also known as an "inter vivos" trust, which is Latin for "among the living."

With a living trust, your assets can pass to your beneficiaries immediately after you die without having to go through probate. You can manage the trust yourself, or name a successor trustee to do it. Living trusts are also completely private, unlike wills.

Living trusts are more flexible than wills. If you become incapacitated, for example, the successor trustee automatically manages your assets, avoiding legal proceedings that can eat away at your estate. (Durable powers of attorney, which we discuss later in this chapter, can do much of the same.)

If you decide to establish a living trust, you may also want a special type of conventional will called a pour-over will to guarantee that any property remaining in your estate after you die is distributed to the trustee of your living trust. The property transferred from the pour-over will, however, still requires probate. And the trust must predate the will to be valid.

Living trusts have drawbacks. *Claro, nada es perfecto.* Although they help you avoid probate, they have absolutely no tax advantages. They're also more complicated and expensive to arrange than wills. And there may even be a transfer tax imposed in some states if you transfer real estate to a living trust.

Do you need a living trust? Probably not if you can use joint ownership, affidavits, or simplified court procedures to settle your estate. And if you're young and healthy, a will is an easier and cheaper way to accomplish your goals. But you may want a living trust if you're single, own lots of real estate, live in a state with a cumbersome probate process, or want to make sure a beneficiary doesn't squander his or her share.

 Seek the advice of a financial planner and attorney who's licensed in your state before establishing a living trust.

Beware of so-called "trust mills" where salespeople with no legal or estate planning expertise target retirees at free estate planning seminars. An improperly drafted living trust will be considered invalid, and could leave your *familia* with a big estate tax bill. You may not need a living trust at all, and tax laws affecting estate planning are always changing.

 Write a will.

¿Por qué? A will lets you do a lot of things that you can't with a living trust, joint ownership, affidavits, or simplified court procedures. A will lets you name a guardian for minor children and an executor to manage your estate. You may be able to disinherit a child or spouse. You can forgive debts. And you can dispose of assets not included in the living trust, or assets acquired after the living trust was established.

But one of the most compelling reasons to have a will if you're married is to be able to take advantage of the marital deduction (*deducción impositiva matrimonial*), which allows the passing of an unlimited amount of assets to your spouse without estate or gift taxes. These taxes are due, however, upon the death of the surviving spouse. Non-U.S. citizens can't use the marital deduction unless a special trust is established. (More on trusts later in this chapter.)

Before writing a will, you need to calculate the size of your estate to get a sense of what you're worth and what your potential estate tax strategies might be. Start by subtracting your total liabilities from your total assets. (See "Figuring Your Net Worth" in Chapter 5, pages 126–27.)

Your estate typically includes cash, investments, retirement funds, and personal assets such as your home, collectibles such as art and antiques, cars, furniture, furs, jewelry, and foreign assets. When calculating the size of your estate, use the current fair market value—not the original purchase price. (See "Calculating the Value of Your Estate," pages 220–21.)

To legally write a will you must be at least eighteen years old in most states, you must be of sound mind, the will must comply with state rules, it must be handwritten or typed, you must appoint at least one executor, and you must sign the will in front of witnesses.

Wills can be handwritten (holographic), videotaped (nuncupative), or formally drawn up by a lawyer. But handwritten wills can be contested and declared void if they aren't handled properly, and not all states accept video-taped wills. Our advice: Have a lawyer draw up a formal will.

Some states—California, Maine, Michigan, New Mexico, and Wisconsin—offer statutory wills, which are authorized by state law. These types of wills are preprinted documents with boxes to check and lines to fill out. The problem is, they can't be customized to fit your situation, so it's best to avoid them.

Wills can be extremely simple or complicated, depending on the size of your estate and your final wishes. But they all have three basic components: direction on how to dispose of your assets, the name of an executor, and the name of a guardian if you have minor children.

The person who makes out the will is called the testator (or testatrix if a woman). A gift made by the terms of the will is known as a bequest or a legacy (legado) if it's gift of personal property or a gift paid out of the estate's general assets, or a devise (legado) if it's a gift of real property.

When making gifts, you can divide your estate among your heirs by percentage, leaving your spouse 50 percent, and divide the other half among your children. You can also make special bequests, such as leaving your daughter your engagement ring. Or you can use a combination of both.

When naming beneficiaries, you may want to name contingent beneficiaries (beneficiarios contingentes) in case your original choice dies before you do. You may also want to specify the names of people you don't want to leave anything to, along with an explanation for your decision.

When choosing an executor (the term is executrix if it's a woman)—try

CALCULATING THE VALUE OF YOUR ESTATE

We suggest that you indicate by initials how assets are held (J for jointly or I for individually). Also, indicate if you have designated a beneficiary (B) for the asset. Remember to use current fair market values, not original purchase prices.

PERSONAL ASSETS:

Primary residence	$____	Jewelry & art	$____
Vacation home	$____	Automobiles and/or	
Furnishings (furniture &		motorcycles	$____
electronics)	$____	**Total Personal Assets**	**$____**

RETIREMENT ASSETS:

IRAs	$____	Annuities	$____
Keogh or SEP IRA	$____	After-tax 401(k)	$____
Qualified Retirement Plans		**Total Retirement Assets**	**$____**
[e.g., 401(k), 403(b)]	$____		

LIQUID AND INVESTMENTS ASSETS:

Life insurance death benefits		Stocks and stock mutual	
including cash values	$____	funds	$____

to name someone who's young and healthy enough to outlive you. Family members who are also beneficiaries can be executors, and often waive the executor's fee (the amount of which is established by each state).

If you have minor children, you need to name a guardian for them in the will. This can be the child's godparent, a close friend, or a relative. You should also name an alternative guardian in case your first choice can't do it. You can even specify the names of people whom you don't want as guardians.

Both you and your spouse or partner should have wills that name each other as beneficiary. If one dies, typically the surviving spouse or partner inherits the estate. There should also be a simultaneous death provision in

Liquid and Investments Assets (continued):

Cash/Money Market accounts	$____	Tax-free municipal bonds/ funds	$____
CDs, other savings	$____	Precious metals or collectibles	$____
Bonds and bonds mutual funds	$____	Limited partnerships	$____
U.S. Government obligations	$____	**Total Liquid and Investment Assets**	$____

Business and Investment Real Estate

Notes Receivable/Business Assets	$____	**Total Business and Investment Real Estate**	$____
Investment Real Estate	$____		

◎ Total Gross Estate

Total Personal Assets	$____	Total Retirement Assets	$____
Total Liquid and Investment Assets	$____	These totals when added together equal:	
Total Business and Investment Real Estate	$____	**Total Gross Estate**	$____

the unlikely event you both die at the same time in an accident.

The signing of the will must be witnessed by two or more people, depending on which state you're in (to play it safe, you may want three witnesses). The witnesses don't have to read the will; they just have to see you sign it. In most states, blood relatives or anyone named in your will aren't allowed to serve as witnesses to avoid a potential conflict of interest later on. There's no need to notarize the signatures unless you're using a "self-proving will," which in some states can eliminate the need for witnesses to testify at probate proceedings.

Be sure to keep the original will in a safe place. A safe deposit box is one possibility, but only if you're sure the executor will have access to it after your death (more on safe deposit boxes later in this chapter). You can also place the original in a safe or fireproof box at home. Either way, be sure your executor knows where it is. Some states will also store your will at the local county clerk's office for a fee. You can make photocopies of your original will and give them to family and friends. These copies aren't legally binding, however, so you must work from the original will to make changes.

Your will should be reviewed every three to five years, or after a major life change such as the birth of a child, a divorce, a death, a remarriage, or a move to a new state. You may require a new will. But minor changes can be made with a codicil, a written amendment that's witnessed and attached to the original will.

You should also have a letter of instruction, which is an inventory of assets not itemized in your will. You can specify how to distribute these assets, describe what kind of funeral arrangements you want, or donate your organs. Attach your original letter of instruction to your original will.

There are many do-it-yourself will forms in books, software programs, and Web sites, and many people are perfectly capable of writing their own simple wills. But given the vast differences in state laws, we recommend using a lawyer, or at least having a lawyer look at your final version, to avoid any mistakes.

ACCIÓN For free brochures on wills and living trusts, call the American Association of Retired Persons (AARP) at 800-424-3410.

Be sure you leave enough cash to pay for estate taxes, debts, and the living expenses of your survivors.

If you're the primary breadwinner, consider a payable-on-death account or a life insurance policy to cover immediate living expenses of your dependents.

Get a living will and durable powers of attorney for financial decisions and medical care.

Medical technology is allowing the terminally ill or debilitated to live longer than ever before. But spending weeks or months on life support systems can quickly wipe out a lifetime of assets or conflict with a person's moral or spiritual beliefs. Living wills and durable powers (*poder*) of attorney, which are written instructions regarding medical treatment, tell your doctor and family what to do in such a situation.

Living wills. A living will states that you don't want to continue on life support if your condition is terminal or you're in a coma with no chance of recovery. You can also specify whether you want to donate your organs. A living will doesn't require a lawyer, and it's revocable, but it must be completed or revised at least thirty days prior to death to avoid any challenges.

At least two adults should witness the signing of your living will, but they can't be blood relatives, spouses, doctors, or anyone else who could benefit from your death. The living will should be notarized, and copies should be given to your doctor, lawyer, and close relatives and friends. Keep the original in a safe, accessible place.

Durable powers of attorney. There are two kinds of durable powers of attorney. One is for finances, and the other is for health care and is also called a health care proxy. With a durable power of attorney, you can name someone to act as your "attorney-in-fact" to make financial and medical decisions for you.

Unlike a living will, which only authorizes medical care with respect to life-sustaining treatment, a durable power of attorney lets you specify what types of medical treatment you want or don't want. And it lets your attorney-in-fact make these decisions if you're incapacitated.

At least two adults should witness the signing of the durable power of attorney. You can select anyone to be your attorney-in-fact. Just make sure the person understands your wishes and is willing to carry them out. The durable power of attorney should be notarized, and copies given to your doctor, lawyer, attorney-in-fact and close relatives and friends. Keep the original in a safe, accessible place.

There are other durable powers of attorney as well. With a durable power of attorney for real estate, you can name an attorney-in-fact to make decisions about your real estate holdings if you become incapacitated. There's also a conventional power of attorney for real estate, which is temporary.

You may want a durable or conventional power of attorney for real estate if you can't be present when important real estate documents need to be signed, you can't look after your property for a period of time, or you don't live near the property and want to authorize someone else to manage it.

A durable power for child care authorizes someone to care for your child in your absence. You may want a durable power of attorney for child care if you'll be separated from your child for a long period of time, you are ill and can't care for your child, or your child is staying with friends or family for an extended period.

Durable powers of attorney for real estate and child care should be signed in front of a notary public in your state. Witnesses may not be required, but it's always a good idea to have them. Give the original documents to the attorney-in-fact, and copies to financial institutions, schools, and doctors.

Recording of a durable power of attorney is required in some states. But even if it isn't, you may want to do it just to be safe. Places to record durable powers of attorney are typically your County Recorder's office, the Land Registry office, or perhaps the Registry of Deeds office.

Should you get both a living will and a durable power of attorney for finances? If you've got a living trust, you've already named a successor trustee to handle your financial affairs if you become incapacitated. But if all you have is a will, then you should get a durable power of attorney for finances.

You should have both a living will and a durable power of attorney for health care because they accomplish two different objectives. A living will focuses entirely on life-sustaining treatment, while a durable power of attorney for health lets you name an attorney-in-fact to make medical decisions for you.

ACCIÓN State specific living will and medical power of attorney forms and instruction booklets can be obtained from doctors or hospitals. You can also get them for $5 from the nonprofit group Choice in Dying by calling 800-989-WILL. In addition, a group called Aging With Dignity has created a very simple living will document called *Five Wishes*. However, this document is only valid in 33 states and the District of Columbia. To find out where it's valid

call 850-681-2010, or go to the Web site at www.agingwithdigni-
ty.org/, where you can also download the document for free.
Ordering the document by mail will cost $4.

 **Unmarried couples need to take special estate
planning precautions.**

Unmarried couples don't have the same legal protections that married
couples do. If you're unmarried, but want to name your life partner as a beneficiary or attorney-in-fact, you'll need to have wills, living wills, durable
powers of attorney, and joint ownership.

But you need to take special care with real estate and life insurance if
you're unmarried. You won't, for example, be allowed to take out life insurance policies on each other. But you can buy policies for yourselves and each
name the other as beneficiary.

If you and your partner buy real estate together, you can own it as joint
tenants *(copropietarios)* or tenants-in-common *(tenedores en conjunto)*. If one
joint tenant dies, the other gets his or her half of the house without going
through probate. With tenants-in-common, the deceased partner's portion
of the property goes to the beneficiary named in the will or living trust; but
if there's no will or living trust, the portion of the property automatically
goes to the deceased partner's nearest relative.

ACCIÓN For more information read IRS Publication 559,
Survivors, Executors and Administrators, which can be obtained
by calling 800-TAX-FORM.

 **Use deductions, gifts, and charitable contri-
butions to reduce estate taxes.**

If the value of your estate is less than $650,000 (less than $1.3 million for
married couples), you won't owe any federal estate taxes. But if it's worth
more than that, you could owe estate taxes ranging from 37 percent to 55
percent on every dollar over $650,000.

The 1999 exemption of $650,000 for individuals rises to $675,000 in 2000,
and will continue to increase until it reaches $1 million in 2006. The 1999

exemption of $1.3 million for married couples rises to $1.35 million in 2000, and will continue to increase until it reaches $2 million in 2006. (See the chart below.)

Some states also have inheritance taxes, which vary depending on the state, the size of your estate, what you've left to your beneficiaries, and the relationship between you and your beneficiaries. Certain kinds of property are sometimes exempt from inheritance taxes.

With proper planning, however, you can take advantage of many deductions that reduce your taxable estate and leave more to your beneficiaries. Among the most widely used are:

Gifts and charitable contributions. You can give up to $10,000 each year ($20,000 if you're married) to as many people as you like without having to pay gift taxes. They must be gifts of present interests, which can be enjoyed now or soon. Gifts of future interest that can't be used until a future date don't qualify. (The annual limits of $10,000 for individuals and $20,000 for married couples was indexed to inflation beginning in 1999.)

Educational and medical expenses. You can pay for someone's medical or educational expenses and claim a deduction for the entire amount if you make the payment directly to the institution providing the service. In other

FEDERAL ESTATE TAX EXEMPTIONS

Exemptions will increase from $650,000 for individuals in 1999 to $1 million in 2006 and from $1.3 million for married couples in 1999 to $2 million in 2006.

YEAR	EXEMPTION FOR INDIVIDUALS	EXEMPTION FOR MARRIED COUPLES
1999	$650,000	$1.3 million
2000	$675,000	$1.35 million
2001	$675,000	$1.35 million
2002	$700,000	$1.4 million
2003	$750,000	$1.5 million
2004	$850,000	$1.7 million
2005	$950,000	$1.9 million
2006	$1 million	$2 million

words, don't give the money directly to your son, daughter, grandchild, or other beneficiary. *Mejor que pague la escuela u hospital directamente.*

Miscellaneous deductions. You can deduct many other expenses from your estate including funerals, debts, unpaid mortgages, personal bank loans, car loans, credit card bills, utility bills, executor fees, attorney fees, accountant fees, appraisal fees, and court costs.

ACCIÓN For more information read IRS Publication 950, *Introduction to Estate and Gift Taxes,* which can be obtained by calling the IRS at 800-TAX-FORM.

 Use trusts to reduce or defer estate taxes.

Trusts can also reduce or defer estate taxes. There are many different trusts, which can be used alone or together. Here's a description of some of the most popular trusts:

Marital Deduction Trust. With a Marital Deduction Trust, the first spouse can give the surviving spouse a life income interest in the trust's assets, and the ability to leave the trust's assets to anyone when he or she dies. A trustee is also named to control and manage the trust during the surviving spouse's lifetime.

A Qualified Terminal Interest Property Trust (QTIP). With a QTIP Trust, the surviving spouse is given a life income interest in the trust's assets, but a trustee is named to control and manage the trust during the surviving spouse's lifetime. The QTIP Trust lets the first spouse determine who gets the property after the surviving spouse dies.

Bypass Trust. With this type of trust, also called a Credit Shelter Trust or Marital Life Estate Trust, estate taxes are due when the first spouse dies. A trustee manages the Bypass Trust, but the surviving spouse can receive income from it. No estate taxes are due when the surviving spouse dies because he or she never legally owned the trust's assets. That leaves more money in the trust for the final beneficiaries named by the first spouse in the original trust document.

Child's Trust. You can leave assets to a minor child by establishing a Child's Trust in your will or living trust. You name a trustee to manage the assets for your child, and you specify the age at which your child receives the property outright. If a Child's Trust is established as part of a living trust, the assets avoid probate. But if a will is used, the assets must go through probate.

Uniform Transfer to Minors Act (UTMA). In most states you can also use an UTMA to leave assets to your child. The person who manages your child's assets is called the custodian. Your child receives the property outright at the age of majority, which is either 18 or 21, depending on the state. (For more information see Chapter 6.)

Special Needs Trust. If you're the official guardian of a child, parent, sibling, or anyone with special needs, you may want to establish a Special Needs Trust. You can place assets in a property control trust, and name a trustee to gauge the beneficiary's needs and decide how and when to spend the money.

Charitable Trusts. Charitable Remainder Trusts and Charitable Lead Trusts provide income to you or your beneficiaries while making a gift to a charity. These trusts are irrevocable and can only be established for IRS-approved, tax-exempt charities.

With a Charitable Remainder Trust the charity receives the donated assets after you die. But in the interim, one or more beneficiaries, including yourself if you choose, receive a set payment from the trust or a set percentage of the trust's assets. You get an income tax deduction the year of the donation. And after your death, the assets you donated aren't included in your taxable estate.

A Charitable Lead Trust is the reverse of a Charitable Remainder Trust. With a Charitable Lead Trust, the income from the trust's assets is given to the charity for a set period of time. Once the period ends, the trust's assets come back to you or someone you've named as beneficiary. There are fewer estate tax benefits with this type of trust because the only thing that's deducted from your estate is the income the charity receives over time.

Life Insurance Trust. Life insurance proceeds paid to your beneficiaries are free from income taxes. But the death benefits on your policies are included in your estate and are subject to estate taxes. You can reduce these taxes by transferring ownership of a life insurance policy to a Life Insurance Trust.

Under IRS rules, the transfer of ownership to a Life Insurance Trust must be made at least three years before you die. Future premium payments can be made by giving the money directly to the policy's beneficiaries and having them make the payments. This is what lawyers call a Crummey Trust provision.

 Take special care if you own a family business.

Many Latinos own businesses they'd like to pass on to their families. There are many strategies you can use to do so and reduce estate and gift taxes. Because of the complexity involved, we recommend getting advice from an estate planning professional who specializes in small businesses. But here are some things to consider:

Estate tax exemption. Small businesses and family farms are eligible for a $1.3 million federal estate tax exemption. Eligible businesses must be 50 percent owned by the decedent and members of his or her family, 70 percent family-owned in the case of a two-family business, and 90 percent family-owned in the case of a three-family business. The beneficiaries must keep the business for at least ten years. If the business is sold before the seventh year, the full value of the exemption becomes taxable. If it's sold in the seventh year or after, the full value of the exemption drops by 20 percent annually through the tenth year.

Buy-sell agreement. A buy-sell agreement is a contract where one party agrees to buy ownership shares in a business at a pre-determined price. This prohibits the business from being sold to an outsider after you die, ensures a fair price for the shares, and helps with the appraisal of the business for estate tax purposes.

Family limited partnership. You can transfer assets into a family limited partnership, and retain substantial control by serving as the general partner. Typically, parents contribute the assets, and give their children shares of the partnership. The partnership shares are typically bought at a discount. Because the shares are purchased and not given away, they aren't subject to gift taxes. The IRS has strict rules that must be met for a family limited partnership to be valid, however, so check with a lawyer before establishing one.

Section 303 Redemptions. If you die and more than 35 percent of the value of your estate is comprised of your business, your heirs can redeem stock to pay for taxes and estate administration expenses. But the distribution won't be taxed as ordinary income.

 Be aware of special estate tax rules if one spouse is a non-U.S. citizen.

The United States taxes non-U.S. citizens based on whether or not they're U.S. residents. However, U.S. residency for estate and gift tax purposes differs from U.S. residency for income tax purposes (For more information about income tax residency see Chapter 9.)

Residency for estate tax purposes is based on whether the non-U.S. citizen has established the United States as his or her domicile. The IRS looks at where your primary home is located and what kind of social, economic and family ties you have in the United States, among other things.

No marital deduction is allowed from one spouse who is a U.S. citizen to another spouse who isn't a U.S. citizen. Of course, if your estate is worth less than $650,000, you won't owe any gift or estate taxes anyway. But if the estate is worth more than $650,000, there are other ways to reduce estate taxes:

Qualified Domestic Trust (QDOT). With this type of trust, no estate tax is assessed on the property in the trust when the citizen spouse dies. The non-citizen spouse receives all income from the trust during his or her lifetime. But estate taxes must be paid when the non-U.S. citizen spouse dies.

Citizenship. A spouse who is a non-U.S. citizen is also entitled to the full marital deduction if he or she becomes a U.S. citizen before the deceased citizen spouse's estate tax return is filed, which is required nine months after death.

Inheritance. If you received foreign gifts worth more than $100,000 in 1998 (the amounts are adjusted for inflation every year, so check with the IRS for the most recent figure), you must report the full amount to the IRS as an inheritance to avoid taxes. Otherwise, Uncle Sam may presume it's taxable income. Also, the penalty for failure to provide this information to the IRS is 5 percent of the gift amount for each month the information isn't furnished up to 25 percent of the total gift.

Foreign tax credit. Foreign-owned assets are subject to estate taxes. However, a tax credit is allowed against your U.S. estate tax for any death taxes paid to a foreign country.

Joint ownership. If a married couple—one a U.S. citizen and the other a non-U.S. citizen—own assets jointly, then all of those assets will be considered to be part of the citizen spouse's estate for tax purposes instead of just 50 percent of the assets.

Tax-free gifts. Any U.S. citizen who's married to a non-U.S. citizen can give the non-citizen spouse up to $100,000 a year without having to pay gift taxes.

ACCIÓN To obtain IRS Publication 519, *U.S. Tax Guide for Aliens*, call the IRS at 800-TAX-FORM.

 Consider pre-arranging your funeral.

Most of us don't want to think about our own deaths, let alone the death of a spouse, parent, or child. But making funeral arrangements in advance, or at least knowing where to go in an emergency, can save you and your loved ones much time, stress and money.

The average funeral cost $4,782 in 1996, not counting the vault, cemetery plot, monument or marker, flowers, burial clothing, or newspaper notices, according to the most recent figures available from the National Funeral Directors Association. These prices are rising an average of 5 percent a year. (See page 232 for a list of average funeral expenses.)

The earlier you talk about funeral planning, the better. You'll be able to comparison shop at your leisure and think about what you want, what you don't want, how much you want to spend, and which mortuary to use. You can get prices on your own, but the easiest thing may be to rely on a memorial society.

Memorial societies are nonprofit groups that conduct price surveys and negotiate inexpensive, high-quality funeral and cremation services for members. Today, there are about 125 memorial societies across the United States, and one-time membership costs range from $5 to $25. A few memorial societies accept "at-death" memberships if you have a sudden death in the family.

FUNERAL COSTS

Average price ranges* for goods and services provided by funeral homes:

SERVICE	LOWER RANGE	UPPER RANGE
Non-declinable professional services**	$863.99	$1,194.36
Embalming	$315	$415.54
Other preparation (cosmetology, hairdressing, casketing)	$103.75	$147.86
Visitation/viewing	$175.22	$362.51
Funeral at funeral home	$274.65	$357.17
Memorial service	$291.64	$382.61
Graveside service	$173.75	$345.34
Transfer of remains to funeral home	$115	$142.30
Hearse (local)	$135	$170.62
Limousine (local)	$88.15	$157.65
Service car/van	$60	$95.39
Acknowledgement cards	$9.67	$35.50
Direct cremation, container from funeral home	$1,060	$1,448.62
Direct cremation, container provided by family	$980.44	$1,335.84
Immediate burial, container or urn from funeral home	$1,244.92	$1,824.84
Immediate burial, container provided by family	$1,081.85	$1,470.06
Cloth-covered wood casket	$564.07	$650.64
18-gauge steel casket with sealer, velvet interior	$1,925.69	$2,522.22
Select hardwood casket, crepe interior	$1,972.22	$3,046.65
Two-piece concrete burial container for casket	$386.25	$584.66
Concrete vault with non-metallic liner	$607.67	$963.19

* Price ranges as of January 1997, the most recent figures available.
** Includes overhead and fees for planning funerals and gathering information for death certificates.

Memorial societies, which have been around since the 1930s, also make referrals to businesses offering price breaks on options such as viewing, memorial services, scattering of ashes, flowers, monuments, and cemetery plots. The savings that can be obtained by joining a memorial society can add up to hundreds, even thousands, of dollars.

There are two basic options for funerals: burial or cremation. Full-service burials or cremations typically include a funeral and a viewing. Direct burials or cremations have no viewing, although family and friends can arrange memorial services on their own. (Check with your church to find out what its policy is with regards to cremation.)

The costs of these services vary widely, which is why it pays to shop around. Buying a casket or urn from a discount outlet, for instance, can reduce costs by as much as 50 percent. But it's also important to know your rights as a consumer. Under the "funeral trade" rule, funeral directors are required to give you an itemized price list for all goods and services both in person or over the telephone.

The list includes everything from embalming (which is almost never required, by the way) and hearse services to nondeclinable fees. Nondeclinable fees are overhead and the time it takes to plan a funeral and gather information for the death certificate.

The funeral rule was created in response to complaints by consumers who were being pressured to buy expensive "package deals" they didn't want. Unscrupulous undertakers, for instance, will refer to low-cost items as "welfare caskets" or tout caskets with expensive, unnecessary seals.

A growing number of people are bypassing expensive, full-blown funerals and caring for their own dead by washing and dressing the body, setting up a viewing at home, and handling the paperwork themselves. This is the way it's done in many parts of the world, including Latin America, and there's no reason it can't be done here. For more information, contact the Natural Death Care Project.

 Avoid pre-paying for a funeral.

Pre-arranging your funeral is a good idea; pre-paying for it isn't. *Note bien la diferencia.* Funeral directors claim that pre-paying "locks in" today's prices.

The problem is that the funeral home you sign the contract with may not be around when you die, it may be sold to another owner who won't honor the agreement, your funds may be nonrefundable, or you may be penalized if you withdraw or transfer funds.

Avoid paying by installment, because you'll be charged interest. Remember, funeral costs are rising an average of about 5 percent annually. If you take the money you would have used to pre-pay a funeral and invest it instead, you can earn a return higher than 5 percent.

Also, prepaid funeral costs aren't tax deductible on your income tax return (although they're tax deductible from estate taxes if they're paid within nine months of death). If you're young, the money would probably be better used to pay off high-interest credit card debt or to save for retirement.

There are many other ways to make sure you have enough money to pay for a burial or cremation. You can put money aside in a payable-on-death bank account, for example, and specify that it's to be used for funeral expenses only. You can also use proceeds from a life insurance policy.

But if you use a payable-on-death account or a life insurance policy, never name the funeral home as the beneficiary. If you do, chances are the funeral home will use the entire amount for the funeral, leaving nothing for your family. Keep the money in your estate's control by naming a trusted family member, friend or executor as beneficiary.

ACCIÓN To locate the memorial society nearest you call the Funeral and Memorial Societies of America at 800-458-5563, or go to www.funerals.org/famsa. To contact the Natural Death Care Project, send a self-addressed, stamped envelope to P.O. Box 1721, Sebastopol, CA 95473. For more information about funerals, call the AARP at 800-424-3410, or the National Funeral Directors Association at 800-228-6332. For free pamphlets on cremation send a self-addressed, stamped envelope (77 cents postage) to the Cremation Association of North America, 401 N. Michigan Ave., Chicago, IL 60611.

 Keep all your estate and funeral planning information in one place.

The death or serious illness of a loved one is always devastating. But it's even worse for those left behind if they have to scramble to gather the necessary paperwork and information. If you've gone to the trouble of planning your estate and funeral, keep a well-organized set of personal and financial records.

A so-called personal record keeper isn't a legal document. It's simply information put together in a loose-leaf binder or computer software program that's designed to tell your beneficiaries where to find everything from your medical record, will, and tax returns to your doctor, lawyer, and financial planner.

You can probably compile everything yourself. But if you're a procrastinator, or freeze when looking at a blank piece of paper or computer screen, a book or software program that prompts you to answer specific questions can make the process easier.

You can create your own personal record keeper with a three-ring binder or in your computer by creating different "chapters" such as personal and family information, accountants and attorneys, financial advisers, financial institutions, income, insurance, investments, loans, philanthropy, and miscellaneous.

Each chapter should have detailed information. For example, under personal and family information include the names, telephone numbers, and addresses of immediate family, friends, other relatives and religious leaders you want contacted when you die or become incapacitated.

Under financial institutions, list your safe deposit boxes, savings and checking accounts, certificates of deposit, money market funds, and individual retirement accounts (IRAs). The miscellaneous chapter is where you can put your letter of instruction, your computer password, and the combination to your safe.

Keep a copy of your personal record keeper in a locked drawer or filing cabinet at home or at work, on a bookshelf where burglars are unlikely to look, or perhaps with a trusted friend and relative. For security's sake, be sure that only a few people know where to find all the copies.

A personal record keeper can eliminate the need to hire a private fiduciary to investigate your personal finances if you die or become incapacitated, which can cost your estate thousands of dollars.

ACCIÓN There are many good sources for personal record keepers. Nolo Press at 800-992-6656 offers a software program called Personal Record Keeper 4.0 for Windows. Active Insights at 800-222-9125 produces *The Beneficiary Book* in book form and as a Windows version software program.

 Don't keep important papers in your safe deposit box unless it's held jointly. And even then, be careful.

Banks must freeze assets, including a safe deposit box, and await orders from your executor, if the safe deposit box is held in your name only. That means the safe deposit box won't be opened until the executor, the IRS, your attorney, and a representative from the state banking commission can meet. Depending on the state you live in, this may not apply if the safe deposit box is held jointly.

❑ You may be able to avoid probate with "joint ownership of assets with rights of survivorship," affidavits, or simplified court procedures.

❑ Consider a living trust to avoid probate, but only after consulting a financial planner and attorney.

❑ Write a will. Use a lawyer, or at least have your will reviewed by a lawyer.

❑ Be sure you leave enough cash to pay for the immediate living expenses of your survivors, and to cover other bills.

❑ Get a living will, and durable powers of attorney for finances and medical care.

❑ Take advantage of deductions and make gifts to reduce the size of your taxable estate.

❑ Consider different types of trusts to help reduce or defer estate taxes.

❑ Understand special estate tax rules for non-U.S. citizens.

❏ Consider pre-arranging, but not pre-paying, your funeral.
❏ Keep all your estate and funeral planning information in a safe, accessible place.

ADDITIONAL RESOURCES

Recommended Books

A Legal Guide for Lesbian and Gay Couples, by Hayden Curry, Denis Clifford, and Robin Leonard (Berkeley: Nolo Press, 1996; 10th edition, March 1999).

Caring for the Dead: Your Final Act of Love, by Lisa Carlson (Hinesberg, Vermont: Upper Access Book Publishers, 1998).

8 Ways to Avoid Probate: Quick and Easy Ways to Save Your Family Thousands of Dollars, by Mary Randolph (Berkeley: Nolo Press, 1996).

How to Settle an Estate: A Manual for Executors and Trustees, by Charles K. Plotnick and Stephan R. Leimberg (New York: Penguin, 1998).

Make Your Own Living Trust, by Denis Clifford (Berkeley: Nolo Press, 1998).

Nolo's Will Book, by Denis Clifford (Berkeley: Nolo Press, 1997).

Plan Your Estate: Absolutely Everything You Need to Know to Protect Your Loved Ones, by Denis Clifford and Cora Jordan (Berkeley: Nolo Press, 1998).

Staying Wealthy: Strategies for Protecting Your Assets, by Brian H. Breuel (Princeton, New Jersey: Bloomberg Press, 1998).

The Complete Book of Trusts, by Martin M. Schenkman (New York: John Wiley & Sons, 1997).

The Financial Power of Attorney Workbook, by Shae Irving (Berkeley: Nolo Press, 1998).

The Inheritor's Handbook: A Definitive Guide for Beneficiaries, by Dan Rottenberg (Princeton, New Jersey: Bloomberg Press, 1998).

The Living Together Kit: A Legal Guide for Unmarried Couples, by Toni Ihara and Ralph Warner (Berkeley: Nolo Press, 1997; 9th edition, April 1999).

v

CHAPTER 9

Taxes

"HE WHO ASKS A QUESTION DOES NOT ERR EASILY"   —MEXICO

WHEN MIGUEL NEEDED HELP PREPARING HIS TAX RETURN, HE WENT TO one of the many *notarios públicos* in his Los Angeles neighborhood. The *notario* told the Mexican-born musician that he could deduct the $10,000 he'd spent on a demo tape to send to record companies.

The *notario* was half right. While the expenses were tax deductible, they could only be taken over four years—not all in the same year. The reason? It was considered a start-up business, but it had not yet generated any income. The mistake prompted the Internal Revenue Service (IRS) to launch an audit *(auditoría)*, an in-depth investigation of Miguel's return.

Miguel ended up paying a Certified Public Accountant (CPA) to defend him before the IRS. The CPA successfully argued that he got bad advice, but Miguel was still assessed back taxes, interest, and other penalties. "It cost me a lot of time, sleep, and money," he says.

There's a lot of confusion about *notarios* in the Latino community. *Notarios* aren't necessarily trained to prepare tax returns or provide investment advice, although they often do. Their only legitimate function is to serve as witnesses on legal documents.

It's easy to see why some of us turn to *notarios*. In much of Latin America, a *notario* is often an attorney. In addition, neighborhood *notarios* tend to speak Spanish and work long hours, making it easy and less intimidating for consumers to come in and seek advice.

The problem is that many *notarios* are too busy to keep up to date on tax laws. Some *notarios* sell clothes and work as travel agents in addition to offering tax preparation. Others are available only during tax season.

A true tax specialist, whether it's a tax attorney, a CPA, an Enrolled Agent, or an accredited tax preparer or tax adviser, can properly prepare our returns, help us legally minimize our tax bill, and educate us about the tax process. Such a professional is also available for consultation throughout the year.

Although the U.S. Tax Code is incredibly complicated, the concept is pretty simple. *Al Tío Sam, siempre se le paga.* Our taxes are used to pay for services and benefits ranging from public education to Social Security. How much tax we pay is based primarily on our income. The higher our income, the more tax we pay.

We're required to file a return to help the government determine if we've paid our fair share of taxes. If we underpaid, we owe the government money. If we overpaid, we're entitled to a tax refund. Failure to file a tax return can result in criminal and civil penalties.

There are several reasons why Latinos need to file returns correctly and on time. If we're immigrants who plan to apply for U.S. citizenship someday, one thing the Immigration and Naturalization Service (INS) may ask for is our tax returns. We also want to be sure we're getting properly credited for the Social Security taxes that are being withheld from our paychecks. Our future old age benefits will be based, in part, on the amount of money we've contributed over the years.

We've tried our best to include up-to-date tax information. But tax laws are complex and constantly changing. And there are always exceptions to various rules. *Así es la vida, y así son los impuestos.* Unless you have a very basic return, or feel confident doing your own taxes, we recommend getting advice from a tax professional.

Learn some key tax terms.

IRS publication 850, *English-Spanish Glossary of Words and Phrases Used in Publications Issued by the IRS,* can help you understand some key tax terms. For a copy call 800-TAX-FORM. Here's a quick review:

Deductions. These are expenses that can be subtracted from your income. Lowering your income lowers the amount of income tax you must pay. There are two types of deductions: standard and itemized.

The standard deduction *(deducción fija)* is a flat deduction based on your filing status (single, married filing jointly, married filing separately, head of household, or qualifying widow or widower with dependent child). An itemized deduction *(deducción detallada)* is a specific expense such as mortgage interest or state and local taxes. Itemizing may save you more money than taking the standard deduction.

For 1999 the standard deduction is $4,300 for a single person; $7,200 for a married couple filing jointly and qualifying widow or widower; $3,600 for a married couple filing separately; and $6,350 for a head of household.

Exemptions. This is an amount of money you can subtract on your tax return. Each exemption you claim reduces your taxable income by $2,650. There are two kinds of exemptions: personal exemptions *(exención personal)* and exemptions for dependents *(exenciones para dependientes).*

You can take a personal exemption for yourself unless someone else claims you as a dependent. Your spouse also gets a personal exemption as long as you file a joint return, and he or she can't be claimed as a dependent by someone else.

An exemption for a dependent is allowed if you provide more than half of his or her support for the year. The dependent must also be a member of your household, a relative, a U.S. citizen, a U.S. resident alien, a Canadian resident, a Mexican resident, or an adopted child.

An adopted child doesn't have to be a U.S. citizen, but has to have lived with you all year. A child who isn't a U.S. citizen and lives in a foreign country other than Canada or Mexico can't be claimed as a dependent— neither can married dependents who file jointly unless they meet all other requirements.

There's also a gross income test for dependency. That means to qualify as a dependent, a person's gross income must be less than $2,650 for the calendar year. However, a child's gross income can be $2,650 or more if he or she was either age 19 at the end of the year, or under age 24 at the end of the year and was a student.

Tax credit. This is a dollar-for-dollar reduction of your tax bill. Say you owe $2,500 in taxes. If you have a $1,000 credit, then you pay just $1,500. In general, tax credits are more valuable to the average taxpayer than deductions.

The amount owed with a deduction is much higher: the actual amount saved on your tax bill with a deduction is equal to the amount of your deduction multiplied by your tax bracket (*clasificación contributiva*). For example, if you reduce your taxable income with a $1,000 deduction, and you're in the 33 percent tax bracket, your saving is $330 ($1,000 x .33 = $330).

That means it takes a bigger deduction to give you the same amount of savings you'd get with a straight credit. Another benefit of tax credits is that they're easier to get because you don't have to itemize on your return to use them. Tax credits are discussed in detail later in this chapter.

Phase-outs. Most deductions, exemptions, and tax credits phase out, or decrease, when your adjusted gross income (AGI) reaches a certain level. After your AGI exceeds a certain level, they're often eliminated altogether.

Gross income. This is your total taxable income before you subtract any adjustments, deductions, and exemptions.

Net income. This is the income left after you subtract all adjustments, deductions, and exemptions.

Adjusted gross income (AGI). This consists of all your income including wages, salaries, tips, and taxable interest, minus allowable adjustments. It's calculated before subtracting deductions and exemptions.

Taxable income. Your taxable income is the amount of income that you get taxed on. It's calculated by subtracting deductions and exemptions from your AGI.

Tax bracket. A tax bracket is a range of income levels that are grouped together, each with its own tax rate. There are five tax brackets and rates: 15 percent, 28 percent, 31 percent, 36 percent, and 39.6 percent. (See the chart at right for 1998 tax brackets/rates.)

1999 Federal Income Tax Rate Schedules

STATUS	TAXABLE INCOME (BRACKET)	TAX RATE
Single	0 – $25,750	15%
	$25,750 – $62,450	28%
	$62,450 – $130,250	31%
	$130,250 – $283,150	36%
	Over $283,150	39.6%
Married Couples Filing Jointly or Qualifying Widow or Widower	0 – $43,050	15%
	$43,050 – $104,050	28%
	$104,050 – $158,550	31%
	$158,550 – $283,150	36%
	Over $283,150	39.6%
Married Couples Filing Separately	0 – $21,525	15%
	$21,525 – $52,025	28%
	$52,025 – $79,275	31%
	$79,275 – $141,575	36%
	Over $141,575	39.6%
Head of Household	0 – $34,550	15%
	$34,550 – $89,150	28%
	$89,150 – $144,400	31%
	$144,400 – $283,150	36%
	Over $283,150	39.6%

Tax rates. There are two types: marginal and effective. If you're single and your annual income for 1999 is $25,750 then your tax rate is 15 percent. But if your annual income is $30,000, then the first $25,750 will be taxed at 15 percent, and the remaining $4,250 will be taxed at 28 percent. This is your marginal tax rate *(tasa impositiva marginal)*.

FILING REQUIREMENTS*

Generally, your filing status for the entire year is your status on December 31.

STATUS	AGE	YOU MUST FILE IF YOUR GROSS INCOME EXCEEDS
Single	Under 65	$6,800
	65 or older	$7,800
Married filing jointly	Both under 65	$12,200
	One spouse 65 or older	$13,000
	Both spouses 65 or older	$13,800
Married filing separately	Any age	$2,650
Head of household	Under 65	$8,700
	65 or older	$9,700
Qualifying widow/ widower	Under 65	$9,550
With dependent child	65 or older	$10,350

*The amounts listed are for 1998, the latest available at press time. The IRS is scheduled to release 1999 filing requirements in October 1999.

Your effective tax rate is a blended, or weighted, average of the tax rates that apply to your income. Using the example above, a blended average for tax on income of $30,000 gives you an effective tax rate of about 17 percent.

 Find out if you need to file a return.

Is everyone required to file a tax return? No. Filing requirements are generally based on your income, age, and filing status. (For filing requirements, see the box at left.)

Single. You're unmarried, you're legally separated from your spouse, or are divorced from your spouse. If you're single and have dependents, you may also be able to file as head of household, which gives you a more advantageous tax rate and standard deductions.

Head of household. You're unmarried or considered unmarried, and pay more than half the cost of a home for you and a qualifying person. You're considered unmarried if you have lived apart from your spouse for the last six months of the year.

A qualifying person (*persona cualificada*) is someone who is either claimed as a dependent or related by blood, and has lived with you for more than six months. There are two exceptions. First, if your parent doesn't live with you, but you pay more than half the cost of the parent's main home for the entire year. Second, if the qualifying person dies, you can still qualify as head of household if you paid more than half the cost of the home while the person was alive.

Married filing jointly. You can file a joint return if you're married, if you're spouse died during the year, if you're living together in a common-law marriage, and if you're living apart but not legally separated or divorced. If one spouse is a nonresident alien at any time during the year, a joint return can be filed only if both parties agree to be taxed on their worldwide income.

Married filing separately. If you're eligible to file jointly, you can choose to file separately. Most couples choose this option if they're thinking of separating or believe they can save on taxes (in some cases, money can be saved if one spouse has larger itemized deductions and smaller income than the other).

But there are disadvantages to filing separately. You can't claim a deduction on an Individual Retirement Account (IRA) on behalf of the non-working spouse, and you may not be able to claim tax credits for child and dependent care, among other things.

Qualifying widow or widower with dependent child. If your spouse died last year or the year before, you're entitled to use a joint return tax rate and standard deduction if you were entitled to file a joint return the year your spouse died; you did not remarry this year; you have a dependent child; and you paid more than half the cost of keeping up the home during the entire part of the year your spouse was alive.

For more information on filing status for citizens and non-citizens read IRS Publication 501, *Exemptions, Standard Deduction, and Filing Information*, and IRS Publication 519, *U.S. Tax Guide for Aliens*.

 Use the correct form to file your return.

There are three federal tax forms: the 1040EZ, the 1040A, and the 1040. Which one you use depends on your filing status, income, and whether or not you plan to itemize or claim any tax credits.

1040EZ. This is the simplest form to fill out. Generally, it's for single people, or couples filing jointly, with total taxable income not exceeding $50,000, and less than $400 in taxable interest. You can't itemize your deductions, claim dependents, or take the additional standard deduction for being blind or age 65 or older, so use this form if you're better off taking the standard deduction.

1040A. This form is also pretty simple. As with the 1040EZ, it's intended for singles or couples filing jointly with total taxable income less than $50,000 but with more than $400 in taxable interest. You can't itemize, but you can deduct your IRA contribution and the child or dependent care credit, among others.

1040. This form is required if your income is more than $50,000 and you receive income from rent or capital gains. It should also be used if you think you'll be better off with itemized deductions than with the standard deduction. In order to itemize charitable contributions or business expenses, you'll need to fill out an additional form called Schedule A.

State taxes. Most states also require that you file a personal income tax return. Nine states—Alaska, Florida, Nevada, New Hampshire, Texas, South Dakota, Tennessee, Washington, and Wyoming—don't have any personal income tax on wages (although some states like New Hampshire and Tennessee tax income from interest and dividends). Check with state officials to find out what, if any, return is required. (For a list of where to call for state tax forms, see pages 248–49.)

Tax forms should be mailed to you if you previously filed a return. You can also get federal forms directly from the IRS by mail, fax, or via the Internet, or by walking into a local IRS office or Tax Assistance Center.

Some libraries and post offices also provide forms, and 24-hour copy centers may have tax forms that you can copy.

ACCIÓN To obtain federal income tax forms by mail, call the IRS at 800-TAX-FORM. To obtain forms by Tele-Fax call 703-368-9694 (you must phone directly from a fax machine). To download forms via the Internet go to www.irs.ustreas.gov/. Tax forms and publications from prior years are available on CD-ROM for $17 plus postage by calling Government Printing Office at 202-512-1800.

 Obtain either a Social Security Number or an Individual Taxpayer Identification Number.

All U.S. citizens or legal immigrants who hold jobs are required to have valid Social Security numbers provided by the Social Security Administration (SSA), as are people who are claimed as dependents on tax returns.

To obtain a Social Security number, you need to fill out an application and provide a birth certificate along with another form of identification. This ID can be a driver's license, school records, military records, medical records, a passport, a marriage or divorce record, an insurance policy, a government employee ID card, a health insurance card, hospital records, adoption records, a record of baptism, or documents from the Immigration and Naturalization Service (INS).

These documents must be originals or copies certified by the county clerk or other official who keeps the record. Certified copies can be sent in the mail. Originals should be taken to your local Social Security office in person. (If you're aged 18 or older and applying for your first Social Security number, you're required to apply in person, anyway.)

Undocumented workers with jobs need a valid Individual Taxpayer Identification Number (ITIN) instead of a Social Security number. And no matter what your citizenship status, you'll need an Employer Identification Number (EIN), which is your Social Security number, if you're a sole proprietor, own your own business, or are self-employed.

You'll need to fill out IRS form SS-4 to get an EIN, and IRS Form W-7 to get an ITIN. Original or certified copies of documents such as a driver's

STATE TAX HELPLINES

For state tax help, use the following numbers:

STATE	FORMS	INFORMATION
Alabama	334-242-9681	334-242-1099
*Alaska	907-465-2320	907-465-2320
Arizona	602-542-4260	602-255-3381
Arkansas	501-682-7255	501-682-7250
California	800-852-5711	800-338-0505)
Colorado	303-232-2414	303-232-2414
Connecticut	860-297-5650	860-297-5650
Delaware	302-577-3310	302-577-3300
District of Columbia	202-727-6170	202-727-6104
*Florida	904-488-6800	904-488-6800
Georgia	404-656-4293	404-656-4071
Hawaii	800-222-7572	800-222-3229
Idaho	208-334-7660	208-334-7660
Ilinois	800-356-6302	800-732-8866
Indiana	317-486-5103	317-232-2240
Iowa	515-281-7239	515-281-3114
Kansas	913-296-4937	913-296-0222
Kentucky	502-564-3658	502-564-3028
Louisiana	504-925-7537	504-925-4611
Maine	207-624-7894	207-626-8475
Maryland	410-974-3981	800-638-2937
Massachusetts	617-887-MDOR	617-887-MDOR
Michigan	800-367-6263	517-373-3200
Minnesota	800-657-3676	800-652-9094
Mississippi	601-923-7000	601-923-7000
Missouri	573-751-4695	573-751-4450
Montana	406-444-0290	406-444-2837
Nebraska	800-742-7474	800-742-7474
*Nevada	702-687-4892	702-687-4892

**New Hampshire	603-271-2192	603-271-2186
New Jersey	609-292-7613	609-588-2200
New Mexico	505-827-2206	505-827-0700
New York City	718-935-6739	718-935-6000
New York State	518-485-6800	800-225-5829
North Carolina	919-715-0397	919-733-0300
North Dakota	701-328-3017	701-328-3450
Ohio	614-846-6712	614-846-6712
Oklahoma	405-521-3108	405-521-3125
Oregon	503-378-4988	503-378-4988
Pennsylvania	888-728-2937	888-728-2937
Puerto Rico	787-721-2020	809-721-2020
Rhode Island	401-222-1111	401-222-3911
South Carolina	803-898-5599	803-898-5761
*South Dakota	605-773-3311	605-773-3311
**Tennessee	615-741-4466	615-741-2594
*Texas	512-463-4600	512-463-4600
Utah	801-297-6700	801-297-2200
Vermont	802-828-2515	802-828-2501
Virginia	804-367-8205	804-367-8031
*Washington	360-786-6100	800-647-7706
West Virginia	304-344-2068	304-558-3333
Wisconsin	608-266-1961	608-266-2486
*Wyoming	307-777-5287	307-777-7722

* These states have no state personal income tax (although some charge taxes on dividends from stocks and bonds). Call these numbers for information about all other types of taxes as well.

** New Hampshire and Tennessee require the filing of an individual tax return if interest and/or dividend income over a certain amount (which depends on the state you live in and your filing status) was received during the tax year.

license, passport, birth certificate, or INS papers must also be provided by mail or in person at your local IRS office.

The IRS can be avoided by using Certifying Acceptance Agents, many of whom are tax preparers. These agents have been authorized by the IRS to help non-U.S. citizens obtain EIN and ITIN numbers by forwarding completed W-7 forms, reviewing documentation, and certifying that the materials are authentic, complete, and accurate.

The IRS strongly encourages taxpayers to file for a Social Security, ITIN, or EIN. The IRS and the INS are two completely separate agencies that don't share information with one another. According to the IRS, that means there's no need to worry that you'll be reported to the INS if you're an undocumented worker.

ACCIÓN To apply for a Social Security number, call the SSA at 800-772-1213, or download the form via the Web site at www.ssa.gov/. To get an ITIN or EIN call the IRS at 800-TAX-FORM, or download the form from the Web site at www.irs.ustreas.gov/. To find a Certifying Acceptance Agent call your local IRS office, or ask your tax practitioner for a referral.

 Use what the U.S. government recognizes as your correct name on your return.

Latinos sometimes get confused over which name to use on a tax return. In Latin America, for example, it's common to use your mother's maiden name at the end of your last name. (Using this style, our names would be Laura Castañeda de Padilla and Laura Castellanos del Valle.)

¡Cuidado! In the United States you must use your father's surname or your married surname only, especially on your tax return. And you need to be consistent. Using your last name one year, and your last name along with your mother's maiden name the year after, can cause a lot of confusion.

Filing a return with the wrong name can lead to big problems. First, the IRS may think you haven't filed all the returns you should have over the years. Second, the money that's withheld from your paycheck for Social Security and other benefits could mistakenly be credited to another person.

Understand the kind of tax help that's available, where to find it, and what it costs.

Some of us lack the time, discipline, and desire (not to mention the English-language ability) necessary to prepare our own returns and learn about all the new tax law changes that may have kicked in over the past year. Fortunately, there are plenty of tax professionals who can help. Where you go depends on the complexity of your tax situation and what you can afford. Here are the four main types of tax practitioners:

Tax attorneys. Tax attorneys are typically the most expensive tax practitioners by far, charging hundreds of dollars per hour. Many don't even deal with tax returns. Instead, they focus on court cases or other complicated legal issues such as the purchase or sale of a business.

Certified Public Accountants. CPAs must typically complete at least 150 hours of study in accounting at a college or university, pass a professional qualifying exam, and in some states obtain a certain amount of professional work experience in accounting. They must also complete an average of 40 hours of continuing professional education every year.

CPA fees vary greatly, but generally they're less expensive than tax attorneys and more expensive than enrolled agents or tax preparers. CPAs are appropriate if your situation is complicated, if you own a business, or if you've had a major change such as a marriage, divorce, a death in the family, or retirement.

Before hiring a CPA, make sure he or she specializes in individual income tax returns (some CPAs handle business taxes only). Get referrals from friends, family, colleagues, and your state CPAs association, and check the Yellow Pages.

The American Institute of CPAs (AICPA) also provides referrals to CPAs, but only those who've earned a Personal Financial Specialist (PFS) designation, which means they can provide financial planning. The American Association of Hispanic CPAs (AAHCPA) can help you find a CPA who speaks Spanish.

Enrolled agents. EAs have been approved by the IRS to represent taxpayers in an audit. They must pass a tough two-day IRS exam on federal taxation, undergo a background check, and complete 72 hours of continuing

252 The Latino Guide to Personal Money Management

professional education every three years. Some people can become EAs after working for the IRS for at least five years.

Fees vary greatly, but they're typically less expensive than tax attorneys or CPAs. Depending on their experience, EAs are capable of handling complex tax returns or providing guidance if your financial situation has changed. And unlike tax attorneys or CPAs, EAs work exclusively in the field of taxation.

Tax preparers. Tax preparers tend to be the least expensive type of tax practitioners because they usually have less training than tax attorneys, CPAs, or EAs. In fact, there's no national standard for tax preparers. Consequently, it's best to use a tax preparer only if you've got a simple return.

If you use a tax preparer, find one who's been accredited. Accreditation is earned by completing a basic tax preparation course administered by the National Endowment for Financial Education, and completing 90 hours of continuing tax education every three years.

Only two states have taken steps to try to monitor tax preparers. California tax preparers must complete 60 hours of approved tax education before registering with the California Tax Education Council (CTEC), and 20 hours of continuing tax education each year. They must also provide clients with their CTEC certificate, the name of their bonding company, and their bond number.

Oregon has two licensing levels for tax preparers. The first is an apprentice level, which requires tax preparers to complete a tax course and pass an exam. The second is an expert level, which requires tax preparers to work for two years under supervision, and pass another exam.

ACCIÓN To find a CPA with a PFS designation, call the AICPA at 888-999-9256. To find a Spanish-speaking CPA, call the AAHCPAs at 659-965-0643. To find an EA, call the National Association of Enrolled Agents at 800-424-4339. To find an accredited tax preparer, call The Accreditation Council at 703-549-2228, ext. 1341. To check a California tax preparer's state registration status, call CTEC at 916-492-0457. To check an Oregon tax preparer's certification status, call the State Board of Tax Service Examiners at 503-378-4034.

Take advantage of free tax help if you've got a basic return.

Much free help is available from the IRS, volunteer programs, and Web sites. Many of these programs have Spanish-speaking volunteers, and the IRS provides some forms and publications in Spanish.

If you rely on free information to prepare your return, jot down the questions you asked, the answers you got, the name of the IRS employee you talked with, and the date of your conversation in case you're given incorrect advice. Here's a rundown of some key programs:

IRS. The IRS offers a toll-free tax information line, Tele-Tax (pre-recorded answers to frequently asked questions); TeleFax (a fax-on-demand system with answers to frequently asked questions); and information on its Web site. The agency also runs free walk-in Tax Assistance Centers that provide forms, publications and advice. Most states provide tax help lines as well. (See pages 248–49 for a list of state tax help lines.)

Volunteer Income Tax Assistance (VITA). The IRS runs VITA out of libraries, community centers, and churches. The program offers free help to low-income taxpayers, the disabled, and non-English-speaking taxpayers with simple tax returns. Many sites also offer free electronic filing.

Tax Counseling for the Elderly (TCE). This program provides free tax help to persons aged 60 or older by volunteers who are familiar with tax issues that are of importance to older people. Tax assistance is provided at locations such as retirement homes, senior citizen centers, or private homes.

AARP Tax-Aide. The Tax-Aide program offered by the American Association of Retired Persons (AARP) is part of the IRS' TCE program. Tax-Aide has more than 10,000 sites nationwide, some of which offering free electronic filing.

Student Tax Clinic Program (STCP). The STCP is staffed by law students and graduate accounting students who receive special permission to represent taxpayers before the IRS during an audit or appeal. It's designed to provide free tax counseling to taxpayers who wouldn't normally obtain counsel.

TAX WEB SITES

Deloitte & Touche Online	www.dtonline.com/
Ernst & Young LLP	www.ey.com/
Federation of Tax Administrators	www.taxadmin.org/
H&R Block	www.hrblock.com/
Internal Revenue Service (IRS)	www.irs.ustreas.gov/
International Tax Resources	www.taxsites.com/
	international.html
U.S. State Tax Resources	www.2best.com/
Tax Prophet	www.taxprophet.com/
Tax Web	www.taxweb.com/
1040.com	www.1040.com/

Software/Web sites. If you're comfortable doing your own taxes and using a computer, a software program can make preparing and filing your return fast and easy. They also help with record-keeping. But these programs don't offer legal advice or accept responsibility for mistakes other than calculation errors in the software. The three best programs are TurboTax, TaxCut, and Personal Tax Edge. You can also get lots of information and forms from the Web. (See the chart above for a list of tax Web sites.)

ACCIÓN To find the VITA, TCE, or STCP site nearest you, call the IRS at 800-829-1040, or the Taxpayer Education department of your local IRS office. To reach the IRS Tele-Tax number, call 800-829-4477. To reach the IRS Tele-Fax number, call 703-368-9694 (you must phone directly from a fax machine). To reach the IRS Web site, go to www.irs.ustreas.gov/. To find the AARP Tax-Aide site nearest you, call the AARP at 888-227-7669. You can also check the AARP Web site at www.aarp.org/tax-aide/home.htm

Don't procrastinate. Get your tax forms and publications, and find a tax professional, as early as possible.

Don't wait until the last minute to call the IRS for tax forms, publications, or basic tax questions. Chances are, you'll get a busy signal for hours on end. And even if you manage to get through to someone, the forms or publications may not get to you in time unless you get them via fax or the Internet.

Similarly, the closer it gets to April 15, the harder it is to find a tax professional who can squeeze you in unless you've been a client throughout the year. To beat the rush, call sometime during January or February to schedule an appointment.

 Keep good records.

If you want to make tax preparation easier, save money, and have ammunition in case you ever need to defend yourself against an IRS audit, keep good records. These records should be kept in a fire-resistant box or filing cabinet. How long you need to keep these records, however, isn't very clear cut.

Generally, the statute of limitations on IRS audits and assessments is three years after the original tax return is filed. But the IRS can go back six years if it suspects that you underreported your income by 25 percent or more, and indefinitely if it suspects fraud. We recommend keeping records at least four years, but preferably longer. Key records include:

W-2 forms. Your employer is required to send you a W-2 form by January 31 of each year. This form must be submitted with your tax return. It shows your gross income and how much tax was withheld over the year.

Paycheck stubs. Keep all your stubs for the year. They include the amount of money that was withheld for Social Security, federal, state and perhaps city taxes, health insurance, union dues, and 401(k) contributions.

Form 1099. This form records earned and unearned income from interest, dividends, or retirement plan distributions paid over the year. Paycheck stubs, W-2s, and 1099 forms should be checked against each other for name, Social Security number, and address discrepancies.

Other records to keep: investment-related documents from brokers, mutual funds and banks; tax returns; business-related expenses; records of charitable contributions; medical expenses; records of losses from accident, fire, natural disaster, theft, or vandalism; moving expenses; travel expenses; or any other records needed to substantiate amounts reported on your tax return.

 Understand your filing options.

To meet the IRS's "Timely Filing" requirement, your return must be postmarked by April 15 at the latest. You can file in many different ways nowadays, including mail (the old standby), over the telephone, electronically, or via computer.

Mail. If you send your return by mail, it must be postmarked by midnight April 15. If you're sending your return at the last minute, don't just drop it in a mailbox on the corner. Take it to a post office yourself (many post offices work extended hours during the tax season).

Alternate carriers and specialty types of mail delivery services can also be used to send your return to the IRS, including Airborne Express, DHL, Federal Express, and UPS. Just be aware that these services will cost you more than regular mail.

Under federal regulations aimed at fighting terrorism, your tax return must be given to a letter carrier or taken to a post office and handed to a clerk for mailing if it weighs 16 ounces or more and bears postage stamps. Otherwise, it will be returned to you.

Telefile. Millions of taxpayers each year use this IRS system to file their returns over the telephone. Telefile targets taxpayers who are eligible to file a 1040EZ form, are single or married filing jointly, have no dependents, filed a tax return for the previous year, and live at the same address from which they filed the previous year.

The advantage of Telefile is that once you file your return, you just push a button and you'll be given a receipt number to prove you made the deadline. But it's an "invitation-only" program, which means you can't participate unless the IRS sends you a Telefile tax package.

Electronic filing. Paid tax preparers such as H&R Block, Jackson-Hewitt, and many mom-and-pop stores can be used to send your return electronically over telephone lines. The preparer will ask you to sign Form 8453, which gives permission to file the return to the IRS Service Center. If the return doesn't get there due to a computer glitch, this form proves you filed on time. The advantage of electronic filing is that you'll get your tax refund earlier than you would if you used regular mail. The disadvantage is that it's expensive. (See the next *Consejo* on refund anticipation loans below.)

Computer filing. A growing number of commercial services let you file your return over the Internet from your home computer for around $10. What you're actually doing in most cases is sending your return to the commercial service, which sends it on to the IRS. After it gets your return, the IRS sends the commercial service an electronic acknowledgment, which is forwarded to you.

 Avoid refund anticipation loans.

Refund anticipation loans, commonly referred to as "rapid refunds" or "fast tax" services, aren't really refunds at all. They're short-term loans with astronomical interest rates offered by banks working with various tax preparation firms.

Banks will usually charge a flat fee to process a refund anticipation loan. These fees seem pretty small—until you calculate the annualized interest rate. For example, if you pay a $29 fee for a twenty-one-day refund anticipation loan of $1,300, that's the equivalent of paying interest of 39 percent per year. *Mal negocio.*

The best strategy, of course, is to avoid getting a refund altogether. Why? If you get a refund, you paid too much in taxes. Although you get back the excess money, the interest the government has been collecting on your money won't be passed on to you.

Try to break even by adjusting the withholding on your W-4 form, and funneling the extra money into a savings account or investment. Generally, you should increase the number of withholdings if you owe taxes, and decrease the number of withholdings if you expect a refund.

Determining your proper withholding isn't easy. If you're computer literate, a software program can help. A good tax practitioner can also do it for you. And IRS Publication 919, *Is My Withholding Correct?*, has a worksheet that can project your correct withholding for the year.

The earlier you file your return, the faster you'll get your refund. If you file in January, for example, you'll get your refund in about three weeks. If you wait until April 15, it can take up to eight weeks. But if you still haven't received your refund by May 31, the IRS must pay you interest.

You can also speed up your refund (and help the IRS reduce costly paperwork) by filing electronically and having the money directly deposited into your bank account. Be sure you or your tax preparer fill out the requested information (routing transit number, bank account number, account type) in the "Refund" area of the return.

ACCIÓN Check the status of your refund by calling the IRS automated refund information line at 800-829-4477.

 When filing your tax return, be sure you take all the deductions, exemptions, and credits you're eligible for.

There are many money-saving tax deductions, exemptions and credits that can help minimize your federal income tax bill. A tax professional will be familiar with all of them, and help you figure out which ones you're eligible for. For a good overview read IRS Publication 17, *Your Federal Income Tax.* Here's a brief review:

Earned income credit. If you have a low income you may be eligible for an earned income credit of as much as $3,656 (the larger your family, the bigger the credit). If the credit exceeds your tax bill, or you don't owe any tax, you'll get all or part of it back as a refund.

To qualify for the earned income credit, your income must be $25,760 or less if you have one dependent child; $29,290 or less if you have two or more children, and $9,770 if you don't have any children, are at between 25 and 65 years of age, and aren't being claimed as a dependent by anyone else.

Alternative minimum tax. At the other end of the spectrum, the government has a second federal tax system, known as the alternative minimum tax (AMT), to ensure that taxpayers who claim a lot of deductions and exemptions pay at least a minimum amount of taxes on their income.

The tax is calculated by refiguring taxable income and tax after eliminating and/or reducing tax deductions and exemptions known as "tax preference items." If the refigured tax results in alternative minimum tax, it must be paid in addition to the regular tax. For more information read IRS Form 6251, *Alternative Minimum Tax—Individuals.*

Adoption credit. You can claim a credit for qualified adoption expenses of up to $5,000 per child ($6,000 for a child with special needs). Credit for a foreign adoption is limited to $5,000 per child in all cases. Qualified adoption expenses include reasonable adoption fees, court costs and attorney's fees. For more information read IRS Publication 968, *Tax Benefits for Adoption.*

Child tax credit. You can claim a child tax credit of $500 per dependent child under the age of 17 every year, and $400 for those over 17. The credit starts phasing out when AGI exceeds $110,000 on a joint return, and $75,000 on an individual return.

Child and dependent care expenses credit. This credit is available if you pay someone to provide day care or household services for a dependent while you work. To be eligible, your dependents must be under age 13, or incapable of caring for themselves. You can claim a credit of $2,400 for one dependent, and $4,800 for more than one dependent. If you received any dependent care benefits from your employer you may be able to exclude all or part of it from your income. For more information read IRS Publication 503, *Child and Dependent Care Expenses.*

Education credit. The HOPE Scholarship credit lets you claim up to $1,500 per year of qualified tuition and expenses for the first two years of a student's education (100 percent of the first $1,000 and 50 percent of the second $1,000). The Lifetime Learning credit equals 20 percent of up to $5,000 in qualified tuition and expenses every year for a maximum of $1,000. The Lifetime Learning can be taken after the first two years of school. (See Chapter 6 for more information.)

State, local, and property taxes. These taxes are deductible in the year they're paid. If you live in a co-op, the property taxes will be paid as part of your monthly maintenance fee. Find out what your share of property taxes comes to because it may be deductible.

Mortgage interest. Home mortgage interest can be deducted in most cases. You may also be able to deduct points, the one-time fee you pay to a bank for the loan, in the year that you buy your home. If you live in a co-op, find out what your share of mortgage interest comes to, because it may be deductible.

House sale exclusion. When you sell your home, profits of up to $500,000 for married couples, and a $250,000 if you're single, are tax-free. To qualify for the exclusion you must own and live in the house for two of the five years prior to the sale. This tax break can be used an unlimited number of times, but only once every two years.

Charitable donations. You can deduct charitable contributions only if you itemize and the charity meets IRS requirements for tax-exempt organizations. The limit on charitable contributions that can be claimed as deductions are based on your adjusted gross income (AGI).

Be sure to get a receipt for any donation with a market value of $250 or more, and an independent appraisal for non-cash donations of $5,000 or more. Smaller cash contributions thrown in to a collection plate at church are deductible without receipts as long as you keep track of them, but it's always better to have a canceled check.

Cash donations aren't fully deductible if you get something in return. If, for instance, you pay $200 for a charity ball and the dinner is valued at $50, your deduction is limited to $150.

¿Y las loterías? Lottery tickets sold by tax-exempt organizations aren't deductible, although you can deduct the price of the tickets from your taxable winnings. *¡Buena suerte!*

If you give away assets that have appreciated in value, such as stock or land, you can take a deduction for the full market value without paying taxes on the gain. But there's one caveat: You must have held the asset for at least a year. If it was held less than a year, you can only deduct the asset's cost basis—the amount you originally invested—not the current market value.

Donations of used cars, computers, real estate, and publicly traded stocks, bonds, and mutual funds are usually valued at market prices on the day you make the transfer. Clothing is typically valued at between 10 and 20 percent of the original cost, depending on the condition of the items.

If you do volunteer work, you can deduct unreimbursed expenses such as telephone calls, stamps, stationery, and other materials, as well as 50 percent of meal expenses. When you drive your car in connection with a volunteer activity, you can take a deduction of 14 cents per mile, plus tolls and parking. Fares for public transportation can also be deducted.

The amount of your deduction for charitable contributions is limited to either 20 percent, 30 percent, or 50 percent of the value of the gift, depending on the type of property you give and the type of organization you give it to. For more information read IRS Publication 526, *Charitable Contributions.*

This publication also describes when you can deduct certain contributions to charitable organizations in Mexico. Typically, these charitable organizations must meet the same tests that qualify U.S. groups to receive deductible contributions, and you must have income from sources in Mexico.

Job-related expenses. You can deduct certain job-related expenses such as career counseling, employment agencies, resume printing and mailing costs, phone calls, and transportation if you're looking for a job in your current occupation, and the expenses exceed 2 percent of your adjusted gross income (AGI).

Moving expenses. Moving expenses are deductible if your move was made because you changed job locations. The new job site must be at least 50 miles farther from your former home than your previous job site. You must also have worked full time for at least 39 of the 52 weeks following the move.

Deductible expenses are limited to the cost of moving household goods and personal effects to your new home, and travel and lodging costs during the move. Reimbursed moving expenses are excluded from income; unreimbursed moving expenses are deductions in computing adjusted gross income (AGI)—not itemized deductions.

Medical expenses. Unreimbursed medical expenses that exceed 7.5 percent of your AGI are generally deductible. This includes out-of-pocket expenses for everything from insurance premiums, co-payments to doctors, birth control pills, and transportation needed to obtain medical care.

Household employees. If you pay annual cash wages of at least $1,100 a year to baby-sitters, gardeners, housekeepers, or nannies, you must withhold and pay Social Security and Medicare taxes. The taxes can be paid when you file your return in April.

If you're the employee, it's in your best interest to make sure these taxes get paid by you or your employer. If you want to become a U.S. citizen, evidence that you paid these taxes will count in your favor. And you'll be eligible for retirement and disability benefits. For more information read IRS Publication 926, *Household Employer's Tax Guide.*

Retirement plans. Contributions to many retirement plans such as 401(k)s, and Traditional, Roth and Education IRAs, Savings Incentive Match Plan for Employees (SIMPLE), or Simplified Employee Pensions (SEPs), are partially or fully deductible. (See Chapter 7 for more information on retirement plans.)

Social Security. If your adjusted gross income (AGI) plus one half of your Social Security benefits exceeds certain thresholds ($32,000 for couples filing jointly and $25,000 for individual returns), you may get taxed on up to 85 percent of your benefits. For more information read IRS Publication 915, *Social Security and Equivalent Railroad Retirement Benefits.*

Capital gains. Profits on the sale of assets that are held for at least 18 months prior to being sold are taxed at a top rate of 20 percent (10 percent if you're in the 15 percent tax bracket). Assets held between 12 and 18 months prior to being sold will be taxed at a maximum rate of 28 percent (15 percent if you're in the 15 percent bracket). And beginning in 2001, assets held for five years or longer will be taxed at a maximum rate of 18 percent (8 percent if you're in the 15 percent tax bracket).

Mutual funds. If you're thinking of buying a mutual fund outside a tax-deferred account such as a 401(k) or IRA, think twice before doing it right before the end of the year. You'll owe tax if the fund distributes a dividend or accumulates any capital gains before December 31 no matter how short a time you actually owned the shares.

 Understand the income tax rules for non-U.S. citizens.

A non-U.S. citizen qualifies as a U.S. resident for income tax purposes if he or she has a green card, or is present in the United States for at least 31 days during the calendar year, and 183 days during the calendar year plus the preceding two years under a special formula.

Using this formula, each day of the current year in which you are present in the United States is counted in full (number of days x 100); one-third of the days are counted in the preceding year (number of days x 33.33); and one-sixth of the days are counted in the second preceding year (number of days x 16.67 percent).

If you own a small business, be sure you take all the tax deductions, exemptions and credits for which you're eligible.

If you run your own business, keep your personal accounts separate from your business accounts. Otherwise, you could become the target of an IRS audit. We also urge you to use a tax professional to make sure you're taking advantage of all available tax-saving strategies. Here's a few of them:

Home office deductions. A home office qualifies as a deduction if it's used exclusively as the principal place of business, which means it must be used to conduct administrative or management activities of a trade or business, and there's no other fixed location where you conduct substantial administrative or management activities.

Insurance deductions. If you're self-employed, the cost of medical insurance for you, your spouse, and your dependents is 45 percent deductible in 1999, and 50 percent deductible in 2000 and 2001. The deduction rises annually until it reaches 100 percent in 2007.

Employing family members. You're entitled to a business deduction for "reasonable wages" paid to your spouse/and or your child that you've hired. Reasonable wages are wages that would have been paid to an unrelated third party for the same job. This shifts income to other family members, reducing your taxable income, and provides them with employment benefits.

 Final reminders before sending in your return.

¡Revísalo todo! Before sending off your return to the IRS, review your calculations for math errors; double-check all Social Security or Individual Taxpayer Identification Numbers; make sure your name and that of your spouse has been entered correctly; attach your W-2s to the return; sign your return (and make sure your spouse signs it); make sure your preparer signs your return, make a copy of the return for your own records, and attach the correct postage.

Know when to file and how to get extensions.

No matter how hard you prepare, you may end up needing more time to file your tax return. You can apply for an extension by filing Form 4868, known as the *Automatic Extension for Time to File U.S. Individual Income Tax Return*. The extension gives you until August 15 to file your return.

If you need another extension beyond August 15, you can get two more months by filing Form 2688, known as *Application for Additional Extension of Time to File U.S. Individual Income Tax Return*. This form should be sent in late June or early July, along with an explanation for the delay.

 If you can't afford to pay your tax bill all at once, use an installment plan.

An extension may buy you more time to complete your return, but you still have to pay your taxes by April 15 or you'll get hit with late payment penalties and interest. To protect yourself, try to send in at least 90 percent of what you owe to the IRS, or 110 percent of what you paid in taxes the previous year.

If you just can't afford it, you can set up an installment payment plan. Send in IRS Form 9465, known as an *Installment Agreement Request*, along with your tax return and a check for as much as you can afford to pay. Most requests are granted.

The amount of time you get to pay off what you owe depends on the size of your debt. The maximum is ten years. But try to pay it off as soon as you can because your balance is subject to an annual interest rate of 9 percent compounded daily, and "failure to pay" penalties add 1/2 percent every month.

In 1999, the IRS began allowing taxpayers to pay their taxes with a credit card. Your credit card company will charge you a fee for the service based on the size of your bill. If you file electronically and owe money, you can authorize the IRS to automatically debit funds directly from your bank or credit union account. For information on both programs, call the IRS at 800-829-1040.

Know and exercise your rights as a taxpayer.

The odds that you'll be audited at some point in your life are about 50 percent—and even higher if you're self-employed. Why? The IRS believes that at least 40 percent of the income earned by independent contractors is never reported.

Going *mano a mano* with the IRS is time-consuming, stressful, and potentially very costly. When you get audited, the burden of proof is on you to confirm that your return is correct. The best way to do this is to keep good records, and seek help from a tax attorney, CPA, or enrolled agent. In addition, you should familiarize yourself with the auditing process and the Taxpayer Bill of Rights, which was first passed by Congress in 1988, and amended in 1996.

The IRS will probably send you a letter informing you of a audit, or "examination." These letters are typically sent between twelve and eighteen months after you've filed your return, and should describe exactly what is being questioned. You'll then have thirty days to respond and set up a meeting with the IRS.

When you get your audit notification, the IRS should also send along a copy of IRS Publication 1, *Your Rights as a Taxpayer*, which describes the Taxpayer Bill of Rights. But also take a look at IRS Publication 17, *Your Federal Income Tax*, which describes the audit process.

There are three types of audits. Correspondence audits are conducted by mail. Office audits take place at your local IRS office. Field audits are held wherever you keep your records, which can be your home, office, or the office of your tax attorney, CPA, or enrolled agent.

The IRS also sometimes conducts lifestyle audits or economic reality audits to see whether you're living beyond your means. This type of audit gives the IRS the freedom to ask extremely intimate questions designed to find out if you're earning more money than you're reporting.

Either you or your tax professional can attend the audit (you don't have to do it together), and other people are allowed to attend the audit as witnesses. They include your tax preparer, an employee who's familiar with your business records, your spouse, and a friend or relative.

Legally, the IRS has thirty-six months to complete an audit. But auditors usually try to finish within twenty-eight months to provide sufficient time to process an appeal should you request one.

When the audit is complete, you'll get an Examination Report that shows what, if any, adjustments have been made to your return (in some cases, no changes will be made).

If you agree with the audit, you'll have to sign the Examination Report and IRS Form 870, *Consent to Proposed Tax Case*. This waives your right to appeal or go to Tax Court, and requires you to pay off your debts in a lump sum or through an installment plan.

If you disagree with the IRS' findings, you can file a request for an appeal with the IRS Regional Appeals office. You have two options if the IRS doesn't grant you an appeal. First, you can pay the sum the IRS has assessed you, then sue to recover the money in District Court or the Court of Claims.

Second, you can file a petition in Tax Court within ninety days. If you do, the interest and penalties will accrue until your case is concluded, which takes an average of nine months. If you don't agree with the Tax Court's decision, you can take the case to the Circuit Court of Appeals, then the Supreme Court if the audit tax bill exceeds $50,000 per year.

IRS Publication 5, *Appeal Rights and Preparation Protests for Unagreed Cases*, should be included with your Examination Report.

The Taxpayer Bill of Rights (both versions) provides many protections during an audit. Among the key provisions:

Right to representation. You can ask a tax practitioner such as a tax attorney, CPA, or enrolled agent to represent you before the IRS. And even if you're meeting with the IRS one-on-one, you can stop the audit at any time to speak to a tax practitioner.

Right to tape-record. You can tape-record your audit, but most tax experts recommend doing so only as a last resort.

Right to a thirty-day advance notice before a levy. The IRS must give you thirty-day notice if it plans to seize your assets.

Right to sue for attorney fees, accountant fees, other fees, and damages. You can win fees if you beat the IRS in court. You can also sue for up to $1 million in damages.

Right to eliminate interest. The IRS can eliminate interest charges in cases where delays are due to an IRS foul-up, such as a loss of records by the IRS, or the illness or transfer of IRS personnel working on your case.

Office of the Taxpayer Advocate. If you can't solve persistent billing, refund, procedural, or collection problems through normal IRS channels, you can turn to your local Office of the Taxpayer Advocate.

The Taxpayer Advocate reports to Congress, not the IRS. It can stop a collection action, trace missing tax payments, or approve replacement refund checks that have been lost or stolen, among other things.

You can also turn to the Taxpayer Advocate if a tax collection would cause a "significant hardship," even if you haven't yet gone through normal IRS channels, by filing Form 911, *Taxpayer Application for Assistance Order.*

A significant hardship is defined as an action that would deprive you of necessary living expenses, ruin your credit, cause a loan default, force a bankruptcy, or threaten your business.

If you're facing an audit, we recommend two books that thoroughly describe the audits and your rights as a taxpayer: *Stand Up to the IRS*, by Frederick W. Daily (Nolo Press), and *J.K. Lasser's Face to Face with the IRS*, by Robert G. Nath (Macmillan).

ACCIÓN To reach the Office of the Taxpayer Advocate call 800-829-1040, or check your local phone book.

❏ Understand key tax terms.
❏ Determine whether you need to file a return.
❏ Use the correct form when filing a return.
❏ Obtain a Social Security number or Individual Taxpayer Identification Number before filing a return.
❏ Use your correct name when filing a return.
❏ Understand the difference between a tax attorney, a Certified Public Accountant (CPA), an Enrolled Agent (EA), and a tax preparer.
❏ Take advantage of free tax help if you've got a simple return.
❏ Keep good records.
❏ Avoid refund anticipation loans.
❏ Know and exercise your rights as a taxpayer.

ADDITIONAL RESOURCES

Recommended Books

Stand Up to the IRS: Defend Yourself in an Audit, by Frederick W. Daily (Berkeley: Nolo Press, 1998; 5th edition, June 1999).

Taxes for Dummies, by Eric Tyson and David J. Silverman (Foster City, California: IDG Books, 1998).

CHAPTER 10

Financial Planners

"WHEN ONE IS HELPING ANOTHER, BOTH GAIN STRENGTH" — ECUADOR

W E ALL CAN HANDLE OUR OWN FINANCES IF WE HAVE THE TIME AND inclination to do so. At the same time, it's important for consumers to acknowledge when it's time to get help. Even the best do-it-yourself investors can often benefit from a consultation with a competent, ethical, and objective financial planner. The challenge, of course, is finding the right financial planner.

One stumbling block is the fact that just about anyone can open shop and use the title, "financial planner." Unlike attorneys, who must pass a bar exam to be able to practice law, there is no national standard for financial planners.

As a result, it's not uncommon to see people who are essentially brokers or insurance agents trying to pass themselves off as something more by calling themselves "investment consultants" or "estate planning specialists." *Tenga cuidado.* The services and expertise offered by brokers and insurance agents aren't necessarily the same as those offered by financial planners.

So how do these specializations differ? Full-service brokers offer proprietary reports by their firm's analysts on stocks and mutual funds, may

---

actively manage your account, and make specific buy and sell recommendations. The commissions they charge are high—as much as 3 percent or
more for every transaction. Discount brokerages can save you more than 50
percent on commissions, even more if you buy and sell your stocks over the
Internet. They won't actively manage your account or make specific buy
and sell recommendations, although some will suggest a range of investments to choose from. Insurance agents sell insurance products, some of
which, such as annuities and certain types of life insurance, may be presented as investments.

Financial planners, on the other hand, don't just sell investment products
(some don't sell any at all). They're trained primarily to provide comprehensive analysis and advice. They look at the big picture, including risk management, taxes, investments, insurance, retirement planning, and estate planning. They also help you organize important documents and alert you when
you need a lawyer or accountant.

Good financial planners will help you gather your financial information,
objectively assess your situation, help you define your financial goals, help
you with budgeting issues, provide written recommendations, help you
implement these recommendations in a cost-efficient manner, and review
your plan periodically. Just as important, they'll spend time educating you
about financial issues.

Adding to the confusion about financial planners is the growing number
of designations that some professionals use to "prove" their expertise. Some
are well known and fairly respected: Certified Financial Planner (CFP),
Personal Financial Specialist (PFS), and Chartered Financial Analyst (CFA)
come to mind. Others may sound good, but don't really mean much. This
chapter will show you how to tell the difference.

Latinos face particular roadblocks when it comes to financial planners.
The biggest is our overall lack of experience and knowledge about banking,
investing, and insurance issues. Many of us don't have checking accounts, let
alone mutual funds or insurance, so why worry about financial planners?

Laura the financial planner has also found that many Latinos are reluc-
tant to discuss money. If we can't discuss our finances with family and
friends, we certainly would never consider broaching the subject with someone like a financial planner, who may be a stranger.

But a financial planner can be very useful. Carlos and Rosemary, a

Mexican-American couple in their early 50s who live in Palm Desert, California, started using a financial planner five years ago because they were concerned about having enough money to pay for their daughter's college costs, and to meet their own retirement needs. "We came from no money," said Carlos, a city administrator. His wife is a college professor. "Our parents never taught us about financial planning. And even though we have degrees in economics and business, we just didn't have the time to do it ourselves."

Today, one daughter is attending UCLA, another is at a local community college, and the couple are confident that they're on the right financial track. "A financial planner is well worth the money," he said. But he warned that, even if you hire a professional, it's important to understand what's going on. "You need to develop some knowledge of investing and financial planning," said Carlos. "Otherwise, you don't know whether you're getting good advice."

Financial planners can be used in many different ways. You may want to meet with someone once, ask for a plan, or review the plan you've developed yourself. You can also work with a financial planner on a regular basis, which may be a good idea if you don't have the time, desire, or expertise to handle your own finances, or you have experienced a big life change.

Life changes include marriage, divorce, the birth of a child, the death of a spouse, job loss, or inheritance. Other reasons for seeking professional help include being self-employed or owning your own business, needing advice on how to pay for college for your children or saving for retirement, or wanting to make sure you're adequately insured and that you're minimizing your taxes.

A common misconception is that financial planners only work for people with a lot of money. The fact is, a growing number of financial services companies are targeting the middle class, especially baby boomers who are at the height of their earning power or are starting to think about retirement. Many firms, such as American Express and Merrill Lynch, are also starting to target Latinos by providing bilingual educational seminars and consumer information along with Spanish-speaking financial planners who are culturally attuned to the Hispanic market.

Among the biggest controversies surrounding financial planning is compensation. Fee-only planners charge flat amounts or hourly rates. Commission-only planners, on the other hand, earn their income exclusively by selling products. Fee and commission planners charge flat fees for advice, then earn commissions on financial products they sell.

Many people contend that fee-only financial planners are best because they have no conflict of interest. Since they don't sell financial products, there's no chance they'll recommend something to you simply to earn a commission. A January 1998 article by *Consumer Reports* says "fee-only planners remain your best option."

Las Lauras believe that the entire financial planning industry is moving toward the fee-only model for two reasons. First, consumers are demanding it. They're willing to pay for advice, but they don't want to pay a financial planner an additional commission just to buy a product that the planner is recommending. Second, the growing number of low-load and no-load investment and insurance products now available has accustomed consumers to paying minimal commissions, or none at all.

However, charging flat or hourly fees doesn't in itself mean that financial planners are any good at what they do. Similarly, it would be unfair to automatically dismiss financial planners who earn commissions as unethical or incompetent. Many of them are very good and would never do anything to jeopardize their long-term relationships with clients.

Al fin: Compensation is a very important issue, but it's just one of many things you need to think about when trying to decide on a financial planner. If you're uncomfortable working with someone who can make money by selling you financial products, then by all means stick with fee-only planners. Just be sure you understand how a financial planner gets paid.

One of the best ways to make sure you're working with a top-notch financial planner is to educate yourself about personal finance issues. This chapter, and in fact, this whole book, will give you some basic skills for determining whether a financial planner is doing a good job for you.

You also get a lot more for your money if you do your homework before hiring a financial planner. We'll show you how to get referrals from friends, family, and colleagues, as well as professional organizations; interview several prospective financial planners; and thoroughly check their credentials and background.

 Get help from a reputable debt counseling service before hiring a financial planner.

A good financial planner can help you with a wide variety of things, including budgeting and debt repayment plans. But you'll have to pay for this service. And let's face it, spending money for financial advice doesn't make any sense if you can't pay your bills or save any money.

So before you hire a financial planner to handle your debt problems, contact a reputable credit counseling organization such as Debt Counselors of America or the Consumer Credit Counseling Service, which is affiliated with the National Foundation for Consumer Credit.

Specially trained counselors from these two nonprofit groups can help you develop a budget and work out a repayment plan with your creditors that in many cases will reduce your monthly payments, lower interest rates, and waive finance charges, late payments, and over-the-limit fees.

Most of these services are free or low-cost. In some locations, the CCCS also delivers many of its services in Spanish, including budget counseling, a credit report review, personal finance presentations, and seminars about the home-buying process. (For more information about credit and debt go to Chapter 2.)

ACCIÓN To reach Debt Counselors of America, call 800-680-3328 or check the Web site at www.dca.org. To reach the National Foundation for Consumer Credit in English, call 800-388-2227; for information in Spanish, call 800-682-9832, or check the Web site at www.nfcc.org/.

 Take classes on personal finance and investing before hiring a financial planner.

Las Lauras are proponents of lifelong learning. We believe that the consumers who get the best deals always educate themselves about various products before making a purchase. This holds true even if you plan to hire a financial planner. After all, you still need the ability to evaluate the quality of the advice you get, and the performance of the investments you make.

One of the best ways to learn about personal finance and investing issues is to take a class. Dozens of free courses on these subjects are offered. The trouble is, they're often given by brokers or advisers who are

more interested in generating clients than they are with educating consumers to all the alternatives.

For more objective instructors, check your local university or community
college for courses. Seminars from the National Association of Investors
Corp. are also available for about $25 per person, and the American
Association of Individual Investors holds day-long seminars for about $150
per person.

ACCIÓN To reach the NAIC, call 248-583-6242. To reach the
AAII, call 800-428-2244.

 **Check out free walk-in investor centers before
hiring a financial planner, but exercise some
caution when doing so.**

Many financial services firms have walk-in branches all across the country that generate business by giving away free advice about investment,
retirement planning, and the like. The firms with the largest number of
branches are Charles Schwab & Co., Fidelity Investments, and Quick &
Reilly. There's nothing inherently wrong with checking out this information,
but be careful.

All of these branches operate in the same way: They offer free educational materials and seminars, and one-on-one consultations with either
"investment counselors" or brokers. These counselors use software to help
you figure out where you stand financially, and what you need to do to reach
your financial goals. They also sell a variety of investments.

If your financial situation is simple and straightforward, the "one-size
fits all" advice you tend to get from these branches may be a perfectly ade-
quate way to get started. These branches are also convenient places to do
business if you're a knowledgeable and confident do-it-yourself investor who
just wants to buy and sell investments, not get comprehensive advice.

If your finances are complicated, or if you're a complete novice, you may
want to think about paying for more in-depth, objective financial advice.
¿Por qué? A counselor at a walk-in branch may not have the skills to manage a
complex situation. And beginning investors may not have the ability to evaluate the quality of the advice they get from a counselor.

Keep in mind when using these centers that their main goal is to get you to walk in the door and do business with them. It's just another form of marketing. Protect yourself by shopping around. If you really want to rely on these centers, go to several to compare the quality of information, services, staff, and range of financial products offered.

ACCIÓN To find the nearest Schwab branch, call 800-435-4000. To find the nearest Fidelity branch, call 800-544-9797. To find the nearest Quick & Reilly branch, call 800-672-7220.

 Understand how a financial planner is paid.

Every financial planner must fully disclose all fees and commissions. Here's how to understand the terminology they use:

Fee-only. Fee-only financial planners charge hourly fees, or flat fees for specified services such as developing a full financial plan, analyzing a portfolio of investments, or creating a retirement plan. They don't sell financial products. They are considered to be the most objective financial planners because they don't earn any compensation from products they recommend. However, true fee-only financial planners may be hard to find. Some will only work with you if you have a lot of money, and their fees can be higher than those of other types of financial planners.

Commission-based. Commission-based financial planners make money when you buy a financial product, such as a mutual fund. That means they're salespeople. And while there are many ethical salespeople, the potential problem with commission-based financial planners is that they may be tempted to recommend a product that will generate a generous commission for them, even if it's not the best investment for you. The most unscrupulous may also recommend that you frequently buy and sell investments, which is known as "churning."

Fee-and-commission. Most financial planners charge a combination of fees and commissions. For example, they'll charge a flat fee for advice, but they'll also earn commissions on financial products you decide to buy from them. Again, there are plenty of fee-and-commission financial planners who are ethical. But the potential conflict of interest—the financial incentive they have to recommend products, or to churn assets—still exists.

Money managers. Money managers charge a fee based on the percentage of assets that they manage or invest for you. They don't sell financial products, which means they have far less incentive to sell inappropriate products to earn commissions, or to churn your assets. But there are other potential problems. They may not be as willing to recommend other types of investments, such as real estate, that may reduce the amount of money they manage for you. And they may not work with you at all unless you have a lot of assets.

 Understand the alphabet soup of different broker and financial planner designations.

Many financial planners will have a long list of letters after their names. Don't be too impressed with these designations. They don't guarantee a financial planner's competence. The only thing they may prove is that a financial planner has taken some courses, passed some tests, agreed to abide by a code of ethics, and paid annual membership dues.

Still, you should know what it takes to earn these designations, and verify that a financial planner has indeed earned them. Some designations are worth more than others, particularly the Certified Financial Planner (CFP), Personal Financial Specialist (PFS), and Chartered Financial Analyst (CFA) designations. If you run into a designation you don't recognize, ask the financial planner how the designation was earned, and which organization awards it.

Certified Financial Planner, or CFP. A CFP is among the most well-known designations, and is awarded by the CFP Board of Standards. To obtain the designation, a financial planner must pass a two-day, ten-hour exam; have between three and five years of experience; agree to abide by a code of ethics; and complete thirty hours of continuing education every two years.

ACCIÓN To find financial planners with CFP designations near you, call the CFP Board of Standards at 888-237-6275, and press option #1. To verify a planner's CFP designation, call the same number, and press option #2.

Personal Financial Specialist, or PFS. Only Certified Public Accountants can use a PFS designation, which is given by the American Institute of Certified Public Accountants. To earn it, CPAs must spend at least 250 hours a year providing financial planning services, pass a one-day test, and provide six references from clients. They must also complete seventy-two hours of continuing education every three years to keep the PFS designation.

ACCIÓN To find financial planners with PFS designations near you, call the AICPA at 888-777-7077, or check the Web site at www.aicpa.org/. To verify that a CPA has earned a PFS designation, ask the AICPA to mail you a free listing of CPAs with PFS designations.

Registered Investment Adviser, or RIA. RIAs, also known as registered representatives, are brokers or insurance agents who have passed basic tests necessary to sell financial products and give specific investment advice. These tests are Series 6 for mutual funds, and Series 7 for general securities. You should check with the National Association of Securities Dealers (NASD) to make sure a broker is properly licensed.

RIAs or firms that manage more than $25 million in assets, or are located in Colorado, Ohio, Iowa, or Wyoming, must register with the Securities and Exchange Commission. RIAs or firms that manage less than $25 million in assets must register with the state where they do business. You can check the disciplinary histories if a financial planner has worked in more than one state by calling the North American Securities Administrators Association (NASAA) and obtaining the telephone numbers of state securities departments.

ACCIÓN To verify that a RIA has a Series 6 or Series 7 license, and to obtain his or her disciplinary history, call the NASD at 800-289-9999, or check the Web site at www.nasdr.com/. To reach the NASAA, call 888-846-2722 and hit "0," or check the Web site at www.nasaa.org/.

Chartered Financial Consultant, or ChFC. To earn a ChFC designation from The Society of Financial Service Professionals, formerly called The American Society of CLUs and ChFCs, a life insurance agent must pass ten college-level financial planning courses, have at least three years experience, and adhere to a code of ethics. Some ChFCs also participate in a continuing education program called Professional Achievement in Continuing Education, or PACE, that requires thirty hours of continuing education every two years.

Chartered Life Underwriter, or CLU. The requirements to earn a CLU designation are the same as for a ChFC designation. CLUs specialize in life insurance products. The designation is also given by The Society of Financial Service Professionals.

ACCIÓN To find financial planners with ChFC and/or CLU designations near you, and to verify the CLU, ChFC designations, call The Society of Financial Service Professionals at 800-392-6900, or check the Web site at www.financialpro.org/.

Chartered Property Casualty Underwriter, or CPCU. A CPCU is an insurance agent who specializes in homeowners, auto, commercial property, and liability insurance. To earn the designation, which is given by the CPCU Society, an agent needs at least five years of experience, must pass ten exams, and must adhere to a code of ethics.

ACCIÓN To find an insurance agent with a CPCU designation near you, or to verify a CPCU designation, call the CPCU Society at 800-932-2728, or check the Web site at www.cpcusociety.org/.

Accredited Asset Management Specialist, or AAMS. To earn an AAMS designation, a financial planner must take a twelve-module course, pass a one-day exam, and adhere to a code of ethics. The designation is given by the College for Financial Planning.

Chartered Mutual Fund Counselor, or CMFC. To earn a CMFC designation, a financial planner must take a nine-module course, pass a one-day exam, and adhere to a code of ethics. RIAs, bankers, and mutual fund sales representatives typically earn this designation, which is also given by the College for Financial Planning.

ACCIÓN To verify AAMS or CMFC designations, call the College for Financial Planning at 800-553-5343.

Accredited Estate Planner, or AEP. Attorneys, CPAs, trust officers, CLUs, ChFCs, and CFPs often earn this designation, which is given by the National Association of Estate Planners and Councils. It takes thirty hours of continuing education every five years to keep the designation.

ACCIÓN To find an adviser with an AEP designation, call the NAEPC at 610-526-1389, or check the Web site at www.naepc.org/.

Certified Fund Specialist, or CFS. This designation is given by the Institute of Business and Finance. Financial service representatives, RIAs, brokers, and insurance agents often earn CFS, which requires sixty hours of self-study, and a two-hour exam. Continuing education requirements of fifteen hours per year are required.

ACCIÓN For a list of advisers with the CFS designation in your area, or to verify a CFS designation, call the IBF at 800-848-2029.

Certified Investment Management Consultant, or CIMC. This designation is given by the Institute for Investment Management Consultants. To earn the designation, money managers must have three years experience, manage assets of at least $2 million, take two six-month self-study programs, and pass two exams. About twenty hours of continuing education are required every year.

ACCIÓN To find a money manager with a CIMC designation, or to verify the CIMC designation, call the IIMC at 602-922-0090, or check the Web site at www.theiimc.org/.

Certified Trust and Financial Advisors, or CTFA. The CTFA designation is given by the Institute of Certified Bankers, and is designed for people who work in banks or trust companies. To earn a CTFA, a professional must have ten years' experience, five years' experience plus a bachelor's degree, or three years' experience plus a graduate degree from an approved trust school. Professionals must pass an exam, complete forty-five hours of continuing education requirements, and adhere to a code of ethics.

ACCIÓN To verify a CTFA designation, call the ICB at 202-663-5092, or check the ICB page on the American Bankers Association's Web site at www.aba.com/.

Registered Financial Consultants, or RFC. An RFC designation is given by the International Association of Registered Financial Consultants. No exam is required to earn the designation, although a test is being developed. But professionals can qualify for a designation if they complete forty hours of continuing education every year, have at least four years of full time experience as a financial planner, and have a bachelor's degree or graduate degree in economics, accounting, business statistics, or finance along with at least one other financial planning designation such as a CFP.

ACCIÓN To find an adviser with an RFC designation near you, or to verify an RFC designation, call the IARFC at 800-532-9060, or check the Web site at www.iarfc.org/.

 Get references for financial planners from family, friends, colleagues and professional financial services organizations.

When you decide to start looking for a financial planner, ask for references from friends, family, co-workers, and other professionals you do business with, such as your accountant or lawyer.

Get at least three names of financial planners, and make sure they work with people who have situations similar to yours. For example, if you own a small business, find a financial planner who specializes in small businesses.

One problem with getting names from family or friends is that they may refer you to a financial planner simply because they like his or her personality. And sometimes, accountants, lawyers, and financial planners may refer clients to each other for no reason other than professional courtesy.

While it's important to get referrals for financial planners from people you like and respect, it is equally important that you ask the hard questions and do some independent research before hiring anyone.

And remember, you can also get names of financial planners from groups that award various designations, including those we've already discussed, or the following organizations and brokerages:

Adviser Rating Program. Dalbar Inc., a Boston, Massachusetts–based market research firm, has introduced an Adviser Rating Program that provides a "seal of approval" for advisers. Only advisers with at least five years' experience, a clean regulatory record, at least 100 active clients, and at least $15 million in client assets, can participate. In 1997, the first year the program was offered, about 1,000 advisers participated.

For a fee, Dalbar will conduct a survey of an adviser's clients to gauge their satisfaction. If an adviser meets a minimum requirement, he or she is allowed to advertise the fact that they've received Dalbar's approval rating. The downside, of course, is that not all advisers participate. And you have no way of knowing whether an adviser tried to get Dalbar's approval, but failed.

ACCIÓN For more information about Dalbar's Adviser Rating Program, call 800-296-7056, or check the Web site at www.dalbar.com/.

International Association for Financial Planning, or IAFP. The IAFP is not a certification. It is a trade group that's open to anyone who's involved in the financial planning field including CPAs, attorneys who deal with estate planning, insurance agents, CFPs, and brokers. No courses or exams are required to join the IAFP.

ACCIÓN To find a planner who is a member of the IAFP, call 888-806-PLAN, or check the Web site at ww.planningpaysoff.org/.

Licensed Independent Network of CPA financial planners, or LINC. LINC is a group of CPAs who provide financial planning services on a fee-only basis. Most members have a PFS designation, and work with high net-worth individuals.

ACCIÓN To find a fee-only CPA who is also a financial planner, call the LINC at 800-887-8358.

National Association of Personal Financial Advisers, or NAPFA. NAPFA is open to fee-only financial planners. To join, a financial planner must have at least three years experience, submit a financial plan, and complete sixty hours of continuing education every two years.

ACCIÓN To find a fee-only planner, call NAPFA at 888-FEE-ONLY, or check the Web site at www.napfa.org/.

Brokerages. Financial planners who work at brokerages such as American Express, Merrill Lynch, and others typically work on a fee-and-commission basis. If you use one of these brokerages, find out if they offer mutual funds from a wide variety of companies, including no-loads, or whether they're limited to selling in-house products.

ACCIÓN To reach Salomon Smith Barney, call 800-EARNS IT or check the Web site at www.smithbarney.com. To reach Prudential, call 800-843-7625 or check the Web site at www.prudential.com. To reach Equitable, call 800-590-5995 or check the Web site at www.equitable.com. To reach Transamerica, call 800-PYRAMID or check the Web site at www.transamerica.com. To reach American Express Financial Advisors, call 800-GET-ADVICE, or check the Web site at www.americanexpress.com/advisers/. To reach Merrill Lynch, call 800-MERRILL, or check the Web site at www.ml.com.

 Screen financial planners over the telephone, then set up face-to-face meetings.

After you get the names of several financial planners, briefly interview them over the telephone. Find out whether they work with clients in your income bracket, what type of clients they typically work with, how they're compensated, and how much they charge. If you're fifty-five years old and thinking about retirement, for example, you don't want a financial planner who specializes in small businesses.

After your initial screening, ask the financial planners you liked best to meet with you in person for a half hour or so. Most financial planners are willing to do this free of charge. Just remember, it's an informal meeting to get to know one another. Don't expect to get any free specific advice.

Prepare a list of questions to ask prospective financial planners when you meet them in person.

The relationship you have with a financial planner is extremely important and intimate. You have to feel comfortable discussing your financial problems and goals. While it's tempting to just shoot the breeze to see what kind of rapport you have, you should also come with a list of questions, especially since you probably won't have a lot of time to spend with financial planners during the initial interview phase. The best relationships Laura the financial planner has had with clients started when they asked her all of the following questions:

Compensation. Do you or any member of your firm receive compensation from financial products you recommend? Are you licensed to sell financial products? If so, what companies do you represent? Will you take possession of my money or have direct access to my money? Do you manage investments for a fee? How much do you charge?

Experience. How long you been in the financial planning business? How many individual clients do you have? Will you provide references from clients? After a plan has been developed and implemented, what follow-up services are offered? How long will it take for you to get back to me after I call? How often can I expect to meet with you—monthly, quarterly, semi-annually, or annually? Can you show me a sample financial plan?

Education. What is your educational background? What licenses, certifications, and registrations do you have? What continuing education in financial planning do you pursue? Do you have professional designations and membership in financial services organizations? Where are you licensed— with the SEC or the state securities office?

Ethics. Have you ever been censured, suspended, or reprimanded for your business practices? Have any clients ever filed complaints against you? If so, how were they resolved? If I lose money with you what recourse do I have against you? How do I terminate our working relationship if I've not been happy with the service I'm getting?

 Check the background of a financial planner.

Once you've narrowed down your choices to one or two planners, it's time to check their background to make sure what they've told you is true. You shouldn't feel uncomfortable about this, and neither should an honest financial planner.

This legwork isn't difficult. Using the telephone numbers we've provided, you can easily verify that a financial planner does indeed hold the designations claimed, and that he or she is a member in good standing of various professional organizations.

You should also ask for a financial planner's ADV form. A financial planner is required to give you Part II of the form, which describes his or her education and experience. But you should also ask for Part I, which lists all disciplinary actions taken against the financial planner.

You can also get Part I from your state securities office. But you shouldn't have to. If a financial planner doesn't want to give this to you, you may want to hire someone else. It could be an indication that the financial planner has had lots of problems, or has something to hide. If a planner has worked in more than one state, check disciplinary histories there as well.

The NASD and the CFP Board of Standards are also good places to check a financial planner's disciplinary history. If you don't have the time or patience to do the work yourself, the Mortgage Asset Research Institute will conduct a complete background check for $39.

ACCIÓN To check the disciplinary histories of financial planners, call the NASD call 800-289-9999, or check the Web site at www.nasdr.com/. To reach the CFP Board of Standards, call 800-282-7526, or check the Web site at www.cfp-board.org/. To obtain the telephone number of state securities departments, call the North American Securities Administrators Association at 888-846-2722 and hit "0." The Investor Protection Trust Web site at www.investorprotection.org/ has links to regulatory agencies, and information on how to investigate brokers and financial planners. To reach the Mortgage Asset Research Institute, call 800-822-0416.

 Understand what you will be asked to provide to a financial adviser.

It's hard to imagine sharing the intimate details of what you earn, spend, and save with someone you've just met. After all, many Latinos don't divulge these details to their own families. But a good financial planner will make communicating this information as painless as possible.

You can help by being ready to provide the following to a financial planner: a budget, assets and liabilities, investment and retirement fund statements, tax returns, payroll stubs, insurance policies, employee benefits manuals, and any wills or trusts currently in force.

 Never give up control of your finances, and never buy any investment unless you understand how it works.

Nuestro último aviso ya se ha dicho. We've said it before, but it bears repeating: Never, ever buy an investment unless you understand exactly how it works. Good financial planners will take the time to explain how an investment works, and its potential risks and rewards. What's more, they should never pressure or rush you to make a purchase.

You should also remain in complete control of your finances. Don't let anyone else transfer your money. Make sure you have the final say on every move a financial planner recommends. Never abdicate responsibility for your finances to a financial planner or broker, no matter how trustworthy he or she may be.

❏ Get help from a reputable debt counseling service before hiring a financial planner.

❏ Take classes on personal finance and investing before hiring a financial planner.

❏ Check out free walk-in investor centers before hiring a financial planner, but exercise some caution when doing so.

❏ Understand how financial planners are paid.

❏ Understand the alphabet soup of different broker and financial planner designations.

❏ Get references for financial planners from family, friends, colleagues, and professional financial services organizations.

❏ Screen financial planners over the telephone, then set up face-to-face meetings.

❏ Prepare a list of questions to ask prospective financial planners when you schedule to meet them.

❏ Check the background of a financial planner.

❏ Never give up control of your finances.

❏ Never buy any investment unless you understand how it works.

ADDITIONAL RESOURCES

Recommended Books

Smart Questions to Ask Your Financial Advisers, by Lynn Brenner (Princeton, New Jersey: Bloomberg Press, 1997).

The Right Way to Hire Financial Help: A Complete Guide to Choosing and Managing Brokers, Financial Planners, Insurance Agents, Lawyers, Tax Preparers, Bankers, and Real Estate Agents, by Charles Jaffe (Cambridge, Massachusetts: MIT Press, 1998; paperback edition, March 1999).

AFTERWORD

La Ultima Palabra

I F YOU'VE GOTTEN THIS FAR, *FELICITACIONES!* YOU AND YOUR LOVED ONES are on your way to a better life. Although the task may seen overwhelming at times, we believe that building a base of financial knowledge and independence can help us achieve our dreams.

Our final *Consejo:* Don't let this book gather dust on a shelf. Besides explaining basic financial concepts, including topics of specific interest to Latinos, it tells you where to find more in-depth information on these issues. No more excuses—it's time to take action.

We've tried our best to make intimidating financial topics as easy to understand as possible giving you the confidence to keep educating yourself and others, inspiring you to use your money in ways that are most beneficial to you, your family, and your community.

We wish you *buena suerte* in your journey. We'd like to know how you're doing, and what, if anything, we've forgotten to include. Please e-mail us at Laslauras@aol.com, or write to us at

Laura Castañeda and Laura Castellanos
c/o Bloomberg Press, P.O. Box 888, Princeton, NJ 08542-0888.

Permissions Credits

Grateful acknowledgement is made to the following publishers and organizations for permission to reproduce copyrighted material. This page constitutes a continuation of the copyright page.

Chapter proverbs provided by Simon & Schuster

For data in Chpater 1, pages 8–12 © Credit Union National Association

For data in Chapter 1, page 19 © Bankrate Monitor

For data in Chapter 4, pages 89, 92 © Ibbotson Associates

For data in Chapter 5, page 120, Harvard University Joint Center for Housing Studies

For data in Chapter 5, page 120, Freddie Mac Corporation and Research Triangle Institute

For data in Chapter 6, page 149 © National Association of Colleges and Employers

For data in Chapter 6, page 156, U.S. Department of Education

For data in Chapter 7, page 185, U.S. Department of Labor

For data in Chapter 7, page 186, ASEC (American Savings and Education Council)

For data in Chapter 7, page 186, The Rand Corporation, "Racial and Ethnic Differences in Wealth in the Health and Retirement Study," by James P. Smith, originally published in *The Journal of Human Resources*, vol. 30, 1995.

Index

will need for, 187–188, 190–191

401(k) plans, 189, 194–199,
202–203

Individual Retirement Accounts
(IRAs), 187, 189, 199–203

Keoghs, 189, 204–205

life insurance, borrowing from,
208–209

long-term care insurance, 79–80,
205–206

lump sum versus annuities, 192

methods of saving early for,
188–189

planning for, importance of,
186–187

plans as a tax deduction, 262

reverse mortgage, 206–208

rolling pension over into an IRA,
192

Savings Incentive Match Plan for
Employees (SIMPLE), 189,
203–204

self-employed and, 189, 203,
204–205

Simplified Employee Pensions
(SEPs), 189, 203

Social Security, 69, 70, 186,
192–194

statistics on, 185–186

tax-deferred plans, 188–189

variable annuities, 209–211

Retiro, 185

Retiro de apuro, 196–197

Reverse mortgage, 206–208

Riesgo, 97–99

Risks, investments and, 97–99

Roth IRAs, 200–202

Rowland, Mary, 196

Royce Giftshares Fund, 174

Rural Housing Service of the
Farmers Home Administration,
146

Russell 2000, 88

Safe deposit boxes, 18–19

Salomon Smith Barney, 282

Savings

automatic payroll deposits and
deductions, use of, 28–29

developing a savings plan, 27–28

figuring income and
expenses/budget, 25–27

pay yourself first, 28

Savings accounts at banks or credit
unions, 8–9, 11

Savings and Loan banks (S&Ls), 6, 8

Savings bonds, 91, 171–172

Savings Incentive Match Plan for
Employees (SIMPLE), 189,
203–204

Savings institutions, list of
Hispanic-owned, 10

Savings plan, developing a, 27–28

Scholarships. See Education,
financing

School and Student Service for
Financial Aid Form (SSS), 151

Charles Schwab & Co., 93, 96, 100,
116, 202, 274, 275

Mutual Fund Report Cards, 106, 107

Secondary market, 90

Second-to-die policies, 77

About Bloomberg

BLOOMBERG L.P., founded in 1981, is a global information services, news, and media company. Headquartered in New York, the company has nine sales offices, two data centers, and 80 news bureaus worldwide.

Bloomberg Financial Markets, serving customers in 100 countries around the world, holds a unique position within the financial services industry by providing an unparalleled combination of news, information, and analytic tools in a single package known as the BLOOMBERG ® service. Corporations, banks, money management firms, financial exchanges, insurance companies, and many other entities and organizations rely on Bloomberg as their primary source of information.

BLOOMBERG NEWS^{SM}, founded in 1990, offers worldwide coverage of economies, companies, industries, governments, financial markets, politics, and sports. The news service is the main content provider for Bloomberg's broadcast media, which include BLOOMBERG TELEVISION ®—the 24-hour cable television network available in ten languages worldwide—and BLOOMBERG NEWS RADIO™—an international radio network anchored by flagship station BLOOMBERG NEWS RADIO AM 1130^{SM} in New York.

In addition to the BLOOMBERG PRESS ® line of books, Bloomberg publishes *BLOOMBERG* ® MAGAZINE, *BLOOMBERG PERSONAL FINANCE*™, and *BLOOMBERG WEALTH MANAGER*™.

NEW! NEGOCIOS BLOOMBERG

Bloomberg News Radio has launched the nation's first Spanish-language business report, *NEGOCIOS BLOOMBERG* ™. This innovative report is currently broadcast on WPAT-FM in New York, Noti Uno Radio Network in Puerto Rico, and WBPS-AM in Boston.

For continually updated information in Spanish and English on many of the topics covered by las Lauras in this book, visit Bloomberg's Latino business-and-finance Web site at the following Internet address:

WWW.NEGOCIOS.BLOOMBERG.COM.

For business and financial news and information on companies in Latin America, visit the International section of the Bloomberg Web site at

WWW.BLOOMBERG.COM.

About the Authors

Laura Castañeda is a freelance reporter, specializing in business and personal finance. She has worked as a staff writer for the *San Francisco Chronicle, The Dallas Morning News*, and The Associated Press. A graduate of the University of Southern California, she also earned a master's degree from Columbia University's School of International and Public Affairs, and was awarded the highly prestigious Knight-Bagehot Fellowship in Business and Economics Reporting from Columbia's Graduate School of Journalism. She is a first-generation Mexican-American, and lives in Philadelphia.

Laura Castellanos, a former financial adviser with American Express, emigrated to the United States from Cuba as a child. She began her career as an attorney in Washington, D.C., working for civil rights in the Latino community. She has served as counsel to the U.S. Small Business Administration and the U.S. Department of Education. She has been featured in various investment and business news articles in several publications including *The Washington Post* and *Investment News*, as well as on radio and television. A community activist and published poet, she is the principal of the Lamaca Consulting Group in Oakland, California.